KT-173-166

MARTIN O'NEILL

ON DAYS LIKE THESE

MY LIFE IN FOOTBALL

PAN BOOKS

First published 2022 by Macmillan

This edition published 2023 by Pan Books
an imprint of Pan Macmillan
The Smithson, 6 Briset Street, London EC1M 5NR
EU representative: Macmillan Publishers Ireland Ltd, 1st Floor,
The Liffey Trust Centre, 117–126 Sheriff Street Upper,
Dublin 1, D01 YC43
Associated companies throughout the world
www.panmacmillan.com

ISBN 978-1-0350-0848-3

Copyright © Martin O'Neill 2022

The right of Martin O'Neill to be identified as the
author of this work has been asserted by him in accordance
with the Copyright, Designs and Patents Act 1988.

The picture acknowledgements on p. 355 constitute an extension of this copyright page.

All rights reserved. No part of this publication may be reproduced,
stored in a retrieval system, or transmitted, in any form, or by any means
(electronic, mechanical, photocopying, recording or otherwise)
without the prior written permission of the publisher.

Pan Macmillan does not have any control over, or any responsibility for,
any author or third-party websites referred to in or on this book.

1 3 5 7 9 8 6 4 2

A CIP catalogue record for this book is available from the British Library.

Typeset by Palimpsest Book Production Ltd, Falkirk, Stirlingshire
Printed and bound by CPI Group (UK) Ltd, Croydon, CR0 4YY

This book is sold subject to the condition that it shall not, by way of
trade or otherwise, be lent, hired out, or otherwise circulated without
the publisher's prior consent in any form of binding or cover other than
that in which it is published and without a similar condition including
this condition being imposed on the subsequent purchaser.

Visit **www.panmacmillan.com** to read more about all our books
and to buy them. You will also find features, author interviews and
news of any author events, and you can sign up for e-newsletters
so that you're always first to hear about our new releases.

To my wife Geraldine, my two daughters Aisling and Alana, my granddaughter Caragh Gene and my wonderful sister Mary, who sadly passed away recently.

CONTENTS

INTRODUCTION

It is the European Cup final of 1980. I have promised myself during the last fortnight that I am determined to enjoy these moments regardless of the result. But I know in my heart that it's complete balderdash. Winning tonight is the only thing that matters; actually, winning is the only thing that ever matters.

Hamburg are strong favourites to beat Nottingham Forest despite us being reigning champions. They have Kevin Keegan in their ranks as captain. And we have lost last year's game-winner, Trevor Francis, to injury. So superstitious have I become that I follow the routine from when I last played really well. Left sock first, that never changes, then right sock. My heart is pounding and I feel entirely different from last year's final in Munich.

Back then I thought that the chances of ever playing in another European Cup final were remote. George Best and Bobby Charlton only ever got to play in one final. And Denis Law didn't even play in one at all. How must he have felt in 1968 when injury precluded him from Manchester United's winning team? If we win, everything that has happened to me in my professional career will have been worth it. The struggles for recognition, for approval, for respect. It's been a long road since setting foot in England that bright Wednesday morning in October 1971, full of self-confidence and bravado. A bright beginning, but also many dark days. I now have a chance to put everything right. But only if we win.

As we climb into the floodlit arena, the cacophonic roar of

the crowd almost splits our eardrums. We quickly get the game in motion. Hamburg dominate possession in the early stages. Kenny Burns puts in a couple of heavy challenges, Keegan objects to the referee and Peter Shilton makes a good save. It's looking tough for us and there's little respite, but if we can survive this period without conceding a goal, it will be some sort of small victory. We do and we start to build a little momentum of our own.

And then we score. John Robertson plays an inside pass to Garry Birtles, gets the return and then rifles a shot into the bottom corner of the net.

We are in front. I'm too drained to run to congratulate him but I join the huddle we have made around our goal-scorer. It's the first goal, a very important goal. However, there is far too long in the game to go to call it decisive.

The rest of the first half seems to blur its way to half-time. In the dressing room, Brian Clough is thinking about making a positional switch. I volunteer to move wherever he wants me to. 'No,' he says. 'I'm not moving you, son, you're doing brilliantly exactly where you are.'

I'm not expecting such high praise to come in my direction. All these years I've searched for his approval, and he waits until half-time in the European Cup final to give it. I have validation at last. And with those words, energy of which I thought I was bereft jolts through my whole body like an electric current. I'm ready for anything these next forty-five minutes can throw at me.

Hamburg press forward again but, urged by our fans to keep going, we repel their attacks. The spirit within the team, always strong, reaches stratospheric levels, and if we can see out the last six minutes, the European Cup will be ours. Six minutes become four, become two, and then a whistle blows. It's all over.

I fall to my knees and clench my fists. It's an incredible moment of triumph.

From landing at East Midlands Airport that October morning in 1971 to this moment in a brightly lit Santiago Bernabéu

Stadium in Madrid, every word of splenetic criticism along the way doesn't matter any more. Last year's personal heartache in Munich is washed away. Soon I will collect a European Cup medal that I have earned on the field.

John McGovern lifts the trophy, holds it aloft, and points in the direction of our fans. They too have played their crucial part in the last few heady seasons.

We get back to the dressing room and excitement still burns within. We now want to hear from the man who made this all possible: Clough. On this evening of all evenings, we need to know his take. We pulled ourselves back from the brink of disaster in East Berlin, we faced a torrid twenty-five-minute barrage in Amsterdam, and we came through. And this evening in the Madrid heat, we have withstood everything thrown at us and emerged victorious.

The most precious prize of club football now sits on the floor in front of us, having been carefully placed there by the enigmatic Brian Clough.

He tells us that we have been magnificent all evening. John's goal may have given us the lead but he emphasizes that this is a team win. He hails how we threw ourselves into tackles regardless of personal safety, how we blocked so many shots inside and outside the penalty box. He reminds us that these are the reasons why this trophy is in our dressing room and not down the corridor with Hamburg.

A year ago almost to the day, I threw a box containing a European Cup medal across a massage table in Munich thinking that a day like this could never happen for me. Well, it has, and it's better than anything I've ever imagined.

Since Brian Clough's arrival, Nottingham Forest have – in the course of three seasons – won promotion to the First Division, taken the title at the first time of asking, won a League Cup the same season, taken on the best in Europe and won the big prize, and retained the League Cup. And then, to cap it all, we have gone back to Europe once again and, on a warm evening in Madrid, won the European Cup for a second successive year. This is the legacy of this East Midlands city. If I could live to be 1,000 years old I would never see this again in football. That is how big these achievements have been. And I was privileged to be part of this football history.

Brian Clough breezed through the city of Nottingham in the mid-1970s. A man on a mission. Stick close to his coat-tails or fall by the wayside – that was his message right from the beginning. He waited a while at the turnstile for his trusty lieutenant, Peter Taylor, to join forces with him. Together, this greatest partnership in football cajoled, encouraged, lambasted and sometimes charmed their charges into following their path to triumph and glory.

I admit I found the lambasting occasionally difficult to deal with, particularly when I felt it wasn't merited. But the smell of success mitigated the censure, warranted or not, especially if the prize at the end was worth it. And the European Cup was certainly worth it – ask any footballer.

I don't believe football management ever really entered my head until a chance meeting with Peter Taylor sometime after he himself had retired from the game.

He prevailed upon me into thinking seriously about it. He and Clough had their own distinct style of management and there was a lot to admire in their method. League championships with two different clubs and two European Cups suggested they didn't get too many things wrong. Would I, if given an opportunity, do things in the manner in which they operated? Possibly, possibly not. Brian Clough preached simplicity at all times. This approach made perfect sense to me. Don't overcomplicate matters when there is little need to do so. Know your job first and foremost; everything else follows. Then do it to the best of your ability. Every game. Yes, every game.

Sometimes it was not what he said but how he said it. Clough was a brilliant orator and he knew his subject inside out.

It's very difficult not to have been influenced by the success, the personalities, that surrounded me as a player. But in management, influences can only take you so far. I recognized early on that my own skills and character would define my managerial career. I believe I have always had the temperament and work ethic to keep driving on. My passion for football is still as fervent today as it was when I was a young boy growing up in Kilrea. So why have I decided to put pen to paper and write about my professional career in football?

I have been half a century in the game and I'm often asked about my life. This was a great chance to recount the stories and collate them in one place. I have straddled the years just after England's triumph in the 1966 World Cup, when I was a teenager, to the game as it is today.

Those who managed me in the 1970s and 1980s would have to make so many more adjustments and allowances if they were propelled into today's game. However, there are many aspects that still remain steadfast. The dexterity needed to manage people in high-octane environments in the glare of the media is as paramount today as it ever was.

I've witnessed huge financial changes in the game too. Very few players back then earned enough money to secure their futures after they had finished playing football. Today an average Premier League player may be able to do so after signing a three-year contract.

Better playing surfaces, a more stringent refereeing approach to reckless tackles, and using data to take a more advanced approach to injury prevention and rehabilitation also mean the game being played today is probably safer and more career-prolonging.

In my domain I have to be in control of the dressing room whatever else is happening at the football club, politically or otherwise. The players have to see that I'm in charge of their immediate careers and progression. Fostering camaraderie and team spirit is vitally important. A disunified dressing room can have a disruptive effect on what the group wants to achieve. It may not always be possible to get a full squad singing from the same hymn sheet, but that has always been the art of management. Creativity must be allowed to be at the forefront. Recognizing that game-changers or match-winners need an environment in which to flourish is an absolute must in trying to win football matches.

But motivation is key, and the power of the dressing room team talk is to me an integral part of my craft. Making players believe that anything is possible while they're on the field of play. No hurdle insurmountable, no travail insuperable, no dream too remote. That is the beauty of this wonderful game and I am privileged to be a part of it.

PART ONE

PLAYER

1

KILREA AND BEYOND

My first memory as a child is of a four-year-old boy waving down to his older sister from the second storey of a house, then deciding that the quickest way to give her a hug is not to use the stairs but to jump out of the window. That four-year-old boy is me. Thankfully, I miss the concrete step by a few inches and land on the grass. Had I hit the step instead, I can only assume that I would be with the angels right now.

A broken arm and a bloody forehead are my most discernible injuries. The arm, put in plaster by the Coleraine Hospital senior nurse, will heal itself in time. The cracked head may partly explain my behaviour from this day onwards.

Ten months later, I poke a stick into my eye, necessitating another fifteen-mile trip to Coleraine Hospital. I am seen by the same senior nurse, who quietly asks my mother when she thinks my third visit will be. Yet, despite such mishaps, I have a wonderful childhood.

I am the sixth child in a typical Irish Nationalist Catholic family. Lying roughly in the middle, I have four brothers and four sisters. My time at home is mostly spent with those siblings who are closest to me in age: Breedge and Roisin and my two younger brothers, Owen and Shane. Kilrea, my birthplace, is a generally close-knit quiet little town in County Derry. Catholics and Protestants live peacefully together. Sporadic Border-town IRA operations grab attention in the papers and on the radio. But even those Border insurrections seem a million miles away from Kilrea and my life.

The town bursts into life on market day, unrelenting from early morning to very late in the evening. My father is one of two barbers in the town. On Saturdays I take his lunch and dinner from our house to his shop, where he eats his food between cutting hair. He can earn enough that day to keep his family (of eleven) for the rest of the week. Other slack days would find him in Rainey's betting shop, owned and run by two spinster sisters, famous in the town both for their devotion to Our Lord and for their equally enthusiastic extraction of money from mug punters. My father is one of them. He does five-bob doubles, or – if in a really adventurous mood – a ten-bob treble. Getting one horse to win is a minor miracle, two winners usually means divine intervention, but three winners on one docket is a step too far. God believes you're just being too greedy and takes the Rainey sisters' side, presumably because they never ever miss Mass even on weekdays.

With a picture of Padraig Pearse – a leader of 1916's Easter Rising – juxtaposed with one of the Sacred Heart of Jesus in our front room, it wouldn't take a visitor too long to know where our sympathies lie. Despite our council house being small, I never feel that we are overcrowded. With the ages of my siblings spread quite widely, not everyone is in the house at the same time except for summer holidays and Christmas. My older brothers Gerry and Leo are at a boarding school in Derry City and will go on to Queen's University Belfast. My eldest sister Agatha is at Endsleigh Training College in Hull. My sister Mary is boarding at a convent school in Coleraine and will go on to University College Dublin. So there is enough space for the rest of us.

As a family we are strong Nationalists, and my father helped form the town's Gaelic Athletic Association club. My older brothers are excellent Gaelic players as well as being terrific athletes, with Gerry winning the victor ludorum twice in St Columb's College, and Leo following in his footsteps by winning it himself a year later. The wireless, parked high on a shelf where only adults can reach the on/off knob, is the most prized item in the house.

I love listening to Michael O'Hehir's famous Gaelic football commentaries on Sunday afternoon, so much so that I start to mimic his voice, much to the annoyance of my siblings. I'm forced into the toilet – the only quiet sanctuary in the busy house – to continue my imagined commentary. When I roar that a goal has been scored and I extend the last syllable to the point of exhaustion, the toilet at 71 Woodland Park is transformed into the commentary box at Croke Park, with 80,000 spectators roaring approval.

By 1958 a couple of families in Woodland Park own televisions and I am invited by those neighbours who own one to join their children and watch some TV with them. I know they are lovely children and that my mother so wants me to be their friend. However, watching *Andy Pandy* and *Bill and Ben the Flower Pot Men*, having just come home from a tough day at primary school, is far from an inspiring half-hour. But when *The Lone Ranger* comes onto the black-and-white screen I never want to leave their house. 'Can we get a TV of our own?' I venture to ask my mother. Her answer is always the same: 'When your father stays out of Rainey's.'

My older brothers are becoming really good Gaelic players – initially for Kilrea and now for County Derry senior team. Leo is younger than Gerry by a couple of years, yet at only eighteen he is still good enough to play for a top-notch County Derry senior team. I am six years old but incredibly proud that my brother is so good at Gaelic. Derry win the Ulster title, which means they are in the semi-final of the coveted All-Ireland Gaelic football championship to decide the best team in the whole of Ireland.

They play and beat Kerry in the semi-final, which means that they will contest the All-Ireland final against Dublin in Croke Park in September. Leo has played very well and, although he is youngest in the squad by a long stretch, his semi-final performance should keep him in the team for the final. My mother and father decide that I can go and watch him play in Dublin. This is momentous, the single greatest thing to happen to me in my short life. I will leave with my mother on a bus from Kilrea Diamond before sunrise to make the six-hour journey to Dublin.

My father, in time-honoured Irish fashion, is not making the journey with us. He will still be going to the match but prefers the company of his cronies, who will have been well fed and watered last night in Dempsey's pub before being driven in the comfort of a car to Dublin rather than suffering the bumpy and cold ride to Ireland's capital city on a fifty-seater bus. Thomas Hardy would have a field day with such characters if he had chosen to live a couple of years in Ireland rather than in Dorset.

Despite the bumps and lack of heating, the trip turns out to be a wonderful experience. A few girls get on in Maghera, our first stop en route from Kilrea. They settle in immediately and begin a joyous sing-song that takes us through some counties of Ireland. The driver drops us off at what seems quite a long distance from the stadium and, since I'm a big boy now at six and a half, I don't want to hold my mother's outstretched hand as we walk along a canal getting closer to Croke Park Stadium.

My mother lifts me up and carries me over the turnstile. We take our seats behind one of the goals in the Nally Stand. At the moment there are quite a few empty seats, and I think this is strange since I definitely overheard my brothers and father talking about the stadium being jam-packed with people for Sunday's game. My mother tells me that we have arrived early and that the stand will soon fill up. We find our seats and I sit down in full expectation that Derry will beat Dublin and Leo will be brilliant. This might be the first time in my life that I find things don't always work out the way I want them to.

A man with crooked yellow teeth comes to claim the empty place beside my mother. He is very pleasant to us, but he's not going to give up his seat for anyone and so I will watch the hour-long game on my mother's lap. When the Artane Boys' Band leads the two teams round the pitch in the famous GAA ritual, I sense the atmosphere lift, cheers get louder around me and people rise to their feet in glorious anticipation of the unfolding main event.

My brother is not playing. He is a substitute, and I do not know whether he knew this some days ago. If it was known in advance, my family never told me about it. 'Where is Leo? Where is Leo?' I pester my mother. Being small, I can't really see the game and am never sure whether a point has been scored or not. 'He'll soon get on,' she assures me, and I content myself with that answer and go back to trying to follow the game from my restricted vantage point. Derry lose the match.

There is disappointment at every turn. But there are certain things I will never forget.

Croke Park is the most magnificent building I've ever seen; the football pitch is epically long and the grass looks so lush and inviting. The electric atmosphere within the stadium itself entrances me, and when the referee throws the ball in to start the game there is not an empty seat to be had.

The bus journey home after the defeat is even longer. The girls from Maghera still sing but their voices are much more subdued. I realize the impact of defeat. I tell my mother that – when I grow up – I want to play for Derry and win the All-Ireland final.

Growing up in Kilrea is easy. I have my older sister by three years, Breedge, to look after me, and two younger brothers, Owen and Shane, to play with. What could be more idyllic? Our primary school, a long distance away when you are six years old, is Catholic boys only. The convent on the other side of town is for girls. Integration comes only at Sunday Mass and, even then, only fleetingly.

We live harmoniously with our Protestant neighbours. Mrs Boyd next door is particularly pleasant and helpful. She has two sons of her own, slightly older than me. Although at different schools, we are very good friends.

Mr McCotter, two houses away, invites me and my brothers to watch the 1958 World Cup final in his home. Curtains are pulled closed to keep sunlight from shining directly onto the television. Brazil, with a young seventeen-year-old called Pelé scoring two goals, beat Sweden in Stockholm to become world champions. We have a good-sized garden at the back and side of our house. Football and cricket are our seasonal sports and sometimes I imagine myself in Pelé's place, the vagaries of the game as yet unknown to me. When we get our own television, the FA Cup final is an unmissable event, Wolves beating Blackburn Rovers being the first one in 1960. We roar at the television in unison.

As is the case with most Catholic families, the evening rosary is a must. My mother would feel that accidents would befall us if we didn't kneel down in the living room and take up positions with faces pressed into settees or chairs, and rosary beads gripped in our hands. If not, then Hail Marys are to be counted on our fingers and prayer books are open in front of us.

Although the rosary only takes about fifteen minutes to recite, it's a long time for a young lad to remain solemn, so occasionally I will pull *The Victor* comic from behind the prayer book, make sure no one is watching me, and start to read what is for me the best football story ever invented. 'The Goalmaker' is about a footballer called Pickford. He is a brilliant player but there is something decidedly strange about him. He seems to have a connection with players and games of a bygone era, which suggest a ghostly figure. This makes for compelling reading, at least for an eight-year-old.

I see less of my sister Mary at home, as she is still boarding at Loretta Convent, Coleraine. It's only about fifteen miles from our home, but she wants to study hard. My mother, a driving force who desires – no, demands it even – that we are all well educated, grants her wish, saying that we will just have to find the boarding fees from somewhere. And regardless of my father's flutters in Rainey's during the middle of the week, he works all hours on Saturday to earn the money.

We see Mary when she comes home, particularly for

Christmas and summer holidays. She has a pen pal in France, and the young girl announces that she wants to come and visit Mary at our home. We are in a bit of a panic because we don't have time to build an extra bedroom just for Marie-Claire with three weeks' notice until her arrival. We are also convinced that she lives in a grand château, so there is a natural concern that she may not find our three-bed semi to her taste. To make space, all us brothers crowd into one room. We manage in the end, but I'm not sure sleeping upside down on the bed with my brothers' toes poking into my nose could be construed as anything other than a health hazard.

My older brothers invite me to watch them play Gaelic seven-a-side matches at townland carnivals during the summer months. Kilrea are terrific in these competitions and so are asked many times to participate. The matches are a big attraction for the people, but so too are the carnivals themselves, each one lasting at least four or five days. The long summer evenings – with football games being played until sunset against a backdrop of children on carousels, and fairground bulbs lighting up the night sky – make for a magical scene. I watch my brothers change into football gear in the car, the shirts still sweaty from last evening's victories over Newbridge and Bellaghy, getting ready to play the final against Ballerin. They win. It's a wonderful ride back home.

I am nine years old and my brother Gerry arrives home from university in Belfast with a tennis ball in his hand. He tells me that he has just read that the magnificent Hungarian footballer Ferenc Puskás, who scored four goals in the European Cup final for Real Madrid in last year's 7–3 victory over Eintracht Frankfurt, practised incessantly with a tennis ball when a young boy. He could keep the tennis ball up on his feet 200 times without it falling to the ground.

He throws the tennis ball to me and says that by the time he comes home again for Christmas, I must be able to perform this feat, just like Puskás had done. I take the tennis ball and try this exercise immediately; the ball falls away before I get to seven. I keep trying all day. Rosary time, I now have a prayer book, *The Victor* and a tennis ball in front of me as I recite my ten Hail Marys to the rest of the family.

When Gerry and Leo arrive home for Christmas, I take both out to the garden and compose myself. The ball falls away before I get to fifty keepy-ups. 'Wait, I can do this!' I say. By the third attempt I sail past 200 times without the tennis ball hitting the ground. My brothers are astounded. That's it, settled. I'm going to be as good as Puskás.

I am two years away from the Eleven-Plus examinations. My older sister Agatha is now one of four teachers at a school in Rasharkin, a village about three or four miles away. Agatha says that the headmaster of her school, Pat McAleese, is a tough cookie but a brilliant teacher and that my chances of passing the Eleven-Plus would be greatly enhanced under his tutelage. So I leave my Kilrea school friends, travel with my sister to Rasharkin and effectively start a new school life. I admit it takes me more than a little while to settle there, but it is a mixed-sex school and I get to see what girls of my age are really like. I'm painfully shy amongst them and it's Halloween before they realize I can actually talk.

I pass the Eleven-Plus and as a consequence obtain a scholarship for grammar school at St Columb's College, Derry. There is a new school opening in Maghera, nine miles from Kilrea, but my mother is having none of it, even though I would be at home every evening. It's boarding at St Columb's College for me, a respected institution which counts the poet Seamus Heaney and Nobel Prize laureate John Hume as alumni. The two years spent at Rasharkin have not been wasted and my passing of the Eleven-Plus gives me an air of misguided superiority. My brothers have been to St Columb's and have done exceptionally well. Now it's my turn and I'm excited by the prospect.

It is September 1963. My hair is cut so short by my father that I will not need another trim until I'm back for Halloween. I am driven the forty miles to the college. I'm in one of sixty cubicles in a large dormitory with students aged between eleven and fifteen. But tonight I want to go home. All the excitement of the summer, unable to wait to get here, has left me completely drained. I think of the boys going to Maghera school. They'll be home every evening and have a chance to play with their siblings before home-work beckons them inside their own house. None of this for me.

When classes start, we take our places in old tin huts that have housed students for years and years. I find out quickly that I'm not as clever as I thought I was. All thirty of us have passed the same Eleven-Plus and most of the others are far smarter than me. We play Gaelic football at the college and soccer is only played at lunchtime, when the day-boys join in, or in the late afternoons when classes are over and only the boarders remain.

Sunderland have become my team. They have two Irish play-ers. Charlie Hurley, my hero, is a brilliant centre half and the heartbeat of the team. The other is a gifted inside forward called Johnny Crossan, who comes from Derry City, not far from St Columb's College. Unfortunately, Sunderland's centre forward, a goal-scoring machine, is making slow progress from a career-threatening injury sustained on Boxing Day 1962, which effectively stops Sunderland being promoted to the First Division later that season. I will meet this very player later on in my life. His name is Brian Clough.

In 1964, Sunderland, in the Second Division, have drawn 3–3 at Old Trafford in the quarter-finals of the FA Cup. The replay at Roker Park is also a draw, 2–2 after extra time. The second replay is set for Leeds Road, Huddersfield. I need to listen to the game, so I ask one of my day-boy classmates if he can lend me his little crystal radio set. He duly obliges and I hide it under my pillow – with crystal sets not being allowed – waiting for night prayers to end and then up to bed.

Lights out. Silence. By the time I get to switch it on, at very low volume, I cannot believe the score. Manchester United are leading 5–1 with little time left. I am heartbroken. I know Manchester

United from the First Division are expected to beat a Second Division side, but this is Sunderland, with Hurley, Jimmy Montgomery and Nick Sharkey all playing tonight. Just when the evening cannot possibly get any worse, the dean of the college, who is on the prowl, walks into my cubicle, and I am not quick enough to hide the little crystal radio set under my pillow. He takes it off me and tells me to report to his room the next morning.

I receive six slaps with a leather belt, have the crystal set confiscated and lose all my privileges until the end of term. I have to give my classmate whatever pocket money I have left to pay for a new radio set. I don't have enough, but he's my best friend.

It has been a terrible evening and a miserable morning. My twelfth birthday was only a few days ago and my hands are still stinging like crazy well into morning classes. But Charlie Hurley must be feeling even worse than me this morning, although I bet his hands aren't as sore as mine. But there is a happy ending. Sunderland regain their poise and Charlie leads them back into the First Division a few months later. And at the end of the summer term, the dean calls me to his room and gives me back the crystal set, accompanied by stern warnings about my behaviour. Sunderland are in the big league and all is well with the world. Some years later, Charlie Hurley will be voted Sunderland player of the century by the fans. Now that's a real honour.

My class, Junior 1B, is crammed with academically bright boys. I think I am reasonably intelligent, but I abhor science. I cannot understand it for love nor money. Experiment time in Father McCarron's classroom. We are divided into groups of four or five. Those budding scientists, destined for future greatness in this field, cannot wait to fill the lab test tubes with all manner of chemicals. My sole job is to light the Bunsen burner without blowing the classroom to smithereens. Even this task is taken away from me after a vote of no confidence is passed by the other lads in my group.

The laboratory is still in one piece when I leave the double science class, and to me that's a victory of sorts. But when Father McCarron asks me two days later to explain what went on in the experiment, I haven't a clue. I refrain from telling him that I have no intention of donning a white coat in my future years and that my talents lie in English, geography and Irish history. He wouldn't care anyway, and instead he produces the strap for my non-attention to his experiments. Strangely, Father McCarron also takes our class for art lessons. I'm extremely good at art and remarkably Father McCarron is extremely pleasant to me in art class. Perhaps he doesn't recognize me as the same person as from science class.

It's apparent pretty quickly that I'm an excellent footballer – Gaelic for my class team and soccer on the junior pitch. And several other classmates are too. I've become good friends with a boy called Raymond White, a couple of months older than me and a day-boy at the school. He is very bright and also very good at football – soccer and Gaelic. A couple of years from now he will go to Nottingham Forest for some trials, but his heart is set on the medical world and he will become an eminent doctor in Northern Ireland. Just now, not only is he the class captain in football, but he can also easily answer all the science questions posed to him by our grumpy teacher, Father McCarron.

The college, austere and foreboding, overlooks part of Derry City, including the soccer stadium, called the Brandywell. We boarders can see it from our vantage point and I fall in love with the football club. The stanchions holding up the nets behind the goalposts are arched, just like I have seen when Barcelona and Real Madrid are playing, and that in itself is something to behold. Derry City have a very fine team and we see the flood-lights on as they embark on some European Cup games, having won the Irish Cup.

Boarders do not get to watch television, except for the Satur-day teleprinter churning out football results from England and Scotland. The Rolling Stones are vying with the Beatles for popularity among us, but I'm transfixed by the Kinks record 'You

Really Got Me'. I want to grow my hair long, straighten it and part it down the middle, just like Dave Davies. In fact, I want to be in their band. Surely I can be a professional footballer with Sunderland and a third guitarist with the Kinks at the same time? Then the Searchers come out with 'When You Walk in the Room' and I think maybe I could join them also. There is a lot going through my twelve-year-old mind.

The year 1965 is an eventful one for St Columb's College. The under-19 All-Ireland college final is won by us. The team have been brilliant the whole year long and the players in the squad are idolized in the college. Father McQuillan is our trainer and mentor, and he is revered by us. He gets his just rewards when the team beat Belcamp, a college outside Dublin, to win this coveted Gaelic trophy. Bus after bus, juniors and seniors, day-boys and the boarders are all there to support the college team, who have brought such unbridled joy to us all. We owe these players everything.

A free day is called by the president of St Columb's, and I'm particularly delighted because I will miss a double period of science. The college basks in reflected glory, but I am also enjoying a little success myself. I play for the school under-15 team and we win the Ulster colleges Corn na nÓg – the Schools Cup – in two successive years, in the second of which I become captain.

The college can be stern and unsmiling, especially on mid-January days, and there is no doubt I could use study time – and there's plenty of that – much more beneficially than I do. But I love football, both soccer and Gaelic, and even in soggy trousers there's simply nothing like rounding two players and placing the ball between the coats and schoolbags being used for goalposts. Celtic's European Cup victory in 1967 only further whets my appetite to become a professional footballer and I make this an ambition that I need to fulfil.

Meanwhile, my mother harbours a long-held dream to move back to Belfast. When she and my father got married they spent some time living there, and she always maintains this was a special time in her life. Maybe she wants to relive some of those lovely moments. Maybe she thinks it will offer more opportunities for her children. Maybe she just misses us not being at home with her all the time because by now my two younger brothers, Owen and Shane, having passed the Eleven-Plus themselves, are with me at St Columb's. We now have a room of our own together in the college and it is Shane's job, as the youngest of the trio, to take the dead mice out of the trap in our bedroom. But come summer of 1968, my mother's mind is made up and we will soon leave rural Kilrea behind for the bustle of Northern Ireland's capital city.

I'm given a place at St Malachy's College, Belfast, to start my A-levels. It's walking distance from my parents' house to the college. And although I'm shy and concerned about meeting new classmates, there is something liberating about being at home in the evenings with my sisters and brothers.

The summer has been full of brilliant songs in the charts. Cupid's Inspiration, a one-hit wonder, have a big song with 'Yesterday Has Gone', which definitely resonates with me just now, and by mid-September 'Those Were the Days' by Mary Hopkins has taken the number one spot from 'Hey Jude' by the Beatles.

In French class I sit behind a young lad sporting a pair of outsized glasses. The average age of our group is sixteen years old. Geoffrey Waters has just turned fourteen. He is a genius. He passed the Eleven-Plus when he was eight years old, but he is no boastful character. A complete chatterbox, he never stops talking to me. I need to listen to what the teacher is going on about as my French needs a great deal of polishing. But Geoffrey insists on talking, even when the teacher is reading a passage from Molière.

He cannot possibly have heard any utterings from the teacher in the last few minutes, so engrossed has he been in his conversation with a very distressed me.

'Waters,' shouts the teacher, 'you haven't been listening to a word I've said, have you?'

'Yes sir, I have.'

'Well, repeat what I've just said, then.'

Geoffrey proceeds to repeat, word for word, everything uttered by the teacher. Astonishing!

I think I need to sit beside someone of my own French capability rather than this loquacious genius. Later on in my life, when managers are handed this moniker of being a 'genius' when what they have actually done is to mastermind a corner-kick routine to score a goal, I often think of Geoffrey Waters.

I soon make friends. Many Belfast lads, like the Derry City boys, are academically clever and talented footballers as well, both in soccer and Gaelic. I join the school Gaelic team and, outside school hours, I join Rosario Club, playing soccer in the Down and Connor league.

One of the teachers at St Malachy's is Phil Stuart, a university colleague of my two older brothers and a very fine Gaelic footballer in his time. He gets to hear that I am at the school and I discover that we share the same big ambitions for the college football team. He has a really good team at his disposal. My younger brother, Owen Roe, only fifteen years old, is our goal-scoring starlet. We embark on an amazing journey throughout the year, winning game after game, until the final of the Ulster Colleges is reached. Our success has reverberated around the school; even those students with no apparent interest in Gaelic football become curious as to the goings-on. We win the McCrory Cup and the ultimate prize, the Hogan Cup, is within our grasp. This is the trophy that St Columb's won a few years ago to huge acclaim.

Bus after bus pulls away from College Avenue to head to Croke Park Dublin, in scenes so reminiscent of those at St Columb's College in 1965. Only this time I am not going to support the team, I'm playing in it. We know we can win against Coláiste Chríost Rí from Cork City. And our football today is breathtakingly brilliant. However, our opponents – to their credit – hang tough when seemingly overwhelmed, and they score a last-minute goal to win the game. It is heartbreaking for us players, the coach, and for the students who have followed our progress. It remains one of the biggest sporting disappointments of my life.

That summer I am invited back to Kilrea by the local priest Father Deery to play under-18 Gaelic football for his team. I'm also playing for the Derry County under-18 team and soccer for Rosario Youth Club in Belfast, so I'm constantly flitting back and forth. Forty miles there, forty miles back to Belfast amounts to almost a whole day travelling, but the football is far too enjoyable to miss.

On one occasion, Kilrea holds its carnival on the outskirts of the town. By chance I meet a young girl there. I have never seen her before, although that's hardly surprising; I have spent very little time in the town since I was eleven years old. She is achingly beautiful and asking her name is as much as I can muster. She's called Geraldine McGrath, and our conversation is not long before she is drawn away by her friends to the dodgem cars. Transfixed, I watch her walk off into the night before being jolted back to reality, realizing my bus back to Belfast is leaving in ten minutes. Little do I know, she will one day be my wife.

Back in Belfast, I'm doing very well for Rosario Youth Club. I'm picked for the Down and Connor select team to play Dublin, the game being a prestigious event in the calendar. I score three goals as we win 7–3 and I'm in dreamland. This game is usually watched by Irish league scouts and you never know, something might come of it. And it does.

There is a knock on the door. My sister Roisin answers it.

'Are your mother and father in?' asks the caller.

'Yes, I'll get them,' answers my sister.

My mother asks the visitor who he is. He says he is Jimmy

McAlinden, the manager of Distillery Football Club, and he would like for her son, Martin, to come to the club for a trial. He wants to know if I'm in the house.

Soon tea and biscuits are laid out in the front room for Mr McAlinden and I am privileged that the manager himself has come over to the other side of Belfast to personally ask me to come to Grosvenor Park, the home of Distillery. I cannot wait. From what he has been told by his scout, who was watching me against the Dublin team, he thinks he can help make me a proper player.

And so the following Tuesday evening I take a bus down to the city centre and decide to walk to Grosvenor Park. The distance is a bit further than I thought, so I run the last quarter-mile to be on time. I knock on the players' entrance door to be greeted by an oldish man called Armstrong. I soon find out that he is the physiotherapist and also the kit man – or is it that the kit man is also the physiotherapist? I tell him that Mr McAlinden has invited me here tonight, and the little frown that I think I detected on his face transforms into a welcoming smile.

He accompanies me to McAlinden's office, knocks, obeys the call to 'come in' and hands me over to the boss.

'Great, son, you're here. You need to sign these amateur forms for us.' I do this willingly and with that he says, 'Get changed and we'll see you outside.'

Now I'm in a dressing room full of young hopefuls. The first team are down the corridor but a million miles away. I recognize one or two of them as they walk past me out the tunnel to the pitch. They will start their warm-up in full view of the rest of us, and we will start ours a little later. I so want to be in that first team.

I am picked to play on Saturday afternoon for the reserves, and told to report to some pitch in East Belfast for half past one. This means I have to get two buses, one to the city centre and then another one out to wherever. When Saturday comes, I am frantically running round the City Hall looking for the elusive second bus. I get to the ground at two o'clock. Dick Williams, the reserve team coach, is obviously not impressed but he squeezes me onto the team – only, I find out later, because Jimmy McAlinden has insisted I play.

By half-time, Dick is wondering what all the fuss is about. So too, I believe, are my teammates, and if truth be known I'm not sure myself. I haven't had a kick. The second half improves, but only marginally, and it's almost a relief when Dick hauls me off with fifteen minutes to go. What's worse, we score twice in the last few minutes to win 2–1 while I'm watching from the sidelines.

Heaven knows what sort of report Dick will give to Jimmy but it certainly won't be flattering.

I improve on my second outing and I'm even better in my third. I'm even brought into a small group who will play five-a-side with the first team on some Thursday evenings in a school gymnasium at the back of Grosvenor Park. This is an eye-opener for me. The games are played with an intensity I haven't yet witnessed. The first-team players look in a different class, and the little winger, George Lennox, is tantalizingly brilliant in these games.

But Jimmy McAlinden has a lot of faith in me. He has been an excellent player himself in the English game, and an FA Cup winner with Portsmouth. He is an exceptionally shrewd man, both in the footballing world and in normal life. He constantly tells me that I'm going to make the grade in England which, coming from him, gives me an enormous boost of confidence.

One Thursday evening after training, he tells me that I will be travelling to Portadown with the Distillery first team and I will play on Saturday. I will play with Peter Watson, Alan McCarroll, Peter Rafferty, Martin Donnelly, Mervyn Law, Tommy Brannigan, George Lennox, Derek Meldrum, Jim Savage, Roy McDonald and Joe Patterson against Portadown. So soon? And I haven't been that hot in the reserves. Still, I think, I'm not missing this, not for the world. And I don't. I play really well, scoring as we win 3–2.

The players treat me better than I could ever have imagined. Yes, they laugh at my inability to tackle properly, being from a Gaelic background, but the manager has fostered an almost unbreakable bond between these lads that shows so clearly on the field. The team is made up of Protestants and Catholics, but politics is not up for discussion when the players meet twice weekly for training. And when matches begin, Martin Donnelly from the Falls Road would die for Alan McCarroll from the Shankill Road, and the reverse is absolutely true.

We start with an Irish Cup run that leads us to the final. It's April 1971. We will play Derry City at Windsor Park. And who will line up against me for the Derry City team? My great friend Raymond White from St Columb's.

The crowd is sparse. The Troubles are decimating Ulster just now and Derry City fans, with their largely Nationalist background, aren't travelling in numbers to Windsor Park, Linfield's stomping ground, so only 6,000 people turn up, even though this is a cup final.

But I do not care. I want to win the Irish Cup, for myself, my teammates and naturally for Jimmy McAlinden. I play superbly, score two goals, and we win 3–0. The Irish Cup is ours and with it the opportunity to play in next season's European Cup Winners' Cup. It's a monumental day for Distillery and a big, big day for me as well.

Back at St Malachy's College, I am greeted with warm applause from my Latin classmates first thing on Monday morning. In a few weeks I'll leave the college and head to Queen's University to study law. But I've turned nineteen and there's a widely held view that if you haven't played in the First Division by now, your chances of making the big time in professional football may be running out. My mother is keen for me to complete my law degree. I know I'll be too old by that time to make the grade but I say nothing.

The draw comes out for the European Cup Winners' Cup. We have a two-legged tie against Barcelona. What about that? It's my big chance to shine. If I do well against them then, surely, I'll be transferred to England, to the First Division.

I score against them in the first leg, although we lose 3–1. The trip to Barcelona is unforgettable. I really get to know the senior players and luckily my pal Raymond White, who has transferred to Distillery, is on the three-day excursion with us to Camp Nou. We enjoy each other's company and the camaraderie is stronger than ever. We lose the game simply because Barcelona are far superior to us, but my experiences with this group of players are something I remember whenever I want to smile at life. I will leave them in a couple of weeks to start a career in England, but they belong in my soul and I'm richer in spirit for having known them.

2

ENGLAND BECKONS

The old Viscount trundles along the runway of Aldergrove Airport, picks up speed and, before I can finish my second Hail Mary, raises itself into the early morning mist, turns in an unsettling arc and drones skywards.

The shimmering lights of Belfast, wakening from another night of shootings, appear intermittently between the grey clouds. The plane shudders as it passes through those heavy billows, straining every sinew to see clear morning light. Then, just when I think that my second journey on an aeroplane will be my last, the sky yawns open and the horizon leaps out. I am leaving Belfast and trouble-torn Northern Ireland behind. The northwest coastline of England is only half an hour away. A professional life awaits me there. A professional footballer's life. This day I'll never forget. It is 20 October 1971. I am nineteen years old.

The fields of England look just like the fields in Ireland, just as green, as I peer out through the window during the last few minutes of the flight into East Midlands Airport. Sitting beside me on the plane is my Distillery manager, Jimmy McAlinden, who has volunteered to accompany me to help scrutinize my contract with Nottingham Forest. He wants me to sign as long a contract as possible, to give me, in his own words, 'some breathing space', in case things don't go well early on. On the face of it, it's not overly inspiring to hear these words of caution from him, but he's been in the game a long time, and he wants the best for me, so I take his advice in the spirit it is meant.

The plane seems to fly dangerously close to the tall chimneys of the power station situated close to the runway, but the landing is as smooth as you could wish. Within minutes we are in the arrival lounge of the rather small airport, strategically placed to accommodate both Nottingham and Derby citizens.

The Nottingham Forest manager, Matt Gillies, is here to greet us. His assistant, a portly gentleman called Bill Anderson, is in tow. Matt greets Jimmy like a long-lost friend, well aware of the latter's excellent footballing career in England.

We climb into Bill's gold-coloured car. Matt is in the passenger seat and Jimmy and I are in the back as we pull away from the airport and head off on the fifteen-mile journey to the City Ground. There's a gentle sadness to Matt's face as he half turns to talk to us. Nottingham Forest are in deep trouble in the First Division, sitting alongside Huddersfield and Crystal Palace at the bottom of the table. He is extremely well spoken, which contrasts with the rather gruff voice of Bill Anderson, who agrees with him on all things football. Last Saturday, Forest lost 3–2 at home to Liverpool. It was disappointing, if not entirely unexpected. Considering I am in the back seat, Matt is quite rightly guarded when talking about his players, but he is very effusive in his praise of his winger, Ian Storey-Moore, who continues to shine, even in the middle of the team's struggle.

I feel as if I know Storey-Moore. Even his double-barrelled surname rings of nobility. He came into my consciousness when scoring a hat-trick against Everton in the FA Cup quarter-final in that glorious 1966/67 season, when Forest went so close both in the FA Cup and the league, which was eventually won by Manchester United. As Matt talks about him, I'm there in my mind with him, both of us turning the season round and beating Manchester United at Wembley in the FA Cup final. Reality sets in rather too quickly, as Matt tells Jimmy that the first team are at White Hart Lane on Saturday. It will be a very difficult game for his men.

We pass the power station on the left and we are soon on the outskirts of the city. Bill Anderson tells us that the Clifton Estate on our right is the largest council housing estate in Britain. We obviously don't yet know that a young lad from this very estate will, in the not-too-distant future, carve out for himself a place in Forest's history books. But at this very moment Viv Anderson is sitting in a school classroom, unaware of the stellar career that awaits him.

As the car turns left off Wilford Lane, I see the floodlights rising, almost imperiously, above the terraced houses, overseeing this extremely pleasant part of the city. Trent Bridge, home of Nottinghamshire Cricket Club and its historic Test match arena, is parked to my right, and Meadow Lane, home to Notts County, the oldest league club in the world, is just across the River Trent. This morning the two clubs are separated by three divisions, although there is a strong possibility that, come May, that may be only one. County are flying high just now and Forest are obviously in a precarious place.

None of that matters to me on this bright October morning as Bill's car comes to a halt in the car park of the City Ground. The tubby assistant manager seems as excited as I am as he takes me inside the ground, through a corridor and left at its end.

'This is the away team dressing room on match days, and you will change here every morning with the other lads your age.' And, just to remind me that this football life is not all plain sailing, he points to the first-team dressing room, only a few yards down the corridor.

'That's your first big aim,' he says in his gruff but affectionate voice. 'Get into that dressing room as quickly as you can.'

The holy grail, the first-team dressing room, stares out onto the tunnel as we walk onto the pitch. The stadium is empty save for the groundsman, who is doing some repair work at the Bridgford End, but it is truly an evocative arena. It is not a strain to look left at the Trent End and see in one's mind's eye Storey-Moore heading past Gordon West for his hat-trick to win the FA Cup quarter-final against Everton in April 1967. That was only four and a half years ago. The pitch invasion, the players lauded like demigods, the whole stadium swamped with adoring fans. What a day that must have been. What has happened since? Why the decline, why the descent into disarray?

The fire in the main stand in 1968 certainly hasn't helped, forcing Forest to play home games at Meadow Lane. Perhaps the players have grown old together too quickly. This morning I have no proper grasp of the real reasons why. I can only make unqualified assumptions.

All too soon I am sitting in the manager's office. Jimmy leads me into a vacant room next door and shows me the two-year contract. They will pay me £45 per week until 30 June 1973 – and then there's another two-year option, which benefits the club, until 30 June 1975. The club can either continue the contract on the same terms or, if things don't go well for me, let me go at the end of 1973. A first-team bonus sheet is attached, and that's it, save for a one-off £250 bonus per season, to be paid if I get one international cap each year. I'm not sure that Jimmy's idea of a long contract correlates with my own, but he gave me my break at Distillery, and he's shown confidence in me right from the start. So when Jimmy says, in the most reassuring voice imaginable, 'They'll be offering you a new deal long before this contract runs out', I sign the four documents in front of me. One is given back to me in a white envelope, and I thank Jimmy for all he has done for me in the last twelve months.

Matt has asked first-team defender Liam O'Kane – who is from my neck of the woods, growing up and starting his career in Derry – to come down to the ground to welcome me to the club and essentially look after me for the rest of the day. Wednesday is the first-team players' day off, and I'm not sure having to chaperone me is how Liam wants to spend it. However, he arrives, and I spend the rest of the day with him, having met him the previous week when I was ushered into the Northern Ireland squad against Russia.

Lunch with Liam and his wife, Marie, a trip to watch the youth team play in the afternoon and dinner back at Liam's house mean that I'm much later checking into my lodgings on Henry Road than I planned. In fact, it's eleven o'clock at night when I finally knock on the door. The irate landlord refuses to let me in before Liam persuades him to do otherwise. I naturally apologize to the landlord but feel his behaviour much too petty for my liking. All he has to do is show me to my bedroom and tell me what time in the morning breakfast is being served. But he won't let it go. I can stay tonight, under sufferance, but I will have to find somewhere else to get lodgings tomorrow, he tells me.

This doorstep haranguing attracts the attention of another lodger, a footballer like me, aiming to get into the first team: Seamus McDowell from Derry City. He has been staying with the landlord, and seemingly on good terms with him, for quite some time. Seamus comes to the door, has the whole commotion explained to him, and then says that if I'm not allowed to stay permanently at this abode, he will also leave in the morning. At the same time, we introduce ourselves to each other. The landlord, becoming more bellicose by the minute, accepts Seamus's offer to leave, closes the door and points me in the direction of my room, telling me the door is open. I call over to Seamus that his actions are warmly felt but well beyond the call of duty. Nevertheless, the morning sees us both walking the half-mile from Henry Road to the City Ground, with suitcases and bags in arms and over shoulders.

Bill Anderson soon gets to hear about last night's debacle and is none too happy about my lateness in arriving at the digs. I am given temporary reprieve at a comfortable bed-and-breakfast, situated near the cricket ground, called the Talbot House Hotel. Seamus, who has only just signed professional terms for the club and is considered a long way off Forest team selection just now, is shunted off to a large room above McKay's Café, which houses quite a number of labourers from all parts of the country. I feel guilty and ask to join Seamus at this none-too-luxurious accommodation, if only because he gave up his comfortable house to take the side of a lad he had never met before.

Within a few days I'm in residence above McKay's Café, in a room – essentially a converted attic – with Seamus and another ten guys, much older than us, who rise much earlier than we do and arrive back at their digs much later than we do. They spend the night chatting about their respective jobs and at the weekend, if they don't go back home, spend the early hours of the morning detailing their conquests of some hours before. Nottingham, I'm told early on, is a city with five girls to every fellow, so the chances of them getting hitched with someone, at least for the evening, are, I surmise, reasonably decent. Even so, I'm not convinced that their bawdy stories – told to each other at four o'clock on a Sunday morning – ring completely true. Some of these men have, in all honesty, not been introduced to a bar of soap in a week. So if these stories have a semblance of truth then Seamus and I feel that we must have a chance ourselves of finding a girlfriend, because we have not only washed, but also have a little aftershave to hand.

I have been at the club less than twenty-four hours. Bill Anderson, as he tends to do when under some stress, reaches for his breast pocket and produces an outsize handkerchief to wipe some beads of sweat from his brow. If my affair at the Henry Road landlord's house is causing him to perspire, heaven knows what Saturday at White Hart Lane might do to him.

Regardless, he brings me into the reserve team dressing room and introduces me to the players. Most of these lads are my age, perhaps a year or eighteen months older, one or two are a little younger. In fact, John Robertson, almost a complete year younger than me, came on as a substitute last Saturday against Liverpool and may well start the game this coming weekend against Tottenham Hotspur.

Robertson is an interesting character. A young Scotsman from the outskirts of Glasgow, he has been at the club since he was fifteen years old. He is a very talented centre midfield player, with two really good feet, and can spray passes all over the pitch. Robertson is extremely well thought of at the club and a player of much promise. He is also extremely popular in this dressing room, despite the fact that he seems to have plenty to say for himself. All this I glean from my first fifteen minutes in the changing room on 21 October 1971. The introductions finished, Bill departs and I put on my Nottingham Forest training gear, with the number 10 sewn into the shirt and tracksuit. This will be my training number for the next decade. I am acutely self-conscious of the large birthmark over my right shoulder, and keep my back to the wall when disrobing. But they will spot it eventually after training when we jump into the communal bath adjacent to the dressing room. I suppose I will have to endure the almost endless ribbing I received from the Distillery players, who seemed to find continuous mirth at my expense.

Robertson is, as expected, called up to join the first team, but we will, as reserves, get the chance to walk down the riverbank with the first-team players to the training ground, and I get my first glimpse of Ian Storey-Moore as he saunters down in the group ahead.

As well as Robertson, a couple of the other young players have tasted some first-team action, I soon discover. Graham Collier, about twenty years old, and Jimmy McIntosh, of a similar age, have both started in the first team. Collier is a tall, very elegant midfield player, who figured last season for a consecutive spell of games but has been cold-shouldered of late. He befriends me on the walk, naturally asking me what position I play. He smiles when I tell him that I think I'm a centre forward, the smile suggesting that I should know what I am rather than thinking it. More in cynicism than outright rancour, he tells me about his own position at the club, feeling that he's been hard done by this season. He's the first person to point out to me that football, with all its adversities, can be a very unfair business to be in. His own words, 'The game's bent', concern me.

I am nervous this morning. The ball seems no bigger than a

tennis ball and I seem to be exaggerating my first touch when having to control it. Frank Knight, the second team coach, is sympathetic in a rather unsympathetic way. 'Don't worry, son, about that pass, I'm sure things will improve.'

Remarkably, they actually do. I dribble round two players but drive the ball into the side netting. It's the dribble rather than the shot that draws some admiration from the players. Not excessively impressive, I admit, but not a complete disaster either. However, I'm still dreading the communal bath in the next twenty minutes.

Back in the dressing room, 'Maggie May' is being belted out by some of the lads. The record, sung by Rod Stewart, blond-haired and husky-voiced, is currently riding high in the charts. Rod has become the lead singer of the Faces now that Steve Marriott has left for a band called Humble Pie. I haven't yet forgiven Steve for leaving the Small Faces and letting Ronnie Lane, Kenney Jones and Ian McLagan to fend for themselves. But I will do in time.

Robertson, back from training with the first team, asks me if I have any interest in music. When I answer in the affirmative, he asks who my favourite bands are. Jethro Tull feature highly, but so do the Kinks, the Who, the Byrds, the Hollies and, naturally, the Small Faces. His favourite band is the Move, whom I quite like, but John knows all the band members' names. I win him over by telling him that just when it seemed as if the Move's powers were fading, they came roaring back with 'Blackberry Way' a couple of years ago. John and I are both unaware that a new band, Roxy Music, will soon burst onto the scene with 'Virginia Plain', and John will persuade a few of us to travel up and down the country to watch Bryan Ferry and his glitzy rock band perform.

It's Thursday, and John asks me if I would like to go to the Union Boat Club tonight. The Union is one of two or three boat clubs situated beside the River Trent and right behind the Trent End.

'Isn't Thursday night a bit late in the week, considering you'll probably be playing on Saturday?' I ask.

'We go down there every Thursday night. It finishes at half past ten, so we're back in our house before eleven anyway,' he responds.

'Who's "we" and what is "it"?'

'A music place where you can have a dance. A disc jockey plays some songs and it's a chance to meet some girls.'

I'm there with him that evening. Seamus McDowell – my eventual fellow lodger at McKay's Café – is also there.

We pay a few bob and walk in. Everyone knows John. He has been coming here every Thursday almost since he first came to Forest. All the girls surround him, possibly because he's an up-and-coming player or possibly because he's actually brilliant at talking to girls. On the other hand, I am painfully shy, with curly hair that I wish was straight and an accent that might not be totally understood when 'Hold Your Head Up' by Argent is blaring out over the dance floor. John introduces me to quite a number of girls, but just now I don't possess his patter and so opportunities disappear.

When the last song is played, John and Seamus seem to be doing all right, but I retreat from the dance floor, telling myself it's been a long day. I will play against Leeds Reserves at the City Ground on Saturday afternoon, and the Union will still be there next Thursday night.

Last Monday afternoon I was sitting in a hall at Queen's University listening to a lecture on jurisprudence. Four days later, I have completed my first day as a professional footballer. I have seen Ian Storey-Moore, albeit from a distance, and even though I'm aware that my £15,000 signing has not exactly made for earth-shattering news, even in the city of Nottingham, I still feel different to the lad I was just a few days ago. The signing of the contract yesterday morning has changed me. I'm not a student any longer. I now earn money. But really it's because

I'm a professional footballer, and that is what I've wanted to be since seeing the 1958 World Cup final in my neighbour's house.

I walk back to Talbot House, perhaps a little envious of John's and Seamus's good fortune. However, maybe not next Thursday, or the Thursday after that, but sometime soon, those girls at the Union will definitely want that last dance with me. The lady running Talbot House greets me at the door and asks me if I want a cup of tea before going to bed. Life back home is forgotten for a day.

Saturday afternoon arrives and I'm playing against Leeds United reserves at the City Ground. It's a sluggish start for me in front of a few thousand fans – apparently more than average for a home reserve game because of my presence. Within twenty minutes, I am elbowed in the jaw by Terry Yorath, who says something like, 'Welcome to the Football League,' although I cannot believe that Terry Yorath would even know who I am, much less know about my joining Nottingham Forest. I actually take the thump on the jaw as a backhanded compliment, particularly from Terry Yorath. By the time our game ends, news at White Hart Lane is not good. Forest have been hammered 6–1 by Tottenham Hotspur.

I am allowed to go home to Belfast on the Sunday for a few days to get some more clothes and spend a day or two with my family. I can stay until Wednesday, Bill Anderson has instructed the office girls. My knee, caught in a very late tackle, is beginning to ache somewhat, but I'm sure it will be fine for next Thursday's training session.

While I am away, the first team have a chance of redemption at Leeds Road on Tuesday night against Huddersfield. They duly take both points, with our right-winger Barry Lyons scoring the only goal. It's a massive boost and spirits at the club are lifted, at least temporarily.

Back in Belfast, I am treated royally at 5 Madison Avenue, our home, although my two younger brothers, Owen and Shane, say that nothing has changed and that I've always been spoiled anyway. But Mum and Dad are shaken by the Troubles. Seeing a way out for the family, they are now adamant that they will leave Belfast and come to Nottingham to join me as soon as possible. It's not really the news I want to hear just now. I've only been in England five days and I need some space to breathe. I've got lodgings for myself and I don't need distractions, assuming that my two sisters and at least one brother will make the journey with them. Shane, my other brother, will need to stay at St Malachy's College until completion of his O-levels. I accept that the Troubles are escalating and that Belfast is now just as dangerous in the daytime as it is in the dark. However, can't they at least wait a few months while I try to establish myself?

The last five days in Nottingham have flown by, so excitingly different have they been. I just want some independence, but if they come over, it means I will have to find and pay for a rented house for everyone, and I don't have a clue where to even start. But they are insisting. They are coming to look after me, and to flee Belfast. They'll be able to cook for me and I know I'll get the best of food as, in truth, I've always had. But I want to eat kebabs outside a Nottingham nightclub at half past two on Sunday morning, having scored the winner earlier in the afternoon against Chelsea, with the lads congratulating me and girls queuing up to be taken home by me.

When I travel back to Nottingham on Wednesday, my sister Breedge, a couple of years older than me, is my companion on the plane. She has been tasked with seeking out accommodation as quickly as possible for my parents and siblings. I acquiesce, but deep down, I'm not happy about the situation.

On the Friday evening I am playing Derby County reserves at the Baseball Ground. There are almost 10,000 supporters at the game. My knee is still sore and the only course of action is a cortisone injection about half an hour before kick-off. I hate needles, having almost passed out on every occasion I have received a jab since my early childhood. The other Forest players gather round the massage table as the doctor administers the 'medicine', taking a ghoulish interest in either the dexterity with which the doctor does his business or, more probably, my anguished face as he drives the needle into my knee. And all this for a bloody reserve game. Sadly, this will not be the last time I'll need a cortisone injection to play a game. It soon becomes part of footballing life.

Our manager, Matt Gillies, is at the match, and I can only assume Derby manager Brian Clough is also in attendance. I actually play very well in the first half, but as the injection wears off I start to struggle somewhat, nevertheless seeing it through to the end.

The next day, Forest are at home to Derby County and I will be able to watch live my first-ever First Division game. Derby are in a strong position in the league and a big crowd is expected at the City Ground.

Forest lose 2–0 and Ian Storey-Moore misses a penalty. Doom permeates the City Ground once again.

The following Tuesday morning the manager organizes a game at the City Ground. The first team versus the reserves. Essentially it's a workout for the Big Boys but it's also a chance for me to play against Storey-Moore, Bob Chapman and Peter Hindley. I play excellently, aware that these games generally give false impressions, but I score a goal after beating two or three players, forcing Storey-Moore to say to Matt Gillies, 'Hey, that's what I'm supposed to do!'

Although I'm not involved with the first team at the weekend, when Forest lose at Stamford Bridge, I am on the following Monday evening. Forest are playing a testimonial game for Jack Wheeler, a long-time servant of Notts County. I didn't expect such a quick breakthrough, but with the team results being so poor, the manager may feel that a testimonial game is an opportunity for him to see what I'm capable of.

I show him. I score in the game, do well, and I am congratulated by a number of the senior players. By Saturday afternoon, I find myself on the bench for Forest's home league game against West Bromwich Albion.

It's twenty-four days since I came to England and I'm on my way. This is happening at breakneck speed. Am I really on the first-team bench after a goal in a testimonial game? The pre-match meal at the Bridgford hotel even has me sitting beside Storey-Moore.

The game itself is getting much media attention, not because a nineteen-year-old from Northern Ireland is in the Nottingham Forest party of twelve players, but because Asa Hartford is back in a West Bromwich Albion shirt after his dream move to Leeds United broke down because he failed a medical at Elland Road. It has been detected that he has a small hole in his heart. It's enough to prevent Leeds paying the large transfer fee to WBA, but evidently not enough to prevent the lad himself from playing.

An hour has gone in the game and the score is one goal each. I have been in the dugout, listening to everything the manager is saying as he converses with his coach, Bob McKinlay. I'm naturally watching the game as well, but my glances towards the manager intensify, hoping that he'll look at me and give me a nod to warm up. And so he does.

My heart skips a beat, if truth be known, but up I get from the dugout, my head peering up over its roof, to rapturous applause from the main-stand supporters directly behind me. They don't know me, save for those who travelled across the Trent on Monday evening to watch Wheeler's testimonial game. However, I'm new, and they will naturally want to encourage me by cheering me onto the pitch. The applause gathers momentum around the stadium, and most of the 20,000 people applauding seem to be on my side. I'm on a high. This is what I have genuinely dreamed about. Yes, in my dreams, I'm wearing the red and white stripes of Sunderland, and Charlie Hurley has raced over to shake my hand as I step onto the pitch at Roker Park, but this is real life. Storey-Moore gives me the thumbs up as a welcome. It's now up to me.

Two simple passes in quick succession find a red shirt and I feel I'm now properly in the game. Ten minutes after coming on, Forest force a corner kick. I don't remember the manager telling me to take up a particular position at corners, but I hold my place just outside the penalty area. The ball is half cleared from the corner and breaks in my direction. I meet it perfectly on the half-volley and it rockets past the West Bromwich Albion goalkeeper and into the net. I have a scored a goal in the English league ten minutes into my debut. Utter joy.

The roar of the crowd, the hugging by the Forest players. The emotion is almost indescribable. It is honestly a million times more special than anything I could have imagined.

Seamus McDowell and I are enjoying our time in 'The Attic' above McKay's Café and we are getting used to the other guys. Their conversations about their lives, sometimes double lives, their work and their families give us strange insights into their peripatetic existence. Naturally they find out a bit about us too. We joke about them being too old to be allowed into the 'Union', although there is one lad – probably about thirty-five years old – who could pass for someone ten years younger.

Seamus and I say that we will take him with us next Thursday evening, but he declines, saying that he has Friday off work and that he is heading up north, back home. He leaves The Attic and we never see him again. A few days later Seamus tells me he was tragically killed in a road accident.

As my family threatened the last time I saw them in Northern Ireland, my mother, my father and a few of my siblings arrive in Nottingham to escape the Troubles. I have had scant time to enjoy my newfound freedom in the city and worry that it will shortly be curtailed once more. Certainly I am expected to leave The Attic and move back in with my family, so I need to find lodgings for them and myself quickly. One of the girls in the Forest office spots a house in Wilford Lane that is available for rent. I take it, as we have no alternative. Within two weeks my dad, mum, sisters Breedge and Roisin and my brothers Owen and Shane have moved in – along with myself.

It is an odd-shaped building, resting on stilts because of

possible flooding from the River Trent, which meanders danger-ously close to the back of the house. My mother is relieved and says, 'We're together again and away from the Troubles.'

Naturally I am pleased to see them too, but there is no more getting back home late from the Union and no more nightly chin-wags with the lads in The Attic. Over dinner one evening, I broach this subject with caution. Although there is a tinge of sadness about leaving Belfast, my family are excited about their new surroundings. The future teems with possibility now their son is a professional footballer. I do not want to hurt anyone's feelings, but my voice definitely indicates that I'm not completely happy with the living arrangements thrust upon me. My father listens to the conversation but says nothing for a full ten minutes. Finally, he breaks his silence with a biting comment: 'I thought you were here to play professional football, son. Don't you think it's about time you started, then?' My father feels that every single minute of the day should be dedicated to my career and that a social life shouldn't exist, at least at present. My inner belief is that independence will make me a stronger character, yet I don't say this, and let it rest.

The following Friday, the team travels up to Manchester on the train, arriving around six o'clock into Piccadilly Station. Thir-teen players make the trip, a list having gone up on the noticeboard after training. We do not know the starting eleven and the substitute, but we do know that John Winfield is the thirteenth man.

John is not happy but accepts his lot. He had been a fine, cultured left back in his good days but now, like the rest of the team, he is finding the season exceptionally tough. He travels somewhat reluctantly, aware that unless a mishap befalls one of the other twelve overnight, he will not play at Old Trafford tomorrow afternoon.

We alight from the carriage and step onto the platform. Bob McKinlay, the coach, once a fellow player, is unloading the skip from the train. He has, amazingly, no helpers – not even a couple of young apprentices to lessen the burden. Bob is looking at us coming off the train and filing past him. He stares at me and then John Robertson, but says nothing. We are the youngest in the squad, and I think he feels that we should help him without being asked. We don't and walk past. The offloading of a football skip on the Piccadilly platform is not for players about to take on top-of-the-table Manchester United tomorrow.

McKinlay, desperate for some help, looks at John Winfield, probably thinking that the thirteenth man – regardless of past status – should help with the offloading. 'Winnie, give us a hand with the skips, will you?' Winfield is a proud man and, regardless of occasion, always immaculately dressed. He looks down at the kneeling McKinlay, fixes an already straight tie and disdainfully replies, 'Fuck off, Bob, I'm a top-class professional footballer, not a fucking skip man.' And walks on.

McKinlay is embarrassed, particularly in front of the young players like John and myself, and he naturally assumes that we think he has no authority with the senior players. I actually feel sorry for the coach but reason that if I walk back to help now, it will only make him feel worse. Anyway, he's played alongside Winfield for a long time, so he should've known what the answer was going to be.

Not the best start to the evening.

The next day we are at Old Trafford. The manager pulls me aside and tells me that I'm substitute today. I have no reason to be annoyed but I am. Last week we lost 2–0 at home to Leeds United. They were efficiently terrific, and I hardly got a kick. Yet I'm irritated that I'm not starting this afternoon against George Best, Denis Law and Bobby Charlton.

I've only been at the club a matter of weeks – or five minutes, as the old professionals might say to an upstart like me. But somehow this news feels like a hammer blow. I'm almost going to argue with the manager, but thankfully sense prevails and I accept the bad news.

Manchester United take the field. Best, Law and Charlton are all playing. When you are leading the league, as United are just now, all seems well at this imposing arena. When Best gets the ball there is a palpable intake of breath, followed by an almighty anticipatory roar from the packed stadium. I watch from the dugout, wanting desperately to be out there.

An early corner for Manchester United. Best swings the ball in, Law races to the near post and gets the first touch. Goal. 'Too easy,' I hear Gillies mutter to McKinlay. 'Far too easy,' and within minutes we are 2–0 down. United are now playing with all the confidence that a top-of-the-league team possesses. But out of the blue, Peter Cormack pulls a goal back and half-time sounds.

Within seconds of the second half starting, United score again. Gillies has his face in his hands, so distraught is he at the ease with which we are conceding goals. With twenty-five minutes to go, he looks right at me. I'm clearly looking at him already, waiting for the nod to get ready.

'Warm up, Martin,' he says, and I'm out of the dugout before he finishes his sentence. I'm coming on at Old Trafford and will be on the same pitch as Best, Law and Charlton. But I'm not really pinching myself in disbelief. It's not a nervous feeling at all. No, I'm going on this pitch to make an impact. I'm ready to play with the big boys, not like last week when I couldn't get a kick against Leeds.

Within four minutes I pick up the ball just inside my own half. I run forward ten or fifteen yards before United sense danger. I squeeze between two players, one of them being Bobby Charlton, and from outside the box, I hit a low drive past Alex Stepney into the net: 3–2. Momentum shifts and we press for an equalizer; it doesn't come but I've made an impact, which is what I'd dreamed of doing. Actually, I've done more than that. I've arrived on the biggest stage in English football. It's a moment to savour.

Surely football at the highest level is not supposed to be this easy. Well, it isn't, as I'm about to find out.

It's January 1972 and I decide to keep a diary. It's essentially a day-to-day synopsis of how my professional career is progressing. One week of notes suggest that not only is my club struggling, but the writer of such scribblings isn't having the best of times either. I make puerile comments like: 'I must impose myself more in training sessions', 'I must come back in the afternoon every day for extra work', and 'Why am I not in the starting line-up?' It's obvious that, to me, I am better than at least three of the players who are being picked in front of me, and of course my go-to excuse in the diary is that the manager doesn't like me.

Despite results for the first team being poor, Matt Gillies doesn't actually abandon me. The manager is desperate to win games. He would put the bus driver into the team if he thought that would improve his chances of winning. Just now he doesn't think that I can solve his problems, but he must think that I have something to contribute because I train mostly with the first team.

A loss to fellow strugglers Crystal Palace at home at the start of January knocks the stuffing out of us all. I come on as substitute with about twenty minutes to go but for some reason I cannot get into the game.

I don't travel to London with the squad the following week, where Second Division Millwall knock us out of the FA Cup third round and put paid to our dream of playing at Wembley. A loss at home to Leicester City follows. Again, I'm not involved, but in an attempt to lift our spirits, Matt Gillies decides that after next Saturday's game away at Southampton, the team will stay over in Bournemouth for a few extra days for some golf and downtime. I will travel with them as thirteenth man. I watch from the stands as Forest are thrashed again by the stripe-shirted Saints and a miserable, miserable night is spent by us all in a hotel some miles outside Bournemouth.

There is strong feeling among the senior players that relegation is inevitable. I want to tell them that there's still time to pull this round. How can I contribute, though? I cannot get into the team right now, so I haven't earned the right to say anything. The next day, catastrophic events put my football life into perspective.

As most of the players make their way back from the golf course, I spot that the TV in the hotel lounge has been switched on. The pictures, shocking as they are, reverberate all round the world. The Parachute Regiment have opened fire on a peaceful civil rights march in Derry, the city where I was at school. People have been killed, and with each new update, the death toll rises. A young boy with blood pouring everywhere is being carried away. A priest alongside waves a white handkerchief in the air. It is excruciatingly painful to watch such events. I may be far away, but I am suddenly transported back to my homeland. Today football has no relevance. With a final death toll of thirteen unarmed civilians, the day will go down in history as Bloody Sunday.

The following week I am substitute for a home game against Tottenham Hotspur. Again, we lose: this time 1–0. I get on in the second half of the game, but I cannot help the team. I actually do well, though, receiving praise in the aftermath from our embattled manager. Time looks to be running out for him and the pain is etched on his face, but he holds his composure when addressing the players. He is a man of the utmost integrity. If he criticizes anyone, you can be absolutely certain it is deserved.

A couple of the lads have a bit of a go at each other, but it never gets remotely close to throat-grabbing. It is not like my time at Distillery, where the wizened Jimmy McAlinden was not only prepared to turn a blind eye to any war of words between players, but in fact actively encouraged it.

All the first-team players really like Matt Gillies, that much is abundantly clear. However, his little phrases that once seemed inspiring – 'hunt in packs', 'don't get picked off in penny numbers', 'no bunkers in the sky!' – have lost their lustre. To a team struggling for confidence and facing defeat after defeat, they now seem rather feeble. But the praise he has bestowed on my cameo performance makes me feel pretty good at least. I have been called up to the Northern Ireland international squad to play against

Spain in the city of Hull. I will travel there feeling that I'm doing pretty well so far, and that Nottingham Forest's perilous position has little to do with me.

The train from Nottingham pulls into a grimy Hull Station on a damp early Monday afternoon, mid-February 1972. I alight from the carriage carrying two bags, one containing my football boots, and the other with some clothes neatly folded for use in the next couple of days. The Royal Hotel, within walking distance, is my port of call. It's a quaint old Victorian building, in need of a little repair but possessing a grandeur redolent of more affluent times. I have never been to Hull before today, but I know a lot about this city. My eldest sister, Agatha, always maintains that those years at Endsleigh College were among the happiest of her life. Recurring visits to Boothferry Park with her colleagues to cheer on the Tigers, albeit with intermittent success, became a Saturday afternoon ritual. Boothferry Park is of course home to Hull City Football Club and, unbelievably, will host our international game this coming Wednesday afternoon.

The Troubles back home have escalated in the last few months to such a degree that Northern Ireland are unable to play home games at Windsor Park, and consequently will play in this northern English city in a European Nations qualification game. I assume that Terry Neill, who is the player-manager both of Hull City and of the Northern Ireland national team, has probably had some say in the picking of this particular venue, and the board of directors at his club have obviously agreed.

Our meeting place is at the Royal Hotel, to tick off one's name and have a bite of lunch, after which a coach will take us to the Grand Hotel in Scarborough, which is to be our base for the next few days. I am naturally excited. I have already scored two goals in the big league, one of them against George Best at Old Trafford only two months ago, and I'm also now part of an international squad that includes this legendary figure. I'm hoping Best will be at the hotel for lunch so that I can be introduced to him personally. But the most talked-about, if not the most gifted player in Europe doesn't seem to have a salad lunch in a Hull hotel on his mind. I'm not entirely surprised to find out that he hasn't turned up. But the rest of the squad are here and, as I am to learn in my time as an international player with Northern Ireland, the camaraderie, regardless of religious divide, is incredibly strong. The welcome I receive from the senior players is both warm and heartfelt.

We wait for a little while after lunch to see if the mercurial Best arrives, but the manager wants to do a little workout at Scarborough Beach before dark, and so the bus leaves the Royal Hotel to make the journey to our headquarters.

As I look out through the window, I think of my sister Agatha and her time in this city over a decade ago. All those visits to Boothferry Park with her friends had made Agatha a Hull City fan for life. In many ways Hull looks like Nottingham. Endless rows of terraced housing have me wondering whether this might be the area where one of my favourite actors, Tom Courtenay, was born. I speculate, then pinpoint a particular house and convince myself that it's where he was raised. From playing Colin Smith in *The Loneliness of the Long-Distance Runner*, to his spellbinding role as Strelnikov (Pasha Antipov) in *Doctor Zhivago*, he is one of the all-time greats. He also got to act alongside the beautiful Julie Christie. It doesn't get any better than that, I reflect, as the bus makes its way out of Humberside.

Soon we reach the Grand Hotel and within minutes we get our room keys, change into tracksuits and are on the nearby beach having a laugh. Still there is no sign of the magician himself. As usual, the Irish journalists are not a million miles away, every bit as anxious as us to catch a glimpse of George Best. So naturally, by dinner time, his non-appearance is causing alarm within their ranks, and ours.

At around ten o'clock, just when all hope looks to have gone, George comes through the hotel front door with a friend at his side. I'm told he is the manager of the boutique in Manchester that Best owns, but who cares, George is here. He looks a little tipsy as he is hugged by his teammates in the foyer. Within minutes he is chaperoned to his bedroom so that photographers and journalists cannot make early contact with him. Like the children of Hamelin in Robert Browning's poem, we follow George up to his room, which he always shares with Pat Jennings.

It soon comes to light that George and his mate have enjoyed a pub crawl this afternoon from Manchester to Scarborough, so it's anyone's guess who did the last bit of driving. At least he's here in one piece, and soon the bedroom is echoing with George's tales of his recent past. I don't think he even notices me in the corner. He is surrounded by a coterie of players who know him well and deserve to sit close to him. I have to keep pinching myself. Four months ago I was in a Queen's University common room talking about the next day's big soccer game for First-Year Law against Third-Year Law. Tonight I am listening to George Best talking, not only about Ron Harris's attempt to cut him in two when Chelsea played United, but what was in his mind as he picked the ball up before coming across the penalty area for that magnificent goal against table-topping Sheffield United. I soon realize that he wasn't actually thinking about anything, it was just sheer genius.

By morning, news of George's arrival has reached every corner of Scarborough, so that by the time we are called for training, the hotel foyer is jam-packed with people desperate to catch a glimpse of the black-haired superstar. The hotel management team, realizing that George may need a little escorting, have acquired two rather portly gentlemen to act as his custodians. And so he is flanked by these men, like Muhammad Ali being led into the ring at Madison Square Garden in March 1971.

If the cordon is meant to prevent fans from touching George, then it's not working. An extremely attractive young girl breaks ranks and plants a kiss on George's cheek. He just smiles as if this is an everyday occurrence for him. The hotel, we are told, was a favourite summer haunt of Winston Churchill's. Somehow, I can't imagine a Vivien Leigh lookalike accosting the wartime prime minister in this fashion, but then again, Winston didn't look remotely like George Best.

It's very difficult not to be envious of the man. I am only a few feet behind him, but I don't think this is the moment to tap him on the shoulder to introduce myself. Regardless of the matching tracksuit I am wearing, he may still think I'm an autograph hunter if he turns around too quickly. Finally, just before our warm-up, I approach him with my introduction. I am hoping that he will remember it was me who scored a goal against United at Old Trafford two months ago. He doesn't, or at least he fails to say so. I'm a new face he barely recognizes, but he does wish me the best in my future career, and that's actually good enough for me.

We do not train for long, and George just wants to have fun with his Irish teammates anyway, particularly Eric McMordie, the Middlesbrough midfielder, who accompanied him on his first-ever trip to Old Trafford when on trial.

Casual conversations with the hacks, I am warned by the senior players, are not casual and never off the record. If only I could be a little brighter, I might heed these warnings. Alas, I'm a rookie who has scored some goals in the First Division and wants to converse with, and boast to, the lads who follow the team both in spirit and in print. I think I have a good chance of playing. Sammy Morgan, plying his trade in the Third Division for Port Vale, has just been drafted into the squad at the last moment, having not even been in the original group announced some days ago. So I'm assuming that I will be ahead of him in the pecking order. How naïve can I be, at nineteen years old, with just one twenty-minute international cap behind me? I am soon to find out.

Terry has just announced the team to us, and later, to an eager Irish press. I will be a substitute for tomorrow's game. I'm devastated and actually quite irate. Sammy Morgan will start in the team.

Just before tea, one of the journalists, Alex Toner, asks me how I feel about not starting. I think this is an off-the-record conversation, so sympathetic does he sound to my disappointment. I tell him that I might as well go home now if I cannot get into the team. I have no idea why I make these comments; brainlessness comes to mind now, but arrogance and self-importance are surfacing in my character at nineteen. I make my way into the dining hall and think less about my conversation with Alex Toner than my resentment about not being in the starting line-up. How can I be so timid and shy when talking to George Best and yet so bullish and foolhardy when speaking to a journalist?

The following morning I am summoned to Terry Neill's room, unaware that he has heard about what I said to Toner last night. Terry is not very happy; in fact, he's apoplectic.

'Who the hell do you think you are?' is his opening gambit. 'You, son, are an exceptionally lucky fellow even to be in this squad. I brought you here in the first place to give you some experience training with senior players and you want to go home? Is that what you said to Alex Toner?' He pauses for breath. 'Actually, I have a mind to grant you your wish,' he adds rather dismissively before waving me out of the room, my apology falling on deaf ears.

I am thankfully not sent packing, but I am put firmly in my place. I see Toner in the foyer about twenty minutes later and I attack him verbally with expletives that I don't think are actually in the dictionary. I hope that the other players, especially Sammy Morgan, have been too busy to find out about my explosion or, more precisely, my implosion. If they do know, they don't mention it to an already chastened, ten-minutes-in-the-game, know-it-all footballer.

The bus trip from Scarborough to Boothferry Park is uneventful, and we arrive in the dressing room about an hour before the afternoon kick-off. I get changed in a corner of the room, which allows me to watch George Best's pre-match routine without him being aware. Delving into his football bag, he removes his match boots and stares at them for a few seconds.

He holds both boots in the one hand and starts to hit them firmly against the floor, in an attempt to remove the dried mud still clinging to the soles from Saturday's game against Newcastle. Whilst doing so he quietly asks for some shoe polish. Unbelievably, the genius that is George Best is cleaning and polishing his own match boots in Hull City's home dressing room less than an hour before kick-off against Spain.

The game itself is played in front of quite a large crowd, primarily there to see George. The first half starts strongly enough but drifts somewhat in the middle, then bursts back into life before the break when Spain score.

Terry Neill, perhaps still seething with me, tells me at half-time to get ready for action. I'm on for Bryan Hamilton in the second half. My big chance, alongside George Best, has come. I can now prove that my indiscretion yesterday to Toner did indeed carry some weight. But the game is tougher to play than any pre-match optimism would suggest, and I falter in the big moments. We actually force a draw, but it isn't me who scores the equalizer. It is, in fact, Sammy Morgan, whose inclusion I saw fit to challenge.

I don't feel too good after the game, and I feel even worse about my outburst to Alex Toner. I'm sure Terry Neill wants to rip into me in front of the players, as I might do myself later in my career, but he comes over and says, almost in a whisper: 'You'll learn, son.' I hope I will. I say goodbye to the best player in Europe and hope that I will see and perhaps play alongside him again in the not-too-distant future.

The trip back to Nottingham that evening has me ruminating on the incredibly eventful last three days. I don't know it now, and perhaps neither does the player himself, but George Best will never again scale such Olympian heights as he has done so far in his incredible career. Perhaps the self-destruct button has been pressed long before this trip. Or maybe Monday's pub crawl was just the first marker on the downward slope of one of the most brilliant footballers the world has ever seen.

*

Sadly, the international break does not beget a change in our fortunes at Nottingham Forest. At the weekend, high-flying Derby await us. They are on the march. Their brash young manager with a lot to say for himself, Brian Clough, has put together a great squad, and momentum is building with their every victory. They will continue their drive and clinch the league championship at the end of the season. Nottingham Forest are Derby County's most hated opponents. That loathing is mutual.

The Baseball Ground is a proper footballing arena. The stands seem to lean onto the playing surface, so close is the crowd to the players. The playing surface is excessively muddy. It's still February, and dried-up football pitches are a good month away.

The mud seems to be no inconvenience to the Derby players, but it feels like quicksand to me. I receive the ball just inside the Derby County half with my back to their goal. I glance around before the pass arrives. I have clear space in which to collect and drive the ball forward. I think I'm moving pretty quickly, but from nowhere Colin Todd dispossesses me and sends the ball on another Derby attack. What has happened? Where has he come from? There was no Derby player close to me seconds ago. I am stuck on the spot. The game is too quick for me. For the first time since I joined Nottingham Forest, a fear – a real fear – runs through me: a fear that I'm not going to make the grade at the very top level.

The rest of the game passes me by, and in fairness it does the rest of the Forest team also. Even Ian Storey-Moore, starved of the ball because of our inability to get it to him, becomes a peripheral figure. A couple of years ago, when Forest got so close to claiming the coveted league and FA Cup Double, Derby weren't even in the First Division. Life is so different now and Nottingham Forest, beset with all sorts of problems, do not look a match for their fiercest rivals. It is no contest. The score is 4–0 to Derby.

'Terrible pitch,' we moan afterwards. 'How can you play football on that surface?'

Well, Derby County did, and they scored four goals, and they are on their way to the First Division title. As a team we are on our way to the Second Division, and if I don't get a grip on this thing called professional football, God knows where I personally might be heading. Our best player, Ian Storey-Moore, soon leaves the club. Originally, he seems set for Derby County. He is joyously paraded around the Baseball Ground as their new player, but the deal does not get the sign-off from the Nottingham Forest committee. And to the utter chagrin of the Derby County manager, Brian Clough, Ian goes to Manchester United. The departure of Storey-Moore is the final straw for the Forest fans. Transfer deadline has passed and one of Nottingham Forest's greatest-ever footballers has gone with it. He will team up with Best, Law and Charlton and we will feel the full force of the fans' backlash.

Fewer than 10,000 people come to the City Ground for the game against Ipswich. No one seems to have any interest in what's happening on the pitch. 'Gillies out, Gillies out!' and 'Sack the board, sack the board!' echo round the stands in splenetic roars as the fans show their utter disdain for the club. In fact, Gillies will survive until next season. But the club is duly relegated.

There are three home international games in the space of a week at the end of the season. Terry Neill puts me into the Northern Ireland squad, but I don't play in the matches. I'm sure he still has February in Hull on his mind, but he can at least rest assured that I am chastened. I enjoy being with the players, although George Best does not turn up for any of the games, perhaps because his club Manchester United have spiralled down the league table in the last few months.

The summer of 1972 finds me spending a lot of time back in Northern Ireland even though my parents are in Nottingham. I get a chance to see my older brothers Gerry and Leo and my sister Agatha, who are all still living there. Father Deery also gets a message to me asking that I visit him in Kilrea. He has done so much for me in my formative years that I cannot leave without seeing him. He organizes dances in the Marian Hall and I agree to go to one. These Friday nights attract not only large crowds of young people but, because of Father Deery's influence, the best show bands in all of Ireland. When I head to the dance hall, I see that girl, Geraldine McGrath, whom I met at the carnival a few years ago, in 1969.

She is there with her sisters and friends. I am spellbound once again. I pluck up some learned Union Boat Club courage and ask her to dance. If she refuses, I'm out of here immediately. But she accepts and our conversation lasts a little longer than before. I walk her home that evening and we make arrangements to meet the following week. A relationship begins and I ask her over to Nottingham in early September. She will come and our time together, even though just for a few days, will be magical.

As the new season begins, our fortunes on the pitch are mixed. I start well with a couple of goals in early matches, but results for the team are not brilliant. The crowd's frustration and anger at last season's relegation lingers in the air at the City Ground and Matt Gillies pays the price, losing his job in October 1972.

The Troubles in Northern Ireland have escalated further since Bloody Sunday in January, with bombings and shootings an everyday occurrence. It is probably only now that I realize that the moving of my family, particularly with brothers and sisters close to my age, has been a godsend. I have bought a nice house in West Bridgford, which I can barely afford, but at least we now have a proper home and my family are safe. By the time Gillies loses his job at Forest, back home in Northern Ireland Derry City have withdrawn from the Irish league because of insurmountable security problems.

Dave Mackay becomes the new Nottingham Forest manager. Mackay has been one of the great players of the game: hard as nails, and with great courage. He was a member of the fantastic Tottenham Hotspur team that won the league and FA Cup

Double in 1961. Now, moving upstairs, he joins us from Swindon Town where he was learning the managerial ropes.

He takes an almost instant liking to me and throws a few paeans of praise in my direction, particularly in the dressing room in front of the senior players. I respond to these confidence boosters in a big way on the pitch, with John Robertson also benefiting from Mackay's managerial style. We both flourish under his guidance. Towards the end of the season, John and I play brilliantly when we beat Sunderland at the City Ground. Our opponents will go on to win the FA Cup a month later when they beat hot favourites Leeds United at Wembley.

In March I am picked to play for Northern Ireland against Portugal at Highfield Road, Coventry. Belfast is still considered a security risk because of the Troubles. Mackay tells me that if he gets a chance, he'll try and get over to Coventry to watch.

'Do you think you'll start the game?' he asks.

'I don't know,' I reply, 'but if I do it will be my full debut for Northern Ireland.'

'Given the form you're in at the minute, you should play,' he remarks, with an assurance that suggests he is the one picking the team. But actually, he is right. I do start the game against Portugal, and score a goal on my full debut. We draw 1–1 in a game in which the great Eusébio is playing. He is not the lithesome footballer he was in the 1966 World Cup in England, but he is still a brilliant player.

All the Northern Ireland players want his shirt and, when the whistle blows, Bryan Hamilton, who has for the last six minutes of the match followed Eusébio everywhere on the pitch, cannot wait to exchange shirts with the great man himself. I'm really disappointed, thinking that Eusébio might want to exchange shirts with me, the goal-scorer, a new kid on the block.

He walks bare-chested up the tunnel with Bryan's Northern Ireland shirt draped over his shoulders. I quickly follow him and, before Eusébio reaches the dressing-room door, I tap him on the shoulder, point to his football shorts and, using hand signals, ask if I can have them. He doesn't understand my meaning at first, then realizes what I want. He takes off his shorts and gives them to me. The last three strides of Eusébio's walk up the Highfield Road tunnel see him with no shirt, no shorts, and just his underpants, socks and boots left. His shorts become beachwear for my next four summer holidays.

Back at Forest the next morning, Mackay is the first to congratulate me on my goal and performance. At the end of the season, I play for Northern Ireland in the Home Internationals series. As a result of my form, in one British newspaper article I'm touted as one of the five young players to look out for over the next season. I am on my way now, or so I think.

In October 1973, Brian Clough resigns at Derby County after a disagreement with the board. Dave Mackay leaves Nottingham Forest to become their manager. I am heartbroken. I hope that he will take me with him, but Derby County are awash with great players, so that is not going to happen immediately. Allan Brown, another Scotsman, but totally different to Mackay, becomes first-team manager. We don't gel and, instead of continuing my progress now that I can stand on my own two feet, my form lapses and so does Robertson's.

Duncan McKenzie is the new hero at the City Ground. He will go on to have the most fantastic season, scoring loads of goals and spearheading an FA Cup run that is only stopped at the quarter-final stage by the most ridiculous decision possibly ever made by the FA committee. Forest are drawn away to Newcastle United in the quarter-final. We are leading 3–1 with less than twenty minutes to go. The Newcastle crowd invade the pitch and one of our players, Dave Serella, is accosted by Newcastle fans. The game is stopped by the referee and the crowd dispersed by the police.

We restart some twenty minutes later and Newcastle score three times to win. There is a media uproar. Newcastle may be thrown out. The FA decide to delete the game from the record books and order a replay at Goodison Park, a neutral venue, as some form of compromise.

We draw the game but, instead of the second game going to the City Ground, the FA decide that Forest should not have a home tie, which on the face of it is complete lunacy. Instead we are at Goodison Park for the replay, which Newcastle win 1–0 to reach the semi-finals. The saga makes no sense as far as we are concerned.

Had the Newcastle fans not invaded the pitch at St James' Park that March afternoon, Nottingham Forest would have won the match. Allan Brown actually blames John Robertson and me for losing the game at St James' Park after the match is restarted. TV footage of the game suggests a totally different picture of events, but that kind of comment from the manager only serves to fuel the flames of the rows I'm having with him.

In one practice match before playing Luton Town, I don't chase back a couple of times. The manager stops the game and makes me do some press-ups. The game restarts but my intransigence leads me to play up. He stops the game again and tells me to change places with one of the reserve players, and I finish the game playing against the team I started with.

Brown goes back to the City Ground, takes the team sheet off the noticeboard and pins another one up in its place. I'm not on this team sheet for the game against Luton on Saturday. I was on the previous one. Should I be surprised? If I was the manager, I would probably do exactly what Brown has done this morning. In fairness to him, the club go very close to promotion, losing to Carlisle with a couple of games to go. Carlisle will get promotion to the big league, we will falter just at the end.

In 1974, Britain enters its first post-war recession and a three-day week is introduced by the government to conserve electricity during the coal miners' strike. Allan Brown summons me to his office to tell me there is an enquiry about me – not an offer as yet – from Cardiff City, now managed by Frank O'Farrell. He was Manchester United's manager when I scored that goal at Old

Trafford in December 1971. I tell him that I want to stay at Forest and fight for my place. He tells me that I'll have to 'buck up and be less belligerent'.

That old saying 'try and see yourself as others see you' could have resonated with me, but since it's Allan Brown who's telling me, I'm probably going to ignore it. John Robertson lets me know that Brown is trying to offload him to a Second Division team in Scotland. Thankfully for Nottingham Forest, John refuses to go too.

Before we know it, the new season of 1974/75 gets under way. I continue to struggle, and now our results are variable too. I am drifting. There is no more talk in the newspaper about the new kid on the block, as there was when Mackay was manager. And sadly, he has no need for me in his high-flying Derby team either.

The goodwill that Brown had built on the terraces by getting close to promotion and from that incident-packed FA Cup run quickly ebbs away. He sells fan favourite Duncan McKenzie over the summer to a beleaguered Brian Clough during his forty-four-day stint at Leeds United. And as we sink lower in the league, discontent rises from the boardroom and the stands. By Christmas, the writing is on the wall. On 3 January 1975, Brown is sacked.

What happens next, absolutely none of us could have foreseen.

3

CLOUGH

A cold, winter Monday morning has brazenly set in over the city of Nottingham. A new year has begun, with Christmas just a fading memory. Two general elections last year saw the country lurching from crisis to crisis. Labour leader Harold Wilson is back at Number 10, and Edward Heath has departed the political landscape, bludgeoned into defeat. A ceasefire between the IRA and the British government is just a few weeks away, heralding a new dawn. It doesn't last.

For me, it's just another bleak morning in early January. Training has finished abruptly early and we, the players, have been herded into the first-team dressing room at the City Ground. A fresh-faced thirty-nine-year-old Yorkshireman will, at any moment, burst into this changing room, throw his jacket onto a nearby peg, blow hard on his nails as he clasps his hands together to keep the winter at bay, and irrevocably change my life. For ever.

Like an apostle in the upper room, I am transfixed by his presence.

In the subsequent decades, he has entered that room so often in my mind, in both my dreams and my nightmares. Brian Clough, maverick and footballing genius, is now in our midst. He is the new Nottingham Forest manager.

There are probably only two players he will know as he scans the faces staring back at him. Barry Butlin, our centre forward, has been together with the manager at Derby County. Clough sold him to Luton Town, deeming him not good enough to play for that magnificent team he and Peter Taylor had built less than twenty-five miles from this very room. But we are definitely not Derby County, so Barry may well get another chance. Bob 'Sammy' Chapman, our centre half and captain, is the other one he recognizes. I know this because Clough's first words ever spoken in that dressing room are addressed to Chapman.

'Freeze the balls off a brass monkey, eh Sammy?' he says, somewhat rhetorically, as he looks to his left. Sammy smiles in agreement, delighted that the manager has singled him out in front of us all.

His talk is very brief but his voice is unmistakable. The nasal tone, made even more famous by the popular TV comic Mike Yarwood, pervades the room, now sitting in rapt attention.

'Jimmy and I would like to stay in this job a little longer than the last one we were in,' he continues acerbically, the Jimmy in question being Jimmy Gordon, his first-team coach. Both men had been sacked by Leeds United a few months earlier, after a tempestuous forty-four days at Elland Road.

'And the best way to stay in a job is to win a few football matches. But, for a while, you'll do the playing and let me worry about the results. Those who played last Saturday will travel with me on Wednesday morning. Tell your wives and girlfriends, if you have any, that you won't be home until Saturday night. That's right, Saturday night,' he repeats, just in case someone didn't get the message.

'We'll be staying at Bisham Abbey until after the Fulham match on Saturday. Take tomorrow off, get your feet up, we might need some energy at White Hart Lane on Wednesday night.' Wednesday night is the third-round replay against Spurs in the FA Cup.

And with that, he reaches for his jacket and starts to walk out. But, almost as an afterthought, as if he had just remembered something like where he had left his keys, he turns again to face us and asks, 'Is young O'Neill in the room?'

I put my hand up in the air, rather reluctantly, like a pupil not totally sure whether the answer he has just given the teacher is correct, and say, 'Yes boss, over here.'

He stares across at a group of nameless faces, sees my hand in the air, then looks at me, somewhat sternly I think, but then his gaze softens as he says, 'You'll be coming with us on Wednesday morning as well.' And he's gone before I can get the words 'Thank you, boss' out of my mouth.

So stupefied am I that I'm hardly aware of the congratulatory voices of some of the players beside me.

'Welcome back,' says John Robertson.

I have not been in Allan Brown's plans for some time. But he has gone now. Maybe this is a new beginning. Just now it's difficult to take it all in. Surely, I haven't imagined the last few moments. Brian Clough has just spoken to me. He is aware of my existence. What a morning this has been. Roll on Wednesday!

'The outside scenes of *Oh, Brother!* were filmed here a couple of years ago,' says the manager of the complex proudly as we collect our bedroom keys at the reception desk in Bisham Abbey. I am not sure too many of the players are particularly bothered about being gifted this piece of trivia, but it's interesting to hear this is where the BBC clerical sitcom, which ran from 1968 to 1970, was shot.

Bisham Abbey, as the name might suggest, is a historical Buckinghamshire manor house, which was given to Anne of Cleves by her husband Henry VIII as part of their divorce settlement. With the River Thames flowing idly upstream towards the equally historical hamlet of Marlow, it is an idyllic setting. I'm sure Henry's fourth wife didn't have to think too long and hard about where she might rest her head when unceremoniously dumped by her rotund spouse.

As he outlined on Monday, Brian Clough has fixed for Bisham Abbey to be our base for the next three or four days. It's Wednesday lunchtime, and this evening – 8 January 1975 – we will play Tottenham Hotspur in the third-round replay of the FA Cup at

White Hart Lane. We will follow that on Saturday with a game against Fulham at Craven Cottage, in a Second Division league game, hence the four-day stopover.

Tonight's match has attracted much attention in the media, it being Clough's return to football management after his dismal tenure at Elland Road. We lunch in the abbey refectory, which used to be the chapel in medieval times. It may well be steeped in history, but today it is forebodingly gloomy and, like the lunch itself, rather unappealing. However, it bothers me not one jot. This is because, just half an hour ago as we got off the bus, the manager told me in a tone I will hear almost daily for the next six years: 'Hey son, you're playing tonight.' He added, 'You can only do your best.'

'Thank you very much, boss,' I replied, I think three times in all.

Clough sits at an adjoining table for lunch, lifting his head occasionally to address us.

'I suggest you lot get your heads down for a couple of hours this afternoon. You might need some energy this evening.'

But I cannot sleep. I'm starting tonight, and in the manager's first-ever game for Nottingham Forest. Why me, I ask myself? We haven't even had a training session with him yet. Has he ever seen me play? Of course, I played for Forest at the Baseball Ground when he was Derby County manager. But that was three years ago. Derby hammered Forest 4–0 and went on to win the First Division championship. Forest were relegated. Worse still, I was hopeless that day, and Derby County have been dining in different restaurants to Forest ever since. I tell myself to put all of that firmly to the back of my mind, to focus entirely on tonight. Nothing else matters.

There is still some light left in the day when we board the bus, but Bisham Abbey is a long way from North London and darkness has fallen by the time we draw close to the famous stadium at White Hart Lane. The players' voices, hovering just above whispers for most of the journey, fall silent as we pull up to the main gates, which swing open on their hinges like the parting of the Red Sea. A steward on duty guides the bus to its resting place, outside the door over which hangs the sign 'Players' Entrance'.

Clough climbs down from the coach to be greeted by a rapturous ovation from those fans gathered around the bus. As far as I can see, they are mostly Tottenham supporters. He accepts this welcome with a wave of his hand, rather understatedly, before disappearing through the door. We follow him, pulses racing faster now, but somehow feeling that we can win tonight. Perhaps it's because Clough is here in person to lead us, and that's enough in itself. Whatever the reason, we gain much confidence from his presence as we walk towards our dressing room. We strut down the corridor with more pomp and bombast than our footballing status should permit.

This is my first time at White Hart Lane. History oozes from every inch of the ground. The iconic three-tiered East Stand towers overhead. Names like Bill Nicholson, Danny Blanchflower, Dave Mackay, John White, Bobby Smith, Cliff Jones and Jimmy Greaves roll off the tongue, all heroes here.

Our team is confirmed by Jimmy Gordon and we start to get changed. But the manager, overcoat under his arm, exits the dressing room and we do not see him for quite some time. Anxiety seeps in. We need him here to settle nerves, boost confidence and tell us how to play.

Ten minutes before kick-off he walks through the door, much to our relief. The room falls silent as he begins to speak. I am startled when he addresses me directly.

'Son, this is a simple game. It only becomes bloody complicated if you make it complicated. Try and get the ball for a start, 'cos we can't play without it. And when you do get it, just pass it to a red shirt, and make an angle for your mate to give it to you if he needs you. Couldn't be simpler, could it?'

I nod in agreement.

'And one more thing, don't be shooting from thirty or forty yards out,' he adds, 'that's a waste of your time and it's definitely a waste of mine. Do as you're told, son, and we might become friends, got it?'

I nod again.

Then, addressing the whole team: 'Nothing out there to be scared of this evening. Get your heads up, look smart, and get the ball. You can do nowt without it.'

There is no mention of Tottenham Hotspur. No mention of Martin Peters or Steve Perryman. Tonight's opposition doesn't seem to matter to him. Within a minute the bell in the dressing room sounds, the door opens, and we stride out single file into the corridor. Within ten seconds I run out into the glare of the White Hart Lane floodlights.

In the footballing world, little can compare to a cup tie played at night in an atmospheric stadium. Tonight is all that, and more besides.

We are put under severe pressure by Tottenham from the get-go. But there is a strong resilience about our team this evening. Every tackle, pass and header is being closely scrutinized by the man in our dugout. When Neil Martin guides the ball into the Tottenham net, we feel that – regardless of what happens tonight – they will not score. And they don't.

Jubilation fills our dressing room as we celebrate our shock victory. Archive photographs catch an exuberant Clough smiling, not directly at the camera, but at a group of us in his midst. The photographer has been allowed into the inner sanctum, presumably with the approval of the manager himself. We players have fought irrepressibly, more for him than for ourselves. The pain from his forty-four-day sojourn at Elland Road seems to ebb from his face. He is back in the game again. On a stage he knows best, although it is not quite the arena in which he feels his talents belong. Not just yet.

It's late by the time we get back to Bisham Abbey, but time doesn't really matter tonight. I've done enough in the match for the manager to say 'well done, son', both in the dressing room and again as we descend the stairs of the bus. Tonight is absolutely wonderful. The most talked-about manager in the British game has given me his approval. Well, that's how I want to read it. It will, in fact, be the last morsel of praise I receive from him for some considerable time.

In my bedroom, I take off my shoes. My ankle, caught in a tackle late in the game, is beginning to swell and throb. I put my foot in a basin of cold water for a while, dry it and try to get to sleep. In truth, a combination of pain and ecstasy makes this impossible. No matter, who needs sleep tonight?

Back at White Hart Lane, the photographer stows his camera in a bag, his work done for the night. Perhaps he is unaware that those photographs he has taken in the away team dressing room will be forever etched into the history of Nottingham Forest Football Club. They will serve not only as a reminder of Brian Clough's first game in charge, but as a harbinger of historic change at the Trentside club. Very few of those photographed with him this evening will be around to witness Clough's triumphal march down the corridors of the Santiago Bernabéu Stadium five years from now.

Morning comes round and my ankle is still swollen, but I dare not miss the manager's warm-down session on one of the many football pitches surrounding the abbey. It doesn't help that it is taking place on the furthest pitch from the complex, and so the long walk is very uncomfortable, even with a lot of cotton wool stuffed into my boot. The manager put me straight into the team last night, displaying some sort of confidence in me. I have to repay that faith somehow. Now is not the time to pull out of Brian Clough's first-ever training session.

The practice consists of a keep-ball exercise, with two players in the middle of a ring trying to get the ball off those on the circumference of the circle. I am one of the players positioned on the edge. The ball comes to me quickly and I try to pass it to a teammate, but my ankle is woefully sore and the pass falls well short of its intended target.

'Hold it right there,' barks the manager, and the training

session stops immediately. I do not see that happy face of last night. Instead, an angry-looking stare has taken its place and is directed straight at me.

'Hey you, play the ball correctly. Don't short-change your mate.'

And then, the coup de grâce: 'You look like the type of person who would drop your mate in the shit.'

I want to tell him that my boot is full of cotton wool, but I don't. I accept the criticism, but the manager's change of attitude towards me is disturbing. It's less than twelve hours since he praised me, not once, but twice.

I'm thinking it's quite a large judgement call to make on someone's character just because his pass to a colleague falls short in a warm-down session. And that is with a very bruised foot, I might add. What's worse, I have no time to redeem myself, even if I could. The manager calls immediate closure to the training session and I make my long walk back to the abbey with his stinging rebuke still ringing in my ears. Of course, Clough's reproof is the talk of my teammates.

Jimmy Gordon asks to have a look at my ankle. When he sees it, he is surprisingly sympathetic.

'Son, you shouldn't have trained this morning. Why didn't you say something to me?' he asks pointedly.

'I couldn't miss this morning, not after last night. The manager would have thought I was soft. And I want to play on Saturday, so I needed to be there at training,' I explain.

'Get some ice on that foot now and three or four times before teatime. I'll have a word with the boss and tell him about your ankle.'

'Thanks, Jimmy' is all I can muster, so deflated do I feel.

This afternoon Brian Moore, the renowned ITV football presenter and commentator, arrives at the abbey to interview Clough. They have known each other for a long time, and the manager will often describe Moore as the best commentator in the business. Cameras are set up and the confab between them takes place on a grassy slope dangerously close to the river. A few players watch the interview from a safe distance, hoping to catch the manager's words but not his attention.

We should know better. Clough's peripheral vision is astounding. Without looking sideways, he summons Tony Woodcock and tells him that he, the manager, wants his shoes cleaned. Tony will find them outside Clough's bedroom door and the task is to be done immediately. Tony is a young professional footballer with Forest. Clough is unaware at this stage of Tony's fledgling talents. He has been brought along on the trip ostensibly to gain experience within the first-team ranks, but he will spend this four-day stopover as the manager's lackey. Tony is not exactly pleased with his role but keeps quiet. He will have his moment in the not-too-distant future, but today he obeys Clough's instructions and ambles off to polish his shoes.

'Jimmy tells me you have a swollen foot?' the manager states brusquely as we sit down for dinner. He continues, somewhat caustically, 'You couldn't have done it last night, you never made a tackle.'

Before I can say anything in my defence, he relents: 'Jimmy is saying the bruising is coming out. Good. Don't do anything tomorrow and if you're fit for Saturday you're playing.'

'I'll be fit,' I say quickly, in case he changes his mind.

He gestures towards me with a pointed finger and states 'good lad' before taking his place beside Jimmy at the refectory table. All this in less than twenty-four hours from our first meeting.

By Saturday 11 January, my foot is much better. We travel to Craven Cottage where the legendary Bobby Moore, in the autumn of his career, is now playing. We win by a single goal and the manager is once again delighted with the victory. I think I have done well in the game but there is no compliment from the manager this time. In fairness, he doesn't signal anyone out for special praise, so I don't feel so bad. Two wins in three days, and still in the FA Cup competition. What a start for the manager; his magic potion is taking effect already.

The bus pulls away from Craven Cottage and Brian Clough takes his place at the front of the bus, close to the driver. I sit a while with Barry Butlin, who has scored the only goal of the game. Barry is effusive in his praise of Forest's new boss; this is despite the fact that Clough sold him to Luton when both were together at Derby. The experience has made him phlegmatic about his own chances of staying at the City Ground when things settle. We are both aware that changes are inevitable.

'What do you think he'll do?' I pose to Barry. I mean about the team in the weeks ahead.

'I doubt if I'll be part of his long-term plans,' replies Barry, rather regretfully but perhaps philosophically, 'and if Thursday morning's training session is anything to go by, you might not be either,' he adds, laughing as he does so. 'I'm just joking, Martin,' he goes on to say reassuringly, although the thought is already planted in my head. Perhaps Thursday's ear-bashing is more telling than the three or four decent passes I'd made an hour or two earlier at the Cottage. Barry continues: 'Strap yourself in, buckle up, and get ready for a bumpy ride ahead. One thing I do know with this manager: if you survive the cull, you'll be successful.'

Barry's words are to prove incredibly prophetic. Two hours later, the bus swings into a Derby layby to let the manager off.

'Well done, you lot. Have a lovely weekend with your wives and bairns or girlfriends. I'll see you Monday. Don't be late.'

With those parting words, he disappears into a waiting car to take him home. But my conversation with Barry, both serious and in jest, swirls around my head all night. I must survive the cull. The four days spent with the manager have either been like four minutes or four years, I cannot decide which. I want to enjoy the weekend and stay in this winning team.

The fantastic start we enjoyed with Brian Clough makes it hard to imagine that Nottingham Forest will not win another match for sixteen games, with just two victories out of the last twenty. But that is what happens. It is not a record that this brilliant manager will be proud of. He takes his time to get to know the players he is working with and, because he is Brian Clough, these poor results do not overly concern either the board or the terraces.

If he himself is perturbed, he only occasionally shows his displeasure in the dressing room. The real Brian Clough is lurking inside, waiting to reappear and dominate all before him. However, his mood will not have improved when, as we narrowly escape relegation, his old club Derby County – the very club he and Peter Taylor built so splendidly to win the First Division a few seasons ago – do just that again. Dave Mackay has delivered.

We do some preseason training around Wollaton Park on the outskirts of Nottingham before the first-team squad is announced to go on a trip to Germany.

I am not included, and nor are John Robertson or Ian Bowyer. All three of us are holding out for better contracts. John is not yet the star that he will become in the next few seasons. Bowyer is a very good footballer, signed from Manchester City a few seasons ago. He can play any position on the field, can score goals and is courageous. Yet somehow, at this juncture, Clough doesn't recognize his talents.

I've been on £50 a week for the last three years and the manager is offering me another year on exactly the same terms as previously. If this happens, Forest keep my registration, which means I am unable to go to another club unless a transfer fee can be agreed. I've sent a letter to the Professional Footballers' Association, my union, asking for advice, and I'm waiting to hear back from them. I've also asked to see the manager on numerous occasions this preseason, so far without success.

In desperation I bypass his secretary, Carol, and walk into the offices with a racing pulse. I knock on his door.

'Come in,' he bellows.

I open the door and there he is, behind his desk, in a conversation with our captain Sammy Chapman. 'What is it?' he asks abruptly, obviously not happy at my interruption of his tête-à-tête.

'It's about my contract,' I say nervously.

'What about it?' he barks. I look towards Sammy, who in all fairness starts to rise from his chair, realizing that contract talks are private affairs. 'Stay there, Sammy,' Clough says firmly, reaching over the desk to hold him back from leaving. I am taken aback but not confident enough to say that this conversation should not involve the club captain. Incredibly, I continue whilst Sammy is still in the room, looking embarrassed.

'I've been on the same money for three years. I've got a mortgage to pay and—' I realize immediately I've said the wrong thing.

'Your mortgage is not my problem, son.'

Sammy, sensing my anguish, has had enough. 'I'm leaving, boss. I'll see you after training tomorrow.' I also want to leave. I am mortified, and irritated with myself for not speaking up to point out that another player should not be listening to my contract details without my say-so. But I keep quiet.

'I'm not inclined to change your contract. Now get out of my office,' Clough says, pointing to the door.

And so, after three and a half years as a professional footballer, this is where I stand. I head off to McKay's Café for tea and maybe some words of comfort from Old Bill, the owner. What I do there is reflect. I think about the upsides: my debut goal against West Bromwich Albion, my goal at Old Trafford, my excellent spell of football under Dave Mackay, and my international goals for Northern Ireland.

But then my thoughts quickly move to my arguments with Clough's predecessor, Allan Brown. The football world is a small one and news travels. Has my past now come back to haunt me? Not long ago Clough warned me, 'You've had a lot of run-ins with the previous manager. Don't think for a moment I'm going to stand for all that crap!' It's clear that if I want to stay at Forest, I have to win his favour.

I draw comfort from the fact that John and Ian are also not going to Germany. We will train with the reserves.

When the squad arrive back from Germany, they travel

almost immediately to Northern Ireland to play two games, Coleraine and Ballymena, both towns about fifteen miles from where I was born. I am not on the trip when the list goes up, but John and Ian are. I am left behind again. The manager knows I would love to be going back home for a few days. It would be a chance to catch up with the brothers and sisters who still live there, even if only for a cup of tea. But I'm not taken.

I have to assume that John and Ian have agreed new terms, but I don't know for certain. I've heard nothing from the manager. And it turns out John and Ian play brilliantly in the two games in Northern Ireland, with Ian scoring a bagful of goals and John making most of them.

According to the newspapers, the manager has been keen for some time to sign a young winger called Terry Curran from Doncaster Rovers. Rumours abound that I might be part of the deal. I get a call from Carol to report to the office. Doncaster's manager, Stan Anderson, is apparently very keen to sign me as part of a possible swap. I've never met him but I know all about him. He was an excellent player for my favourite team when I was growing up, Sunderland.

But I do not want to go to Doncaster.

I'm waiting outside the office for Carol to call me in. Just now, Neil Martin, who has left Forest to go to Walsall, walks down the corridor. I think he's there to pick something up. He sees me sitting there and in his broad Scottish accent says, 'What are you doing here, sah?'

'I think the manager wants me to go to Doncaster,' I say, with much resignation in my faltering voice.

'Don't do it, sah! You're far too good for that division,' he notes. And with that the office door opens. It's Brian Clough and he has heard Neil's remarks.

'Hey, it's none of your business,' he says to Neil dismissively. Neil is a seasoned professional, now in the autumn of his career and unafraid of anyone, including Brian Clough.

'Just telling him he's too good for that division,' he reiterates, looking directly at Clough. He then turns to me again and says in an even stronger tone, 'I wouldn't do it if I were you.' And with that parting shot, he opens the front door and exits the ground.

Clough tells me that he'll see me later that evening. I'm assuming Stan Anderson has not arrived yet and I'm pleased with the stay of execution. In the afternoon, I rehearse the words I'm going to say later to Clough. 'I want to stay at Forest,' I repeat in my head. Carol calls my home, the meeting is off. I'm not needed this evening at the football club. A possible reprieve? Who knows. But tonight I am not going to Doncaster.

Terry Curran will later come to Nottingham Forest, with Ian Miller and Dennis Peacock going to Doncaster Rovers in a part-exchange deal worth in the region of £75,000. Meanwhile I am finally seen about my contract. Clough tells me that I can have £60 a week, but only if I drop the one-off £250 payment if I play an Irish international game in the season. The maths doesn't actually work but I'm past caring now. I sign the deal and believe I'll do much better in the coming season. However, the signing of the contract has made no appreciable difference to my football-ing status in the manager's mind.

In a training ground incident, I pick a fight with, of all people, our captain Sammy Chapman. It's an obvious mistake on my part, with Sammy probably being the toughest player on the books. During our scuffle I feel and hear two heavy thumps. One, Sammy hitting me, and two, me hitting the ground. I'm down for about five or six seconds but it seems an eternity.

'Don't try that again,' warns Sammy, standing over me. John O'Hare wipes away the blood and probably rearranges my nose. He whispers, 'Very brave, squire, but very, very foolish.' Sammy later apologizes. 'No need to,' I say. 'I started it but couldn't finish it.'

I'm a substitute at Fratton Park for the second league game of the season and start the home game against our neighbours, Notts County. We lose 1–0. I am out for the following week away to Chelsea, the only change to the team. It will be mid-October 1975 before I get a look-in again, probably because results are not so good in the league, but maybe because I get my head down and try to improve in training. However, I hardly miss a game playing in midfield from here till the end of the season. Curran is playing wide and I'm playing inside him. Robertson goes to wide left.

We finish eighth in the table, about six or seven points off promotion, but we have been too inconsistent all year. I have not contributed enough goals from midfield for us. Perhaps another half-dozen could have bridged that gap to the promoted teams.

Season 1975/76 is a disappointing year for the club, and the manager has so far not been able to effect a big change in our fortunes. He is often snappy and irritable in the dressing room, and his post-match comments to the press, which were once brilliantly witty, now seem more caustic. But he must know that the players' belief in him is absolutely unwavering. His achievements at Derby were legendary.

Around this time I am called to collect some items from the secretary's office. Just outside in the corridor there is a lad sitting in a chair, staring at the manager's office like a puppy waiting to be allowed back into the house by its master. A few days later I see the same young man sitting exactly in the same position as before.

'Have you been camping out here since Tuesday?' I joke. 'If it's the manager you're waiting to see, good luck.'

'Yes it is, as a matter of fact. He told me on Tuesday to come back today, so I'm here again.'

We introduce ourselves. He is a young reporter just starting his first job with Radio Trent, the local commercial radio station. Fresh out of Nottingham University, he has determination and resilience in abundance, characteristics needed when interviewing Brian Clough. Clive Tyldesley is taking his first steps on the road to being a superb TV commentator. Within two years he will be headhunted by Radio City Liverpool, but will travel to Merseyside the wiser and richer for afternoons with the Forest manager. Waiting in that corridor for days on end just to get Clough's voice on tape will not have been in vain.

Summer break is coming up, whether I've deserved it or not. 'The Boys Are Back in Town' by Thin Lizzy has broken into the charts. I tell Geraldine that I must go and see them when they are on tour. In November they will play the City Hall, Sheffield. We will both drive up to watch them. When Phil Lynott opens with 'Jailbreak', the hall erupts, and we are carried away, almost literally, by the energy on stage.

News spreads that the manager will have his sidekick with him this season. After a two-year hiatus, Peter Taylor will leave his post at Brighton and become Clough's assistant manager once more – a partnership that proved incredibly successful at Derby County a few seasons ago. Our striker John O'Hare, who played under the manager at Derby, thinks that we will see a rejuvenated Clough in the months ahead with Taylor's arrival. It proves to be a very sound prediction.

Peter Taylor is a tall man, strongly built, as befits a one-time goalkeeper. And although he's now a bit overweight, one would hardly describe him as paunchy. He gesticulates a great deal with his hands to explain his sentences. He can make you laugh very easily one moment, but he can unnerve you just as easily the next.

I don't necessarily believe that he mistrusts absolutely *everybody*, but he definitely has a nature that borders on the suspicious, born, I assume, from his life experiences. Occasionally, when we have all been gathered for a team meeting in the directors' boardroom, he will call for quiet and then check all the windows to see if anyone is eavesdropping outside.

He joins our preseason camp in Germany and starts to make an impression. He sends John Robertson back to the hotel from the training ground for being grumpy or slovenly, perhaps both. We all take notice. Even the manager himself seems content to let Taylor have the opportunity to impress his own personality upon us. It's a natural assumption that Taylor will have a big say in proceedings from here going forward.

As the days in the camp roll on, there is definitely a visible change in the manager with Taylor by his side. Not for one moment do we believe that Clough has lost any self-confidence over last season's league results – after all, we finished eighth in the table – but backed up by Taylor there is a renewed vigour and forcefulness in his tone.

It's unlikely that Taylor has seen this group of players perform too many times over the last eighteen months – he has been in the division below whilst at Brighton – so I'm assuming he will be getting all his information about our squad from the manager himself.

I play well in the preseason games abroad, but when we arrive back home I don't get a look-in. The 1976/77 season begins at Craven Cottage against Fulham. Sean Haslegrave is in the team and I'm left at home. Forest draw the match. A few days later I make it onto the bench at home to Charlton Athletic. Forest draw again. On Saturday, it's the same story and I'm on the bench. Forest lose heavily at home to Wolves.

It is certainly not the start the manager – now with his friend beside him in the dugout – would have been hoping for. And, personally, I'm frustrated at my lack of starts.

Something has to change, and although Taylor has not been an encouraging force for me in these early days (he hasn't spoken to me since the second game in Germany), I find myself in the team against Walsall for a midweek cup tie at Fellows Park. I have a strong riposte for both of them. I score twice in a resounding victory and shift their viewpoint. I press forward with confidence and prepare myself mentally and physically for the season ahead – a season in which we are aiming to make the big breakthrough and win promotion to the First Division, the promised land.

But it's a bumpy old road, and much happens in the months between late August 1976 and May 1977.

Tony Woodcock, almost sold to Lincoln City and Doncaster Rovers for less than £10,000, breaks through into the team, starting up in Scotland in the Anglo-Scottish Cup competition against

Ayr United. Clough doesn't really know what to make of Woodcock. Slightly built, but with whippet-like pace and an excellent left foot, Tony has been at the club since Clough's first day, having polished the manager's shoes at Bisham Abbey some eighteen months earlier. Taylor isn't sure about Tony either; otherwise he wouldn't have considered allowing the player to be transferred for such a paltry amount. Luckily for everyone, the proposed move broke down, and Tony is given a start at Ayr. Within eighteen months he will be playing for England. But Somerset Park, on a cold, crisp, early November evening, is the setting for Woodcock's entry into Nottingham Forest folklore as he scores in the 2–0 victory.

Taylor, despite his initial scepticism about Woodcock, will prove to be pivotal for Forest, not only in our promotion drive, but also in our eventual quest to be the best in the country, by signing two players: Peter Withe from Birmingham City for £40,000, and Larry Lloyd, initially on loan and then permanently for £60,000 from Coventry City.

Withe, a much-travelled Scouser, is a centre forward. He is nicknamed 'Googie' – I have always assumed, but never had it verified, after Googie Withers, the famous actress. Peter is just a brilliant centre forward and a perfect foil for the emerging Woodcock. Strong and powerful, he holds the ball up with feet or chest and can also do that other job pretty well: score goals. And in the next two seasons for Forest, he will prove himself to be the most underrated centre forward in Europe.

Larry Lloyd has been a big player at a big club, Liverpool. A dominant centre half to match his dominant personality, he left Liverpool to go to Coventry for £240,000 – a lot of money for a centre half. But, seemingly unhappy at Coventry, he is allowed to come to Forest on loan. And with his arrival on Trentside, Clough and Taylor have sent out signals of intent for their grand plans. We will sign some phenomenal players over the course of the next few seasons, but – more than any other – Lloyd's arrival at the club at this time portends Forest's road to greatness.

Robertson, myself, Woodcock and Viv Anderson enjoy Lloyd's footballing stories, and he is not shy about sharing them. His glorious days at Anfield, his arguments with the immortal Bill Shankly. Of course, according to Larry, the mercurial Scottish manager never gets the better of him. That Brian Clough can bring someone of Lloyd's status to the club and persuade him to drop down a division makes us believe that we are on the move.

I know in my heart that I want a number of things in this glorious game, and I'm prepared to do anything to achieve them. Acknowledgement from Clough and now Taylor that I can perform at the highest level would be a welcome tonic, but I'm now a regular in their team and that must say something.

There is definitely a change in mood. The clouds are lifting over the City Ground. Taylor's arrival has put down a marker and I start to see the bigger picture, what the management team are driving at. They want to replicate their success at Derby County here in Nottingham, and I desperately want to be a central part of that.

I want to be on that mountain when the climbing has been done. However, problems exist throughout the coming months. We can win big at home but we keep losing away. Four-goal, five-goal, six-goal victories at home are blighted by three consecutive losses on away trips. One step forward and one step back, it seems. But we don't know that a 5–2 victory over Burnley will become a watershed in the history of Forest, and one that's tinged with heartbreak. Terry Curran, enjoying a golden spell and vindicating Clough's belief in him, unfortunately gets injured. In the course of the game, Terry is stretchered off the field with a very serious knee injury which will afflict his Forest career from here onwards. I move to wide right and now the focus of our attacks goes out to John Robertson on the left. These positional adjustments for Curran's injury are fundamental to what will unfold in the next few years.

When Terry was on the right wing, most of the play went in his direction, with John Robertson on the other side, wide left, doing what is termed as the 'graveyard shift', up and down the pitch, spending copious amounts of time in defensive positions as much as getting forward. This role is unbelievably tiring. When you eventually get the ball, chances are you will have covered many yards, leaving you with much less energy to dribble past players than you would desire. With Curran's injury, this position is now afforded to me, and John becomes the focal point of attacks. It's not a position that many relish but, in truth, I'm the only player at the club capable of taking on this demanding role.

In mid-February 1977, a force majeure comes just in time to keep our season alive. I'm watching from the stands at the City Ground, having picked up a hamstring injury at Molineux against Wolves some ten days earlier. We are losing at home to Southampton and do not look like getting an equalizer, let alone a winner. Time is pressing.

Suddenly, as if a large forest fire has been started behind the Bridgford End, what looks like smoke billows over the City Ground and the game is stopped. But it's not a conflagration. It's fog, and it is hanging over the stadium. We are all joining in a prayer that it will remain there for the entire night. The referee can do nothing else but wait for the fog to lift. But it hangs around persistently, so he abandons the game. A big break.

We win the rescheduled game the following month, which is no mean feat considering that Southampton won the FA Cup against Manchester United at Wembley last season. This result sparks a series of victories which take us closer to the promotion picture. However, disaster strikes just when things are gelling. We lose a big game at home to Cardiff 1–0 and Clough loses his temper completely in the dressing room afterwards, calling us all a bunch of losers. For the first time we detect not just annoyance but a loss of faith. The First Division seems light years away. We have three games left and we feel we need to win them all. We will travel south-west for two away fixtures in two days: Bristol Rovers on the Saturday afternoon and Plymouth Argyle on the Monday evening.

In the first game, Bristol Rovers take the lead and hold it for a long time. John Robertson scores an equalizer for us late in the game, but the match ends in a draw. This time there is no fury from the manager, rather an air of resignation that our hopes have gone. I actually apologize to him for missing a chance to score in the game. He seems to accept the apology with some equanimity, saying the damage was done earlier against Cardiff City.

The journey to our hotel in Tavistock, where we are staying before our Plymouth match, is marked by much introspection among the players. There is much for Clough and Taylor to ponder at the top of the bus. We are all quiet, and spirits are as low as they have been at any stage in this long season. We reach the hotel late in the evening. Supper awaits us in our allocated room not far from the hotel foyer.

News that the American actor and singer David Soul is staying in the same hotel reaches us, and sure enough he comes into sight just as we take our places for dinner. David Soul is box office. He has taken time out from his role as Hutch, in the massively popular American detective series *Starsky and Hutch*, and is making a film in Britain. His song 'Don't Give Up on Us' had been at number one in the UK charts for several weeks earlier in the year.

We are dressed in blue club blazers and grey slacks, so it's obvious to any observer that we are a team of some description. John Robertson leaves the table, approaches him with a pen and paper and asks very politely for his autograph. Soul is not happy. However, he reaches rather grudgingly for the pen and paper, almost tearing it from John's grasp, and starts to sign the sheet. Unfortunately, in the process, he adds a few angry words under his breath but audible to John: 'This is the thousandth time I've signed an autograph today.' He hands the same paper back to John, who is now angry himself with the manner in which he has been spoken to, even if it is David Soul. John proceeds to tear the signed paper into quarters, adding a stinging rebuke: 'If that's your attitude I don't want it now – stick it up your arse.'

John walks back to the table, leaving the actor to at least ponder what he has just done, if not to rue his comments.

I assume someone must tell David that we are a soccer team and we have a famous manager in our midst, because he comes back to the table twenty minutes later and apologizes for his rudeness. He actually invites us, if we have time, to come and watch some filming on Monday morning – if the manager allows it, of course. We accept. Now we are David Soul's best pals. Clough permits us to go to the film set not far from the hotel. The weather is cloudy, with spots of rain making the camera work difficult. 'Action' and 'cut' are the order of the morning, and an hour passes with some humour. But tonight's game is on our minds.

Plymouth are having a difficult season themselves, but that's their problem. Promotion may be on again for us if we can win this evening, and we do, coming from behind to take victory. The gate opens just a little wider. At least we take it to our final match of the season. We beat Millwall the following Saturday and finish the season. Bolton still have two games left, at home to already promoted Wolves, and away to Bristol Rovers. Three out of four points will get them promoted at our expense.

A trip to Majorca is arranged for the following Saturday. We will be in the air from East Midlands Airport when Bolton kick off against Wolves. We can only hope that Wolves do us a favour by beating Bolton. However, this could be difficult since they have nothing to play for, having already been promoted themselves along with Chelsea. We are powerless. In the aeroplane, we find ourselves in the hands of a pilot to guide us to Majorca and in the hands of Wolves to win against Bolton. A message from the captain comes across the loudspeaker. He says that – for those interested in football – Wolves have just taken the lead.

When he makes this announcement there have only been twenty minutes played in the game, so there's a long time to wait. There are no more announcements and we are left in limbo. Perhaps Bolton have won and he doesn't want to tell us. If the captain has been able to find out the score inflight after twenty minutes, why can't he find out the final score?

The plane touches down in Majorca. Our chairman, Stuart Dryden, Clough's big friend, walks with much purpose towards the terminal with the manager in close attendance. We follow behind. The chairman makes a call from a public phone box. He's phoning home. The tension is honestly unbearable. Even a draw is probably not good enough. Chances are Bolton will probably beat Bristol Rovers on Tuesday, even if they draw today. We cannot hear what is being said on the phone. Only the chairman's face will tell us the news. He seems to be smiling, although we cannot be sure.

We are trying to lip-read as he puts the phone back in the socket. There is a grin on his face. Does this mean we should be hopeful? He says to Clough, 'I believe congratulations are in order.' Within seconds there is an almighty roar in the terminal: 'Get in there!' Wolves have beaten Bolton. Bolton need to beat Bristol Rovers by about fifteen goals on Tuesday evening to be promoted instead of us. It's not going to happen for them. We will be in the big league come August. Incredible.

However, Clough still takes congratulations in a cautionary manner. Until Tuesday evening passes, until Bolton play the final game and have not won by fifteen goals, he will not accept promotion. At least not in front of us. But we know we are promoted. The city of Nottingham knows we are promoted. And surely Tuesday night will confirm everything. As it does. Bolton draw 2–2 with Bristol Rovers and the celebrations can begin in earnest.

Maybe it's me. Maybe it's my Catholic upbringing, but when you feel that disaster is always just round the corner, success is hard to embrace wholeheartedly. What will the manager do now? Surely they will strengthen the team. Who will they leave behind? They have had their little piece of good fortune with the Wolves result at Bolton. They will capitalize on this for sure . . .

But that's for the future, I remind myself. To hell with this upbringing, at least for the next week. Let me enjoy myself, let me enjoy Majorca. And I do.

4

TOP OF THE GAME

There is great excitement in the city of Nottingham. Forest are back in the First Division and are being led by the most irrepressible manager in Britain. Kenny Burns, a centre forward from Birmingham City, has been signed but will be playing at centre back. Otherwise, there are no additions to our squad. Terry Curran is fit again and, if preseason experimentation is anything to go by, the management team will boldly play two out-and-out wingers in the months ahead. However, a week before the season opener at Goodison Park, they abandon the idea, deciding that I will be better equipped than Terry to do everything that is necessary on the right-hand side of the pitch.

We face Everton on the opening day of the 1977/78 season. Peter Taylor senses our nerves and regales us, in the dressing room, with some hilarious stories of his past playing career. He is uproariously funny and as a result we definitely feel less tense. When looking round the dressing room, he might feel that just one signing in the summer is not enough for what we are about to face. But he doesn't show it.

The opening twenty-five minutes are a shock. We cannot get out of our half, so dominant are Everton. They are playing at a pace we haven't experienced in a long time. I cannot get my breath, never mind a kick, and we are chasing shadows. But then it turns. Somehow, we manage to get a corner kick. Peter Withe heads us into the lead and the game changes completely. We start to play some terrific football, possibly to the surprise of the managerial team.

In the second half I force home a goal for us to put the game beyond Everton, and we take both points away at Goodison Park. In the dressing room, Taylor is taking credit for his influential team talk just before kick-off, as well he might, although the script didn't exactly go to plan in the opening quarter of the game.

Goals are important to most players, but they are particularly important to me at this juncture. Getting left out of the team is significantly more difficult if you have that goal tally beside your name. After all, doesn't the manager tell us constantly that scoring goals is the most difficult part of this fabulous game? He's absolutely right, of course.

Many conclusions get drawn from the pundits, even after one game played. The outlook for Nottingham Forest ranges from 'with Clough and Taylor at the helm, relegation is not an option' to 'with some more additions, Forest can improve on being a mid-table First Division team' to perhaps, with a strong tailwind and a good slice of fortune, we may 'even finish close to a place in Europe'. Unavoidably, comparisons are being drawn with Derby County a few years ago when Clough and Taylor took them to fourth in the table in their first season back in the First Division.

Perhaps not everyone in the city of Nottingham purporting to be big followers of the club is totally convinced that there is something in the air. Fewer than 22,000 people turn up for our first home game. It is admittedly midweek and Bristol City are our opponents. We actually had more in attendance for our final home game against Millwall last season. We win a tightly contested game with a Peter Withe goal, his second in successive games, and with maximum points from two games we head into the weekend's game with Derby County – yes, Derby County, at the City Ground – with much confidence.

This is a game the managerial duo want us to win so badly. Five years ago, they left the Baseball Ground with much rancour surrounding their departure. So, this is a game we really need to win. Which we do, handsomely, 3–0. With two more goals, Peter Withe is showing himself to be a proper centre forward. And John Robertson is beginning to blossom as a playmaker for us. When we demolish West Ham United a few nights later, 5–0 at the City Ground, our reputation is gaining increasing momentum. And so, with the month of August consigned to history, we travel to London to face Arsenal at Highbury in an exultant mood. After that inglorious, twenty-five-minute spell at Goodison Park an eternity ago, we are taking this league by storm. Or so we think.

We are pummelled at Highbury. Malcolm Macdonald and Frank Stapleton, prompted by Liam Brady, are far too good for us. The final scoreline, 3–0, may even underrepresent the Gunners' superiority on the pitch. If we could climb straight onto the bus waiting outside the famous marble hall and not go into the dressing room, we would all choose to do so. But life is not like that, and we incur the wrath of the manager with expletive following expletive. During the second half, Kenny Burns headbutted an Arsenal player, Richie Powling, when the poor lad stepped unwittingly into our defensive wall for an Arsenal free kick. Clough asks Burns what went on and why was Powling lying in a heap and needing medical attention? Burns – unaware that his headbutt has been captured on film for distribution on London Weekend Television on Sunday afternoon – tells the manager that he didn't touch the lad at all. Clough, having to accept what Burns has said without positive proof to the contrary just now, warns Burns that he will not tolerate that behaviour but lets it go at that, continuing to verbally abuse us for our cowardice in London.

I don't think we need to be told how poor we have been this afternoon, but it's a salient reminder of what is required in this league to be half decent, let alone to reach the top of the tree. It's a long trip back to Nottingham. And there is much conversation going on in the front seat between the dual partnership in charge. Despite our great start to the season, that blow today will not go unpunished by the management team. Signings, we feel, are afoot.

On Sunday afternoon, Central TV shows highlights of our match; even in a compressed version, it's every bit as bad as it was in real life. Burns is also caught red-handed on camera as he headbutts Powling. It's very clear that he has made contact with the Arsenal player. That doesn't augur too well for the inevitable meeting tomorrow.

And it duly happens. Training over, and the meeting in the directors' box begins. Clough and Taylor, as is their wont, keep us waiting for ten or fifteen minutes, allowing us to stew for a while. Clough comes through the door with Taylor alongside. The manager has a letter in his hand. We all know what the letter contains. Burns is about to be fined.

'That's for you, Kenneth,' barks Clough.

Burns has the temerity to answer back. 'What for?'

'What for?' Clough repeats quite loudly. 'One for the headbutt on the poor lad. And two, for telling lies that you never touched him.'

Burns takes the letter without further comment.

Clough begins roughly where he had left off on Saturday in the Arsenal dressing room and we have no reply. No excuse is worthwhile. Taylor, feeling that no player is in a position to lift his head, never mind answer back, seizes his moment and addresses Larry Lloyd.

'Larry, that was a poor show from you. And do you know what I think? When Macdonald headed that one into our net, I think your heart failed you.'

The words cut through the room. They are so clear that we cannot possibly misunderstand their meaning. Taylor is calling Lloyd a coward. But, assistant manager or not, Taylor has not anticipated the big centre half's reaction. Lloyd rises, deliberately and slowly from his chair, and with each movement seems to grow taller and taller, asking Taylor to repeat what he has just said.

'If you repeat it, and it means what I think it means, then you're a bigger man than I think you are,' he says, and by the time he has completed the words, he seems to tower over Taylor, who is pretty tall himself.

Taylor is turning white and blue at the same time, unprepared for Larry's reaction. He starts to backpedal, both literally and metaphorically, asking Larry to calm down, and reminding him that he alone was responsible for signing Larry from Coventry and getting the big centre half's career back on track again.

This is all true, but Larry isn't really listening. He is not a coward. He doesn't like being called a coward and certainly greatly resents being called one in front of his fellow players. He is close to getting Taylor by the neck, but Taylor's retreat allows Clough to intervene and Larry calms down a little. But it's the first time that Taylor's position has been threatened. That episode will not sit right with him. However, the manager has made his point with Burns, who leaves the room a little more contrite than when he entered.

After the meeting breaks up, Lloyd is toasted by us all at McKay's Café. He is most definitely our spiritual leader. And he basks in this new-found adoration. But the meeting definitely has its desired effect on us. We travel to Molineux and beat Wolves the following Saturday. Archie Gemmill is signed from Derby County, followed by Peter Shilton from Stoke City. These major signings are more significant indications that Clough and Taylor mean business. Victories over Aston Villa at home and Leicester City at Filbert Street in successive weeks have the country sitting up and taking notice. I score against Leicester, and play exceptionally well in the process. My older brother, Gerry, is the manager of the Armagh County senior Gaelic football team back in Northern Ireland. They are playing Dublin in the All-Ireland final at Croke Park the day after the Leicester City game. I wait until after we have won to ask the manager if I could go to Dublin the next morning to watch my brother's team. I assure him I'll be back for training on Monday regardless.

'Son,' he replies, 'the way you played today, you can take a few extra days if you want.'

I thank him but tell him I want to come back for Monday's training.

'The offer still stands, it's up to you,' he says.

I'm on top of the world. And for this weekend, so are Nottingham Forest.

The arrival of Shilton and Gemmill changes the dynamic. Goalposts are metaphorically repositioned, our brilliant run gains even more momentum and, indeed, our third defeat of the season – at Elland Road against Leeds United in mid-November – actually becomes a landmark in the history of the club. From that day on, we will embark on a record-breaking forty-two league game run without defeat, a record beaten only by Arsenal some twenty years later.

After the loss at Elland Road, the manager takes us off on a midweek trip to Israel and we return refreshed.

Immediately I score important goals in successive games, away at Birmingham City and home to Coventry City. Two victories. Our mesmeric run at the top of the First Division continues, despite losing our talisman; Lloyd is injured against his old club, breaking some bones in his foot. Almost before the X-ray results come through, Forest have signed David Needham from Queens Park Rangers. David had a glorious time with our rivals across the Trent, Notts County, and because of that, moved to England's capital city at Loftus Road. But he's not there long before Clough and Taylor bring him back to Nottingham as a replacement for Lloyd.

Taylor brings David into the dressing room, the ink on his contract hardly dry, to introduce him to his new teammates. David is a genuinely nice lad, a little reserved. As he is individually introduced to us, Taylor – in typical Taylor fashion – picks on our little foibles and exaggerates them for comic effect.

But as David is introduced to Larry Lloyd, the joke falls flat. As David puts his hand out to shake Larry's, the big lad from Bristol doesn't even rise from his seat and dismisses David's hand with some biting comments to accompany his actions.

'Don't think you're here to take my place. I'll be fit again in a couple of weeks and I'll be straight back in the team. This team, let me tell you, actually can't do without me.'

Taylor is more than a little embarrassed. Thoughts of the meeting in September when Larry challenged Taylor after the Arsenal game come racing into my mind. Maybe Taylor has acted so quickly in getting Needham into the club because he genuinely wants Lloyd out of the way. I might be wrong, but my thoughts are also shared by a few of my teammates. Still, we are delighted that Needham is with us, and he does exceptionally well over the next few seasons. We think we are on to something big and the Christmas programme is almost upon us.

Manchester United await on a December afternoon in late 1977. Is it really six years since that goal I scored on this very ground? Law, Best and Charlton have all departed this historic mansion, but a severe test lies ahead nevertheless. The floodlights are on from the beginning of the game. It's four days before the shortest day of the year, so for all the world this seems like a night game. And while we anticipate a tough match, surely the Manchester United players must feel similarly. The opening exchanges are evenly contested, with us having to withstand some intricate wing play from United. But then we score, and the floodgates open. Withe and Woodcock are irrepressible; Needham settles in seamlessly, wondering, I'm sure, if life is actually like this all the time. Gemmill and Robertson are peerless, in an all-round, simply magnificent team performance.

We win 4–0 and it could have been double that. There can be no question now. We are serious contenders for the title of champions. Or are the Gods just having sport with us before casting us down to Hades? Clough can do no wrong. However, within minutes of the final whistle, despite the euphoric elation in the dressing room, Clough reminds us that Mount Olympus has not been climbed yet – not by a long shot.

Deep down we know that, but can we just enjoy the evening, please, boss? And we do.

John Robertson spots a couple of the band members of Deep

Purple in the hotel that evening, and within minutes we introduce ourselves to Ossy Hoppe, their tour manager. Ossy is a German, living down in Buckinghamshire, and he knows his football. John and I maintain a friendship with him for many years afterwards.

The manager has organized a pre-Christmas break for us immediately after the United game. In fact, we will fly to Benidorm out of Manchester Airport the next morning for a four-day trip. Wives and girlfriends are not happy about it but, in truth, we players are delighted. We love the manager's trips. We almost live for them. We see a different side to him, a mellower human being who seems to be able to leave any troubles and anxiety at the door of his City Ground office.

Benidorm before Christmas is not, I might add, Benidorm in the midsummer months. It is less crowded, much less crowded, but it wouldn't matter to us if we were the only people in the place. We enjoy a night out in a bar. We, the players, are all together. There is a genuine warmth within the group. I may not want to share too many evenings in Nottingham with Kenny Burns, but tonight, in Benidorm, the company of the belligerent Scotsman is a joy. On second thoughts, maybe I shouldn't have any more of that cheap Rioja the crafty barman keeps serving us.

Archie Gemmill draws many comparisons between ourselves and Clough's brilliant Derby County side, of which he was a member in 1972. He reminds us that he also won the title with Derby again a couple of seasons ago under Dave Mackay. John O'Hare reiterates Archie's words and of course so does our captain John McGovern. It's so heartening to hear from three big winners. As he finishes his words, Solly (John O'Hare's nickname for years) climbs onto a nearby table and, grabbing hold of a snorkel, pretends to play the bagpipes in an unforgettable rendition of 'Mull of Kintyre'. The irony is not lost on us, considering that this particular drinking hole is called the Robin Hood pub. If team spirit and camaraderie are enough to win the championship, then we have certainly passed that test.

*

Results over Christmas and early New Year continue to defy belief and do wonders for our confidence and self-belief. The manager tells the press that we are naturally enjoying life, but nothing should be taken for granted. Despite our heroics, that remains the message both to the players and to the supporters.

But there is some light relief too. The squad have been asked to make a record and, surprisingly, Brian Clough agrees. Paper Lace, a pop band from Nottingham, are on board. The group had a couple of chart successes a little while ago and 'Billy Don't Be a Hero' is their best-known song. I think they are looking to get back into the limelight. One may wonder if fronting a football club's single is the best way back to stardom, but that's their choice.

Clough leads his merry men to a recording studio, and after perhaps ten takes we're off and running – or singing. The record gets released in February. 'We've Got the Whole World in Our Hands' is not the most original song that could have been chosen, but we have a lot of fun recording it and watching it climb up the charts.

In January 1978, a victory over Bury at Gigg Lane in which I score takes us into the semi-finals of the League Cup. We will play Leeds United, Clough's nemesis, in a two-legged tie. Of all places, Elland Road is the one where he wants his team to perform and win. We don't disappoint him. Peter Withe scores a couple of goals and John O'Hare caps a masterful performance by adding another. A fortnight later we win the second leg. I score, playing exceptionally well, and the manager is as happy as I've ever known him that evening.

Leeds United, the club that discarded him after forty-four days in 1974, have lost the chance of playing at Wembley. Even worse, their bête noire has re-emerged as the leader they were looking for. I am twenty-five years old and playing the best football I've ever played for a team that is in sensational form and pushing aside all before it.

In many ways I'm beginning to think the First Division is easier to play in than the Second Division. Bar the opening twenty-five minutes at Goodison Park, where I thought I'd never be able to cope with the pace of the top division, I've been able to flourish with relative ease. Days like these are simply pure and utter enjoyment.

On 18 March we will be playing against Liverpool at Wembley in the League Cup final. We have managed to get there without three key players – Shilton, Needham, Gemmill – who are all cup-tied. Meanwhile we play West Bromwich Albion in the FA Cup quarter-final at the Hawthorns on 11 March. The most improbable Treble is remarkably close as we are still in the running for top of the league, the FA Cup and the League Cup. Exactly a year ago we were beaten at home by our neighbours Notts County, which seemed to signal the death knell of our promotional chances. How things change.

Unfortunately, West Bromwich Albion put paid to the Treble dream, beating us 2–0. In the dressing room, Clough finishes his deliberations and falls silent for a moment, giving Jimmy Gordon a chance to speak. 'Boss, I've got a shirt here designed for next week at Wembley. If you don't mind, I'd like one of the players to try it on.'

Clough points to me and says, 'Let him try it on, because after today he is first on the team sheet next Saturday.' It's the biggest compliment I have ever been paid by the manager and it comes after a defeat.

This is Wembley Stadium. The big doors open slowly and the bus driver waits patiently until he's given the go-ahead to drive on through. I am in the coach looking out of the window at hundreds of Forest fans on either side of the bus, waving banners of support. A flush of nervous adrenaline runs through me. It's Saturday 18 March 1978 and it's the club's first visit to Wembley since 1959. The media view is that our opponents Liverpool should win comfortably because we are short of a number of cup-tied players. Likewise, a young eighteen-year-old goalkeeper, with not a league appearance to his name, will face the champions of Europe.

The fact that we are leading the league is of no consequence to the pundits, although we have fought tooth and nail to get here. The prevailing narrative is that Forest will put up stout resistance but that the League Cup will travel north to Merseyside in a few hours. No other outcome is considered.

We are in the Wembley dressing room. With the door closed, the noise in the stadium can hardly be heard. Peter Taylor is having a joke with some of the lads in the corner, which reminds me of the first day of the season at Goodison Park, but it still hasn't calmed my nervousness. Time is racing round to kick-off.

There is a knock on the dressing-room door. One of the stewards is asking for me. He informs me that my brother is outside the stadium wanting to speak to me. He can't locate the office where his tickets should be.

I cannot believe it. I walk out of the dressing room in full match kit accompanied by the steward, who then opens up a little slit in the door at eye level. I find myself trying to deal with ticket problems twenty-three minutes before kick-off in the biggest game of my career so far. Moments later, I'm back in the tunnel, opposite the Liverpool players, waiting for our entrance call.

There is an incline in the tunnel. You can hear the noise of the crowd but you cannot see them. Then the signal is given and both teams start walking up the slope. The first thing you see is the roof of the opposite stand, then the top tier, and within another three steps Wembley Stadium in all its colourful, kaleidoscopic glory opens in widescreen. The walk from the tunnel to the halfway line is exhilarating: a chance to soak up the atmosphere before the serious work commences.

Liverpool dominate early possession but, after a few scares, we settle down and slowly get into the game. Chris Woods, the eighteen-year-old goalkeeper, is playing magnificently. On occasions Liverpool show why they have been so brilliant these last few seasons. But there is a resilience to us instilled by the management team that gives us great mental strength in adversity.

And Liverpool raining shots on our goal is surely the definition of adversity.

The ninety minutes are up, the referee blows the whistle, and we will be forced into extra time. The players huddle together about twenty yards from the touchline expecting Clough and perhaps Taylor to come to advise and encourage us through the extra time.

But they don't come out.

They stay in their touchline seats and we are left to deal with the situation ourselves. I am surprised and I'm disappointed. I just need the manager to come forward with his abrasive self-confidence, telling us that all will be well. But he doesn't.

We stay with it and after 120 minutes Liverpool, European champions, have not beaten us. There will be a replay and we live to fight again, on Wednesday night at Old Trafford. Having seen this through today, we really believe that we can win the cup. Liverpool have had their chances today, but it will be ours on Wednesday.

Clough takes us away for a few days in Scarborough. The air is bracing, and we have fish and chips on the seafront. We are like kids on our first vacation. Yet there is something quite wonderful about it all. This is the manager's way of refreshing us for the battle ahead and we are totally with him.

We go again against Liverpool. John O'Hare is upended as he drives into the Liverpool penalty box. The referee points to the spot. Liverpool protest but the decision stands. John Robertson scores past Ray Clemence and we take the lead. We know we will win the game. Full-time is blown. We have won the League Cup. Even with a dozen games still left in the league, this victory, particularly over Liverpool, will sustain us for the rest of the season.

But there is little time for proper celebrations – no open-top bus ride round the city of Nottingham. We just put the trophy on the sideboard and prepare for Newcastle United on Saturday. Of course, we come onto the pitch at the City Ground to thunderous applause. 'Mist rolling in from the Trent' has never been sung more loudly by the fans. But for the players, 'no slip-ups' is the simple directive from the manager. 'Wednesday was brilliant but all that is in the past.' There is a league to be won and Newcastle United are in the way. We don't let it slip. We win 2–0 and continue our unbeaten form.

With each passing match, the title gets tantalizingly closer and closer. On 22 April 1978, we find ourselves at Highfield Road, facing Coventry. Today we just need a draw to win the championship. I know that even if we don't get a point this afternoon, we still have another four games in which to do so, but I dismiss the thought. The fans are here in vast numbers, I'm sure wanting to tell children and grandchildren that they were there for the day it happened. I don't want to let them down.

No one has told Coventry it's supposed to be Forest's day. They are tight with purpose, while we are still trying to recover from our midweek exertions. Shilton makes a wonderful point-blank save. And then it's all over. We are the champions of England. There is unrivalled jubilation among the players and ecstasy among the fans. We have won the league with five games to spare. It's a magnificent achievement for any club, but for a team that scraped promotion in third position last season it is almost miraculous.

Putting the achievement into perspective, we have won the league with sixty-four points, seven points clear of Liverpool and incredibly twenty-eight points more than Chelsea and Wolves, who were promoted in front of us last season. The scenes in the dressing room are euphoric. Then the manager speaks. He hails our achievement, the effort, the key moments he remembers in games: that incredible goal by Robertson or the build-up to another goal, which might have started a full minute beforehand when Viv Anderson or Colin Barrett made a tackle. The league championship will go alongside the League Cup trophy in the Nottingham Forest trophy cabinet. But there will be plenty more glory to come.

5

EUROPE

It's early September 1978 on a Monday night at Field Mill, Mansfield, and Nottingham Forest are playing a friendly. Billy Bingham is the manager of Mansfield. I have never met him before, but I know just about everything about his career, both as a player and now as a manager. Like me, Billy Bingham is from Northern Ireland and, as a player, had been a winger for Sunderland.

We win the game in a common canter again, as you might expect the champions of England to do against much weaker opposition. I'm about to board the departing bus when Billy taps me on the shoulder to make himself known. And in his wonderfully refined Northern Irish accent he asks a favour of me.

'I like the young lad, Garry Birtles, who plays in your reserves. What do you think of him yourself?' he enquires.

'Garry's a really good footballer, but he isn't getting a look-in at the moment in our team,' I answer.

'Do you think he might want to come here?'

'Well, he wants to play first-team football, he's a local lad, and I'm sure he'd love to come and play here.'

I'm not exactly sure this news that I'm imparting to Billy is wholly correct, but I know that Garry is a bit restless, considering that Peter Withe has left the club for Newcastle and yet, despite that, Clough and Taylor have started the season with another young lad with promise, Stephen Elliott.

'Would you ask Garry if he'd like to come to us? If he thinks it's a good idea, I'll move things along,' Billy says.

I agree to do this and get back to him on Mansfield's club number as soon as I can. I see Garry at training and I tell him that Billy Bingham is very interested in taking him to Mansfield. I had forgotten to ask Billy whether this would be a loan or a permanent move, assuming Clough and Taylor agree, but either way Garry welcomes the news. He just wants to play for someone's first team. He had been planning to see Clough about leaving anyway, and this news gives him some extra impetus, knowing that a club not too far away wants him. I phone Billy at Mansfield to tell him the good news.

It is Wednesday 6 September and Garry is going to see the management team on Thursday after training. We beat Oldham Athletic this evening by four goals to two, but young Stephen Elliott still hasn't scored a goal after six consecutive games. What happens in the next twenty-four hours shapes the course of Garry's career. Clough changes tack. He starts Garry Birtles on Saturday at home to Arsenal, and again in midweek against Liverpool in the first leg of the European Cup. Birtles scores and never looks back.

I call Billy to let him know that Garry won't be joining him after all. Billy takes the news graciously, appreciating the call back to him. This is the start of my relationship with this erudite man from East Belfast.

The draw for the European Cup is made. It's a moment to relish and I envisage a trip to Milan, Lisbón or any number of exotic cities that I've never visited. But no, we are drawn against Liverpool. It's the one club we do not want to face. Firstly, it doesn't seem like a European tie this early in the season. Secondly, it's Liverpool and, despite our great results against them last season, they are reigning European Cup holders. We could not be more disappointed, but it is what it is.

In no time Liverpool are at the City Ground for the first leg.

A brilliant performance by Clough's team is epitomized by a magnificent Colin Barrett goal a few minutes from the end. We have a two-goal cushion in our first-ever match in the European Cup, against the champions.

What follows a fortnight later is a defensive display equal to Helenio Herrera's *catenaccio* of a previous generation, the tactical system he made famous at Atlético de Madrid. We ride out a 0–0 draw at Anfield and Liverpool are out. They won't be winning the European Cup for the third time in a row. We later demolish AEK Athens and take our place in the quarter-finals to be played in March.

Back in the league, Liverpool get their revenge, beating us 2–0 at Anfield. It is their first victory over us since our arrival back in the First Division. More astonishingly, it is the first time Nottingham Forest have lost in forty-two league games, an extraordinary achievement.

Now Liverpool are out of Europe, they can concentrate on winning back their First Division title. We will prove we are not one-season wonders and will continue to chase them until the bitter end, but nevertheless, our European campaign takes centre stage. I am playing very well but every game I play feels like a test, a struggle to prove my worth to Clough and Taylor. A lot of my inner thoughts about my place in the team can be way off the mark. But sometimes my observations are pretty accurate. I suppose I'll soon find out.

Our quarter-final opponents in the European Cup are the Swiss champions Grasshoppers Zürich. We don't know too much about them, but Peter Taylor tells us that one or two of them can really play, particularly the centre forward Claudio Sulser.

I do not think that we ever underestimated any team in any league during Clough and Taylor's reign, although we were always given to believe that we could beat anyone with a dose of proper application.

However, the Grasshoppers are very talented, as we are about to find out. Early warning signs on a heavy City Ground pitch go unheeded, and Sulser pops up to give Grasshoppers a deserved lead in the early stages of the match. For the first time in the European Cup, we are behind in a game. And worse, at home, with our opponents having a crucial away goal.

We get ourselves into a nervous state of flux. The manager bellows for us to calm things down and stay in the game until we gain some semblance of composure. Woodcock turns his marker superbly and darts away towards goal, sees Birtles to his left, and plays a little pass to him across the lumpy surface. Birtles controls with his right foot, takes it onto his favourite left foot and slots home the equalizer. There is relief all round. Parity.

Clough isn't happy at half-time. We have been far too anxious, choosing the wrong pass when in possession, and not moving the ball quickly enough. Our biggest sin is giving our opponents far too much time to control the ball and pick passes. The whole first half has been played at their tempo. We need to dictate the play. He's absolutely right.

I do not want to be knocked out of the European Cup. We are English champions! Conquerors of Liverpool in the first round! Come on. I know we can solve this in the second half. We just need to do what Clough tells us and be a lot more positive.

Early in the second half, we get a penalty. The referee makes the correct call but, from Zürich's perspective, it's a needless handball by their defender. John Robertson steps up and calmly side-foots the ball into the corner of the net. I don't know how he does it. I mean, staying calm and slotting it home. I remember him once missing two penalties in one game against Hull City; after the second one I put the rebound into the net to spare his blushes. But here he is in the cauldron of a quarter-final in the European Cup and he strokes it almost nonchalantly into the far corner. Maybe that's why Clough loves him so much.

There are three minutes to go. We lead 2–1 but we definitely need a third goal. The Grasshoppers have played excellently all evening and are still a threat. Then Archie Gemmill drives in a goal after a bit of sloppy defensive play from our opponents. And to put the icing on the cake, Larry Lloyd rises highest to head in a fourth goal with the time almost up. We have won 4–1. The scoreline flatters us. We have been in a proper scrap all evening. We know we haven't deserved such a lead, but we'll take it. Heaven knows we'll take it. Because in a fortnight the second leg is coming. Those two late goals could prove to be absolute gold dust. But there is no time to dwell on that, so dizzying is this carousel that we find ourselves on. Zürich will have to wait. We have a League Cup final against Southampton at Wembley next Saturday.

I came to Nottingham Forest in late 1971 hoping to win medals, which is what the game is all about. Now big game follows big game and I'm having the time of my life. I want to stay twenty-seven for the rest of my existence.

It is Friday evening and we've just arrived at a hotel in Cockfosters, north London. It's about 9 p.m. and the bus ride from Nottingham was an easy two-and-a-half-hour journey. Southampton await tomorrow in the League Cup final of Saturday 17 March 1979 at Wembley Stadium. I remember the last time I played at the home of football. It was last August, and I scored two goals in our 5–0 victory against Ipswich in the Charity Shield before being hauled off by Clough. I never did get to the bottom of why I was substituted that day, but it's water under the bridge now. Tomorrow is our chance to retain the League Cup and get another trophy in the cabinet.

Terry Curran will be playing for Southampton. I'm sure he'll want to show Clough and Taylor that he should still be at Forest, but I'm still here and he's there and that's called life.

The team are summoned to a cosy parlour downstairs in the hotel. There are no tea and sandwiches as we expected. Instead, champagne and orange juice are dispensed and Clough and Taylor are the servers. Archie Gemmill does not think this is a great idea but stays silent for now. David Needham isn't a big champagne lover either, but his mild protestations are dismissed by Taylor and he has to sit back down again in his chair. I'm in the same camp as David, champagne in 1979 being a bit too fizzy for me, but I still want to listen to Clough and Taylor revisit their days at Hartlepool, mimicking the speech and mannerisms of some of the characters they met along the way.

It's actually great fun, and the champagne tastes not too bad when laced with orange juice. Taylor is a funny man when in full flow, and I do not know whether I am laughing loudly at his jokes to ingratiate myself because I'm still scared of him, or because of the anticipation of tomorrow. It is probably a mixture of both. Sometime around midnight, Archie reminds the two hosts that there is a small matter of a Wembley final tomorrow at three o'clock and it is high time we headed off to bed. Taylor says something about Archie being a spoilsport, but the jovial rebuke triggers an end to the night's entertainment. Tony Woodcock is not looking too magnificent just now and we help him up the stairs to his room, although this might also be a show to make the management team feel a bit bad about themselves. Not much chance of that ever happening, even if Tony was to keel over at their feet.

Our pre-match walk around the grounds of the hotel is dominated by talk of last night's champagne reception. Tony is a little groggy, but hopefully will be fine. We know that it is the management's way of relaxing us before a big game. There are maybe less alcoholic ways to achieve that, but their record speaks for itself, so who are we to question their strategy? They have won league championships in the 1970s with two different clubs, so there is likely method in the madness. We get on the bus to Wembley.

Red and white are the colours of the day outside the stadium, these being ours and Southampton's primaries. We must have won the toss because we will wear our normal Garibaldi red shirts while Southampton will be in all yellow. First blood to us, although yellow is no barrier to success: last season we scored a big victory in the League Cup final replay against Liverpool, and we also dismantled Manchester United at Old Trafford, both times garbed in yellow.

Southampton score early and we are on the back foot. We take a long time to get into our stride and, if we don't get an equalizer soon, I'm dreading being in the dressing room at half-time, especially with an intractable manager barking in your ear.

We don't get an equalizer and Clough goes on the warpath. None of last night's jollifications have anything to do with our poor performance. We have not been at it right from the start. Do not leave the stadium this evening without that League Cup. It's ours, has been for a year now, and he wants it back on the bus with a seat of its own and in his house tonight.

'Do you hear me?'

The message hits home. We score three times in the second half, have another two goals chalked off for marginal offside decisions and we win the game. Through utter determination and some terrific football, we will walk back down the most famous of tunnels, letting out roars of unbridled triumph. We get on the bus and think of nothing else but the Grasshoppers away on Wednesday night.

The stadium in Zürich has a 20,000 capacity. But honestly, it seems like there are 60,000 people in the ground, so loud is the noise. I thought that the Swiss were a cultured and civil nation, not prone to excess excitement. I've got this totally wrong. The team they are supporting tonight feel as if they have a score to settle, and if they can get an early first goal, they can still retrieve this tie.

And that is exactly what happens. A penalty is awarded and they take the lead. We are penned back and cannot get out. They are all over us. The next goal is vital. If it falls for them, then one more and they will go through with their away goal. But if we can get it – and at the moment it's a big 'if' – we should see it through to the semi-finals.

I am on the far side of the pitch from Clough and Taylor's dugout, and with the crowd noise I cannot make out anything they are saying. But they are definitely agitated. Can we hold out till half-time conceding only one?

A moment later, Robertson has the ball just inside our half. He helps it down the wing where there is some nice interplay between Woodcock and Birtles. I see all this unfold from my vantage point on the right side of midfield. I know where I must be. I do not need the gesticulations of the management team to tell me to advance to the back post for any possible cutbacks across the box. I run full out to get there. Birtles pulls the ball across and I'm there to bundle it into the net.

It's a big goal in the context of the tie. It's just an equalizer, but it's much more than that and the crowd knows it. The stadium falls silent, my away goal a crushing blow. Half-time follows quickly. In the dressing room, both Clough and Taylor turn to me.

'You weren't going to make that run, were you, until we forced you to? We were roaring at you to get going, get to the back post, you just weren't going to do it?'

I have little idea what they're talking about. I know they were wound up about something, but they had been restless the whole half. I have to answer them back.

'You're wrong. I was always going to make that run, because that's what I do. That's what I've been doing all season.'

They calm down. I've got the goal. And we should see the match out, now that the opposition need at least three more goals again to take it into extra time. The stuffing has been knocked out of the Grasshoppers and they don't come back. We finish the game level. I've made a big contribution, regardless of the management taking all the credit for my run, and we are in the semi-final of the European Cup.

It's a cold spring morning in April 1979. I have been awake half the night. A bit of toast digested, I head into the City Ground from a temporary rented house in East Bridgford. With the game tonight, training will be light and we can choose to do what we want. A walk around the perimeter of the football ground is enough for me. The management will have a team talk in the dressing room in the next half-hour and then we will go to the

Albany Hotel in the city to have some lunch, an afternoon sleep, then back down in cars to the City Ground. Cologne, the West German champions, will be standing between us and a European Cup final.

Clough does not want to spend too much time on the opposition. He leaves Peter Taylor to do the talking this morning. Peter has been to see Cologne recently, so he will fill us in on their capabilities. As usual, they never want us to be afraid of any opposition we might face, whatever the circumstances.

John O'Hare says it was exactly the same at Derby County. Clough and Taylor concentrated on the team they were managing. They paid obvious respect to great teams in opposition, yes, but they never allowed their teams to feel inferior to anyone, irrespective of any internal doubts they might have had themselves.

In his inimitable fashion, Peter tells us that he has watched Cologne play and 'they're a Midland league team' he declares with not a hint of irony in his voice. 'I've seen them. They can't head the ball and they don't have any real pace in the team. And when they see the state of our pitch tonight . . .' He doesn't finish that sentence but we know what he's getting at. They just won't fancy it, he believes. 'You're all going up to the hotel now to have some lunch, aren't you? Well, have second helpings. We'll win this, no doubt whatsoever.'

It's Peter's way of taking pressure away from us. He knows there's tension in our faces. Maybe he really doesn't rate them highly, I don't know. I won't have second helpings, but I might sleep less fitfully this afternoon.

The previous weekend had brought the most tragic news. John Robertson's older brother Hughie and his wife had been killed in a road accident on Saturday night near Glasgow, and naturally he is completely devastated. We are too. Hughie came to a number of Forest matches and we had got to know him quite well. John travelled back to Scotland before our crucial game. Brian Clough said to him that the whole club would want him to play against Cologne, but that it was entirely up to him if he felt up to it. Everyone, including Brian, would understand completely if he didn't. But later on, we hear that John will play.

I am always nervous before big games. I think it's a good thing, or at least I've been telling myself that all my life. Just now, as we travel the couple of miles from the hotel to the City Ground, I try to take proper, deep breaths. I think about the first time I will receive the ball tonight. Pass it off easily or run with it. I suppose that depends on where I am on the field when I get the ball. But I will get to the back post, like I did at Zürich.

If I live to be a hundred and become an addled old man, irking all the nurses in the rest home, I will never forget the next hours of my life. I participate in the most atmospheric game ever played at the City Ground. There is still some light left in the day as the referee signals kick-off. The pitch is an absolute quagmire but what follows in the next hour and a half will be talked about for a long time by those 40,000 people sardined into the City Ground.

We fall behind early. We nearly equalize but are naïvely caught out by a swift Cologne counter-offensive. We concede a second goal. Twenty minutes gone in the semi-final of the European Cup and we are 2–0 down. It's devastating.

Cologne have picked us off so easily they probably cannot believe it themselves. We would like to take those twenty minutes back and start all over again. But God does not allow such things. We need something this very minute.

Once again, Birtles delivers with an exquisite header and it's 2–1. We still haven't learned our lesson. Cologne break again with embarrassing ease. Roger Van Gool, the Belgian international, is clear. He rounds Archie Gemmill and, with the goal at his mercy, he misses and shoots narrowly past the post. It's a big let-off. The game has no respite. Attack follows attack. We need another goal but cannot afford to concede one ourselves.

The manager tells us at half-time that we are well in the game but we are being exposed too easily for his liking. We need to tighten up defensively, not concede, and we can still win.

There are players you get to know when you play often

enough with them that, whatever the situation, you want them by your side. Ian Bowyer, our most underrated midfielder, is that man. Brave, strong in the air and an important goal-getter, he does it for us again, rifling home the equalizer in the second half.

The gaps are still there, and Cologne almost exploit them again, but we survive. And then there is a goal to remember. A twist and turn by Birtles, a cross, and then John Robertson comes flying in to head us into the lead. John never scores a goal with his head. But tonight, in this game of games, anything is possible. The man who had lost his brother over the weekend has no fear in his body. Hughie surely must have guided John's header into the net. We are leading 3–2. But the drama does not end there.

Cologne bring on a substitute, a Japanese player called Yasu-hiko Okudera. Within minutes he fires a shot under Peter Shilton to equalize: 3–3. Like two boxers swinging fists in the last round of a contest, hoping for a lucky punch, Forest and Cologne finish the game out on their feet. The referee calls time on one of the most dramatic European Cup semi-final games ever played.

Our manager sums up his reflections in a post-match TV interview. Considering our position after twenty minutes, we've done brilliantly to finish 3–3. And let no one write us off, he maintains. But those of us who know him, who have been in the dressing room long enough to sense what he's really thinking, reach a different conclusion. We feel that even he believes it's a long way back for us in Cologne. They have three away goals and we need to win.

Back on the domestic front, we have a home game against Leeds United in mid-April. Viv Anderson and I cannot get things going on the right-hand side. We have seen very little of the ball in the first half, and by half-time Clough is frustrated.

His first words when we sit down in the dressing room are directed at me.

'Hey, son, you and I are going to fall out.'

'Why?' I ask.

'Because you haven't had a f***ing kick, that's why.'

I have learned not to answer back. Take whatever is coming and accept it. But I can't always restrain myself. I answer back.

'There's only one ball,' I say. It's not the most revelatory sentence I have ever uttered but it is all I can muster.

'What did you say?'

The manager heard exactly what I had said, but he leans very close to me with his hand cupped round his ear.

'There's only one ball. It's down Robbo's side the whole time.'

'And so it should be. He's a f***ing genius!' And he stares at me but points in the direction of John. I am left with not only a rollicking from the manager but with the residual thought that he doesn't think I'm a genius.

'If you don't buck up in the second half, I'll put the linesman on in your place. He might do as well as you today.'

The second half meanders to a goalless draw. I am not replaced, although a similar pattern to the first half ensues. The manager is within seconds of conducting his post-match brief but says, 'Listen, we'll discuss this on Monday.' We all breathe a sigh of relief, none more so than myself.

Monday, after training, we are told to go to the director's room. Clough's inquisition will be conducted from there. We shuffle into the long, narrow lounge, with a drinks cabinet in the corner. Chairs are set out against a wall in a line. We have had a lot of meetings in this room before, so it isn't unusual for us to be here when the management team wants to discuss something. This morning is obviously geared to poring over Saturday's debacle against Leeds.

We are kept waiting for about fifteen minutes. This is normal practice. Clough and Taylor will come in when they are ready and not before. At present Peter Taylor is full of himself. All of his signings since he's come to the club have had a big impact. Brian Clough's signings, before Peter's arrival, have, with some obvious exceptions, paled in comparison.

Clough starts the meeting by picking up from Saturday's

half-time rancour, repeating to me what he had said. This time, even if I want to reply, I don't get the chance. Taylor interrupts, saying, 'Leave it Brian, I'll deal with this.'

He signals to John O'Hare to go to the drinks cabinet and get him a drink, meaning a small tipple of whisky, or something similar. John passes me and gives me a look, whispering, 'You're in for it now, squire.' He has obviously seen Peter react like this before at Derby County, although I'm still not sure what exactly I'm in for.

There is a thirty-second delay while John gets his drink. Peter gulps it in one go and addresses me.

'You, you, don't open your mouth.' I wasn't going to anyway. 'Let me tell you something. You are only in this team because of him, and him, and him,' he says as he starts to point out my team-mates in sequence. But then he comes to a player who makes him stop and wonder if this player should be included in his approval list. Peter decides in this case the player doesn't make the cut and, incredibly, says while gesticulating, 'Not so much him.'

He proceeds to point to the next player and starts again: 'Him, him,' and then reaches another player he's not sure of and says again, 'not so much him.' It's obvious that Peter wants to make me feel that I should count my blessings that I'm in the team, but now he has made at least three other players uncomfortable when there was no need.

The 'not-so-much-hims' stare at each other as if to say, 'Why has he involved us in the squabble?' Also, we now know exactly what he thinks of us.

Taylor comes back to me, having blown his cover sky-high. It gives me time to respond. 'I don't agree with you. I've scored six goals in the last six games. That's thirteen goals this season from wide right!'

'Thirteen goals, thirteen goals . . . Alan Durban would have scored twenty by now,' he spits. Alan Durban played for Peter and Brian at Derby County. He retired from playing some years ago and is managing Stoke City this season.

'Well go and get him,' I answer back, wishing the 'not-so-much-hims' might intervene and help me out.

'I will, I will,' says Peter in a complete fluster, without realizing what he's saying. I don't think Alan Durban is going to leave his role as manager of Stoke City, take up his boots again and join Forest on the right wing just to prove Peter right in his argument.

Clough sees that the debacle is going nowhere. He may now also have realized that the 'not-so-much-hims' are his signings, not Peter's. He says, 'Hold it, Peter, you are being harsh on the boy. He's done well.' Taylor, annoyed that Brian has intervened on my behalf, cannot resist one last contemptuous look at me and, with that, Clough dismisses the meeting.

A group of us head off to McKay's Café for tea. All the 'not-so-much-hims' don't know whether to laugh or cry. But my thoughts are already returning to the second leg against Cologne, hoping this episode hasn't threatened my place in the team.

Tony Woodcock will spend some glorious years in this beautiful city of Cologne with its famous cathedral. But tonight, he is with us in opposition to his future teammates.

We are strong. We defend well and we conjure some small openings going forward. We must score, otherwise we are out of the European Cup. There is plenty of time to do so. We just can't concede. Gaps that appeared at the City Ground a fortnight ago have been closed effectively.

We get more confident by the minute and Cologne, so effervescent before, are strangely subdued. There is a great chance for them to score, but it is spurned and we grab the initiative. With twenty-five minutes to go we force a corner. This is it: we must make it count. Robertson swings it in right-footed, Birtles gets a touch on it with his head and Bowyer stoops slightly to head the ball into the net. We are in front. Cologne need a goal and our resolve will be tested to the full.

Holding onto a lead is our speciality. It is something at which we are brilliant, just brilliant. Although the twenty-five minutes stretch in time, and we need a good double save by Shilton, the referee ends the game and we are in the European Cup final. Nottingham Forest will be at the Olympic Stadium in Munich next month.

After the match, Clough and Taylor are quite calm. The manager reminds the waiting media that he told them not to write us off. The league championship last season, two League Cup triumphs, and now the final of the European Cup. Stuff of dreams, goes the old saying. We don't think we will catch Liverpool for the First Division title, but the possibility of winning the European Cup? Now that's something else.

It's a lovely sunny May morning in Munich and the manager has taken us into the stadium to have a look at the pitch. Seven years have passed since the Olympic Games took place in this giant spider's-web arena – seven years since the terrible tragedy at the Israeli team's headquarters and the subsequent shoot-out at Munich Airport.

As we walk behind the goal, Clough separates Archie Gemmill, Frank Clark and me from the rest of the squad. They walk on, unsure of what exactly is being said to us but guessing to themselves. The three of us have been injured over the last few weeks but have declared ourselves fit for the final. You would, wouldn't you? Nottingham Forest – provincial Nottingham Forest – are in a once-in-a-lifetime final of the European Cup.

The meeting takes place on the shot-putters' ring, just behind the goal.

'Are you fit?' he asks the three of us. We all say yes.

'I think all three of you are lying, but I can only play one of you. Frank, you will play left back tonight, and you two will be on the bench. It's a tough decision for all of us but I cannot risk three players who haven't trained for three weeks in a European Cup final.'

Archie and I are devastated. But maybe I shouldn't be. Last

Friday I couldn't run properly. My trips to Mapperley Plains to see the physio, Norman Collins, at half past five every morning for over ten days have somehow been in vain. But in truth, without him, I probably wouldn't even have made it onto the plane.

Archie and I don't even console each other. We get up from a sitting position and join the rest of the team, who have walked towards the halfway line, in total silence.

We climb back onto the bus, return to our hotel, and have some lunch. Then it's off to our bedrooms: for Robbo the joy of playing in the European Cup final in a few hours, for me the disappointment, the anger, the resentment that the club had no idea of my battle to even be here this evening. I know I certainly won't walk this way again. Nottingham Forest will not play in two successive European Cup finals. I can only hope that I can get on that field to play a part in victory. In my head, I score twice in the final few minutes to win the cup and I walk those steps to collect my medal, the proudest man in the whole world.

In reality, I don't get on the field. Neither does Archie. We win 1–0 with that Trevor Francis goal, in the very position that I have been taking up these past few seasons, anticipating a Robertson cross.

The final is an anticlimax for me. Not for Larry Lloyd, not for Kenny Burns, not for Frank Clark, and not for Trevor Francis. He is the golden boy this evening. This is Forest's evening. It's the city's evening. It's the country's evening. But it's not mine. Not Archie Gemmill's.

I see my face in the archive footage. It is solemn. I know I shouldn't feel like this. I have been a part of this team, this club for almost eight years. I have experienced everything, from relegation in my first season, to Allan Brown, to promotion, to the First Division championship, to League Cup victories at Wembley and Old Trafford.

All this is lost in the moment of victory, a victory I cannot savour.

I wonder if other players feel this way. Life changes, squads are rotated and players are made to feel part of it all. Those on the bench share the same feelings as those who have just done the playing. But not in Munich. Not for me. An unused substitute is not part of anything. The semi-final against Cologne feels like ancient history. That wonderful, wonderful sensation that night against the double-winning Germans in that beautiful city doesn't exist any more. Forest are champions of Europe and I'm there in body but not in mind. I collect my medal in the little square red box, glance at the medal itself, and then close the box tight. John reaches out to me.

'We've done it, squire, we've actually done it. Unbelievable.' He's done it. He has crossed the ball for Trevor's winning goal.

He has been magnificent all season, and the season before that. He can enjoy the night and the rest of his life. He has played in and won the European Cup. I have not.

In the dressing room the players are exhausted but in phenomenal spirits. I look across at Archie. He is not good either but congratulates the lads once again. He and I have already done that on the pitch. It's worth doing again in the confines of this little room, small for such a massive stadium.

Then Clough speaks. He soon realizes that there are no medals cut for managers or coaches. It's just the playing squad who receive them. I don't think that he or Peter Taylor had thought about this before, but now it dawns on them. They have no medals to bring home. Just the trophy.

'Lads, we would like to have a few more medals cut for the staff [meaning himself, Taylor and Jimmy Gordon], so if the subs put their medals back on the table, you will get them back when we return preseason.'

What? Obviously the cutter would want to have a medal so that he could make a replica, and the manager feels that all five subs should give up their medals rather than just one being forced to hand his over. It seems fair to Clough, but it certainly doesn't seem fair to me. I have family outside waiting to catch a glimpse of that European Cup medal that George Best had won eleven years before at Wembley for Manchester United.

I say to the manager that my family would just like to see the medal and then I'll come back and give it to Jimmy. But he rejects my request. 'We would all like to do that,' he replies, somewhat sarcastically, as if his wife was waiting in the corridor to glimpse one but that he would not even do that for her. The whole conversation, if you can call it that, turns my great disappointment into anger. I throw the box across the massage table in the middle of the dressing room. It dances a few times on the table, like a skimming stone on water, and falls to the ground. Clough doesn't say anything. Perhaps he has realized that my request wasn't as outrageous as he had made it sound.

The club have just won the European Cup. Forest are the champions of the Continent. He will be lauded and feted tomorrow morning. His agonizing semi-final loss against Juventus with Derby has been buried this evening. He says the players can do anything they want tonight, as long as they are at the hotel tomorrow morning for the flight home. But the substitutes cannot show their medals to family and friends. They haven't got them and they will go home with no medal in their blazer pocket.

I expect a reaction from him but he stays silent. I walk five or six paces to pick up the box, and ask Jimmy Gordon for a pen. I put a little mark on the round yellow marker on the cover of the box. 'Jimmy,' I say, 'this is the medal I have won tonight. When I get my medal back, this is the box and the medal that I want to have. No other medal will be good enough.'

'OK, son, I'll see to that,' he replies. A few weeks later the medals are given back. The box with the mark is given to me. To this day, I hold the belief that the medal inside is the one that I was given on 30 May 1979.

*

Anything is possible with Clough and Taylor at the helm. Despite a small lapse in our league form the next season – 1979/80, where we finish fifth – astoundingly we navigate our way to the highest stage in club football once again. A provincial team *can* reach the European Cup final for two years running.

A few weeks before the final, Trevor Francis, having a golden period in Forest colours, snaps his Achilles tendon. Though it brings me no pleasure, the irony is not lost on me after his heroics last year. He will be out for at least eight months. It is a devastating blow to him and to our chances of beating Hamburg, the Kevin Keegan-led German champions in the final at the Bernabéu Stadium in Madrid. The only consolation is that Hamburg have beaten Real Madrid in the semi-finals. Had they not done so, we would have to play the Spaniards in their own stadium. But it's small consolation indeed.

Even with Francis playing, there was a strong probability that I would make the starting line-up. Woodcock is now playing in Cologne. I have played the quarter-finals and semi-finals. I will play in the final. But, without Francis, our hopes look grim to say the least.

It's Saturday morning at East Midlands Airport, eleven days before the European Cup final. We are travelling to Majorca. We will spend a full week there. We will come back the following Saturday to Nottingham, spend that evening and the Sunday with family, and then head back out to Spain on the Monday morning. The final is on the Wednesday evening.

Majorca is fun. Lots of fun. It is no ordinary week and we do very little training. We meet each morning at eleven o'clock in the hotel foyer and go for a stroll with the management team along the beach promenade. That will be the training for the whole week. We will have no curfew in the evening. But are we doing enough? The Germans are at a training camp, with full concentration on the game ahead.

We, the players, know that the manager wants us to relax before games. There is no point in waking up each morning with tension round our shoulders, wasting nervous energy by over-thinking. We enjoy the week, but by Saturday there is a collective feeling among the players that we should have done more training. The final is only four days away.

'What was the trip like? I bet there must have been some nights that the manager allowed you out to midnight,' was the obvious question I received from my wife, back in the county of Nottinghamshire.

'Allowed out to midnight? We were just going out at midnight!' I exclaimed.

Monday morning comes round all too quickly. We fly to Madrid. Trevor, still in hospital, is told by the manager that he cannot come with the team. The manager feels that if he is walking round the hotel on crutches, he will take the focus away from us and our preparation for the game. The previous year's winning goal is forgotten – at least for now. Trevor will not be there.

An eighteen-year-old will take Trevor's place in the line-up to face the team that knocked Real Madrid out of the European Cup a few weeks before. The precocious Gary Mills will be ready for the challenge, despite being the youngest-ever player in a European Cup final.

Our hotel is not in Madrid, not even on the outskirts. It is almost thirty miles into the hills. We know we need some peace and quiet, but it nevertheless seems a long way out. We will have to make this winding journey twice in the next two days.

The morning before the game, we train at the Bernabéu. We are relaxed and the game is still another thirty-six hours away. The groundsmen are re-laying some turf on the pitch. Surely there will not be enough time for those sods to bed in overnight and be ready for the following evening? In broken English, the groundsmen tell us not to worry. The pitch will be '*perfecto*' for the game. The pitch will not be the problem, one of them suggests. Hamburg will.

That same evening, before supper, we leave the hotel on the bus to look for and find some kind of field to have our last workout before the final. We have been told about a local pitch by the waiters in the hotel, but it hasn't been that easy to find.

We spot it eventually and get ready for a full-blooded eight-a-side game. The manager is playing in one of the teams. He takes up his position wide left but not too far from the small goals into which he wants to score. This has always been his position when he has joined in before. Peter Taylor watches the initial skirmishes from the sidelines but soon retreats to the bus.

The game is frenetic, with ridiculous tackles taking place. The Spanish bus driver watches in total bewilderment. He may never before have seen a professional football team try to kick lumps out of each other on the eve of a European Cup final. In fact, it is absolutely certain he hasn't. Clough's team are trailing by a goal. He doesn't want to lose. We have been playing far longer than we should, considering the stakes tomorrow evening. Thunder fulminates around the hills, preceded by sheets of lightning. Hailstones as big as ping-pong balls fall from the heavens. No one seems to notice. The score in the game is the only thing of importance.

Lloyd and Shilton conclude that enough is enough and decide to let the manager's team equalize to call a halt to proceedings. They pass a message round and it happens. Clough's team equalize. 'We'll play a winner,' says the manager, oblivious to the cascading hailstones. We let him score and the game ends. We rush to the safety of the bus, finding Peter Taylor fast asleep. He is woken up, having slept soundly through the game, the thunder, lightning and hail.

'Are you finished?' he asks. 'Yes,' we mutter silently to ourselves. 'We've only been at it for a solid hour.'

Back at the hotel, we shower, change and get ready for supper. The bus driver has already told the waiters what he witnessed in the last few hours. Serving up the food, they whisper to us, 'Your coach, he is crazy, yes?' Our twisted smiles only serve to confirm their assessment.

*

Morning arrives and breakfast is over. The manager summons us to the foyer and from there we climb onto the bus again, this time for a short journey. About two miles down the road, Clough halts the bus and we get off to stretch our legs. It's not a long walk, but long enough to allow us to think about the evening ahead. Peter Taylor has been bullish to the press in the build-up to the game. Hamburg's captain, Kevin Keegan, has naturally attracted national interest and headlines, and as a retort, Peter has upped the banter. 'I think Burnsy and Lloydy are looking forward to meeting him,' he says sardonically, meaning that there might be a few bruises before the night is over. But secretly the management pair are worried. Last year Malmö couldn't beat us. This year is different. Francis is missing and our goal power will obviously decrease dramatically. It will be a long, long evening.

Clough suddenly stops the walk. We gather round. He addresses us. 'Well, Kenneth, what do you think?' He always calls Kenny Burns 'Kenneth'.

'We all know what we've got to do, boss,' replies Burns.

'That's good enough for me, Kenneth.' And with those words, Clough closes the conversation. We turn back, climb back on the bus and return to the hotel. The team meeting is over. But, short though it may have been, it resonates loudly within all of us.

And it does the trick wonderfully. We win 1–0 against Hamburg.

Following our momentous victory, we ask Clough whether we can stay in Madrid with the wives and girlfriends, and not wind our way back to the hotel. We can make our own way out in the morning before travelling back to England. But the manager is having none of it. 'We came here as a team, and we are going back as a team,' he says. And, despite some mild protests, he is adamant that's what we are doing.

We have a few minutes with our families before climbing onto the bus. We have a schoolboy plan which we relay to the girls: 'Don't worry. We will travel back to the hotel as the manager insists. We will wait until he and Taylor go to bed, and we will get some taxis and come back to Madrid to the girls' hotel and enjoy the rest of what remains of the night.'

The bus takes its time. At the hotel we get out Connect 4, which has recently become a phenomenon. We are waiting patiently for Peter Taylor to go to bed, but he's intrigued by the game and stands over our shoulders, watching two of us play each other. Any latecomers booking into the hotel could never possibly guess that a group of young men attired in blue blazers and ties playing Connect 4 had less than three hours earlier won the biggest prize in football, in a stadium nearly thirty miles away. Eventually, Taylor tires of the game and says good night, well done, and see you in the morning.

We know he's an early riser so our time is limited. Taxis are already on standby waiting outside. Some of the lads get cold feet and decide to stay. But a select band known forever onwards as the Magnificent Seven hightail it into Madrid to enjoy the last few hours of the most mind-blowing day one can imagine. Some of the players who don't make the trip will face a grilling back home after a few of the wives ask why their men didn't bother to come to Madrid.

A few hours go by and it's time for us to head back to the hotel before Taylor gets up. We manage this feat by only about three minutes, so by the time Peter comes down to the foyer we are perched, frozen in time, around the same table, with the same Connect 4 game in front of us.

'No bed for you lot, then?' he asks.

'No, Peter, we couldn't sleep, so just stayed here playing Connect 4.'

Peter then makes his way to the breakfast room. Clough gets to hear about our little escapade within hours and threatens fines, but ultimately relents. After all, he's going back to East Midlands Airport with a trophy we've won with him and for him.

Nottingham city centre is thronged again with crowds as large as last year's.

Each of the players takes turns to come onto the balcony of the council building, hold the European Cup aloft and salute the thousands of cheering fans gathered in the city square. Life could not be any sweeter on days like these. Twenty-four hours ago we were in the Bernabéu Stadium playing with heart and soul in order to do exactly what we're doing now. After the final waves to the crowd, we step back into the wings of this large municipal building. The show is over.

The wine bar near Byard Lane seems a perfect place to end this surreal evening. A group of us make our way up the hill and turn right towards our destination, knowing that the pinnacle has been reached. The jubilant cheers of the crowd fade into the night air and the quiet of the lane draws a reflective contrast. At this very moment I believe we all have the same thought running through our minds. We will probably not walk this way again in such circumstances. But today has happened. It isn't a dream, is it? I put my hand into my pocket. The medal is still there.

6

AN INTERNATIONAL INTERLUDE

My European forays with Nottingham Forest were not the only opportunities to widen my game beyond the domestic league. Ever since Terry Neill taught me a lesson in old-fashioned manners in 1972, I'd always relished joining up with the Northern Ireland squad. Those experiences made me want to be part of that unique group of players who were so much fun to be around. I couldn't wait to be picked for the squad. The expectation, particularly when George Best was absent, was not exceedingly high, and so we wore the underdog tag with almost a sense of pride. Nevertheless, a couple of days in the company of Derek Dougan, Pat Rice, Sammy Nelson, Pat Jennings and Eric McMordie was such a thrill for a rookie recruit like myself, and on more than one occasion I had to accept that some of the jokes were on me. And of course if George Best did decide to turn up, then all was good with the world.

There was always a sprinkling of talent in the international squad during the 1970s, but Northern Ireland lacked the overall strength and depth to allow a player like George to display his dazzling footballing skills on the biggest stage – the World Cup finals. The fun, the good-natured banter and strong camaraderie were always at the forefront of any Northern Ireland gathering, but we longed to add a winning run to the good times we had when we were together. Our wishes were about to be granted with the appointment, or should I say reappointment, of Billy Bingham as manager of the Northern Ireland team.

It's late February 1980, about sixteen months since I last had contact with Billy. He is the newly appointed manager of Northern Ireland, taking over from Danny Blanchflower, a one-time teammate of Billy's in a very successful 1958 World Cup campaign in Sweden. Billy gets my home number and he phones. He wants to meet me. This we do in a hotel not far from Nottingham.

'As you know, I've just taken over again as the manager of Northern Ireland. One of the first things I want to do is select a captain, someone who can motivate the players around him, carry out my instructions on the field and be a good communicator on and off the pitch. I would like you to be my captain for the foreseeable future. The 1982 World Cup in Spain is my objective. We have a number of established First Division players already in the squad and personally I think I can get the best out of the team. You know I managed the team ten years ago and I have to say I enjoyed it. Your European experience with Nottingham Forest should be a bonus for us. What are your thoughts?'

'Thank you very much, Billy,' I respond. 'I'm delighted, absolutely delighted that you have asked me. That couldn't have been easy for you considering I'm a Catholic?'

'Yes, I did consider all of that and no doubt I'll take some flak for it, but I'll deal with it, and if we start winning no one will really care that much.'

I would become the first Catholic to captain Northern Ireland. I know that this makes me a target for criticism, but Billy's words are never far from my mind: 'If we start winning no one will really care that much.'

When Billy makes the official announcement about me being captain, he does have to fend off much criticism in the coming weeks. Nevertheless, he insists that I'm the best man for the role and I am encouraged by his steadfastness.

Bingham has little or no time to prepare the squad for the opening qualifying game of the 1982 World Cup. We are in a five-nation group with Scotland, Portugal, Sweden and Israel. Israel are to be our first opponents and we will be playing away in Ramat Gan, a satellite city of Tel Aviv. The World Cup finals have been extended from sixteen to twenty-four teams, which means that two nations instead of just one will qualify from our group. This definitely improves our chances of making it to Spain in two years' time.

Even in this shortened preparation period, a sea change in the squad's management style takes place. Northern Ireland will play to whatever strengths we feel we possess. We will not maraud our way up the pitch, lose the ball and allow teams to attack an unprotected defence, as in recent games. No, we will be solid, allow few gaps to develop, cover them quickly if they do and have our forward players as the first line of defence. I can see parallels between Bingham and Clough. The players are left with no doubt as to what their job on the pitch will be for the entire game. We feel we can win our opening fixture. We know little about Israel, who have been in soccer exile for a period due to the volatile situation in the Middle East. Avi Cohen, who plays for Liverpool, is their best-known player. We don't underestimate them but we don't fear them either.

We fly to Israel in March 1980 and reach our appointed hotel. In each bedroom there are messages greeting us, and a substantial chocolate cake in each as well. It seems a lovely gesture from the hotel staff, but Billy Bingham is not convinced. He reaches his room about the same time as us, sees the cake in his room, and becomes immediately suspicious about its content. He races up and down the corridor knocking frantically on all the doors, shouting, 'Don't eat the cake! Don't eat the cake!' Too late. Tommy Cassidy opens his bedroom door to see what the noise in the corridor is all about. 'What is it, Billy?' he asks as he cleans the crumbs away from his mouth.

*

There is a large crowd gathering outside the stadium as our coach pulls up at the entrance. I was hoping that the Israeli supporters would take little interest in the game and that we might play in a half-empty stadium. No such luck. The stadium is teeming long before kick-off. The fans are definitely up for this and – as I soon find out – so is the Israeli team. They have a midfielder called Rifaat Turk, who is running the show, and we cannot get near him. Most of the first half we are chasing shadows, or at least Turk's shadow. Half-time cannot come quickly enough. Bingham urges us to get closer to our opponents and not give them as much time on the ball. It's a simple instruction, but somewhat more difficult to execute.

The second half starts much like the first ended, with Israel in command of the ball. It's a test for us as a team and certainly for me as captain. At Forest when we were under pressure, we tightened the midfield and pulled our wide players in from the touchline, forcing the opposition to go round the outside of us rather than through the middle. At least we would have numbers back to thwart imminent danger, so I think this is what we should do here. Our attacking options may be limited but a point away from home in the opening qualifying game is an OK start. Just when we are flagging, an act of God comes to our rescue. There is a floodlight failure in the stadium and we are plunged into darkness for about twenty minutes. It is enough time to draw breath, regroup, re-energize ourselves and implement our tactical plan.

The floodlights come back on and we find enough strength and willpower to keep Israel scoreless, but it's been a rocky old start to the campaign. My first game as captain of Northern Ireland is best remembered as the evening when the darkness actually shone its light on Northern Ireland's qualification hopes for the 1982 World Cup.

Billy Bingham tells an unconvinced Irish press that it's a point gained rather than one lost. I agree with him. I have played too many of these games for Nottingham Forest to take any opposition lightly, and anyway the general consensus among the players is that Israel at home will be a tough nut to crack for the other teams in the group, particularly if they play the way they did against us this evening.

The Home Internationals are at the end of the season, with three games within a week. However, in May 1980, Nottingham Forest are still due to play the European Cup final and Brian Clough understandably refuses to release me. He does, however, allow Garry Birtles to play a friendly game for England against Argentina and Larry Lloyd to play against Wales in the same competition. I can't decide whether to be annoyed. Still, no one wants to miss the European Cup final, so I actually feel a small element of relief when I'm not allowed to join up with the Northern Ireland squad.

Bingham certainly makes an impact on the team, who go on to beat Scotland, draw with England at Wembley and beat Wales in Cardiff to pull off a shock British championship victory. Sammy McIlroy stands in as captain in my absence and does a sterling job, but I am reinstated for a four-game tour of Australia in June.

First stop is Sydney, with the famous Sydney Cricket Ground the chosen venue for the game against Australia. Soccer is not the number one sport in this part of the world and Sydney Cricket Ground is used to holding huge crowds for an Ashes Test match. It may not have been everyone's chosen venue for an international soccer game, regardless of the opposition, when there is going to be a relatively sparse turnout for the game. That said, the stadium is a sight to behold. I close my eyes and imagine the cheering as Don Bradman comes out on a sunny morning to bat for his country, or indeed what he must have felt when in 1932 the English captain Douglas Jardine ordered his best bowler, Nottinghamshire's Harold Larwood, to deliver the now infamous 'Bodyline' style of bowling attack at perhaps the greatest batsman in the history of cricket.

Even an empty Sydney cricket ground gives you goosebumps.

Little wonder that Brian Clough brings Geoffrey Boycott into the Forest dressing room at every available opportunity to remind us of the brilliance of the Yorkshireman standing beside him. And if by chance Brian forgets to mention Geoffrey's brilliance, Geoffrey reminds us all by himself, with not a trace of irony in his body. We win the game 2–1 and I get on the score sheet. It's a decent start to the two-week trip.

We get limited time to enjoy Sydney as a city, but even a brief winter stroll on Bondi Beach makes you feel that these young Australian men and women have had a head start on you in life. Melbourne is our next port of call. If I think Sydney Cricket Ground is spectacular, I am completely awestruck by Melbourne Cricket Ground, which houses almost 100,000 people. This time, we draw the match against the Aussies and I score again. I'm beginning to really enjoy this tour! Adelaide is a few days later and there is another victory against our hosts, who must be getting very sick of us by now. Our final destination in Australia is the city of Perth, where we'll play Western Australia. I will go to Vancouver with Nottingham Forest six weeks from now and when I get there I will be undecided between it and Perth in terms of which is the most beautiful city I've ever had the pleasure of visiting.

It has been a whirlwind fortnight and there's been a lot of travelling. However, it has definitely been worth it, and it has served a purpose in terms of team-building too. Camaraderie has always been strong in the Northern Ireland camp, but two weeks of continual companionship has the potential to be claustrophobic. This has certainly not been the case with this group, and we come out of the tour closer than ever. How could it be anything but fun when the likes of Derek Spence and Terry Cochrane join forces with Gerry Armstrong and Billy Hamilton for a singularly Northern Irish type of evening? Derek Spence is not only a fine footballer but is probably the best mimic I know, parodying all of us in turn. Armstrong is a brilliant singer, or so he thinks, and Hamilton and Cochrane could be a warm-up act for any Billy Connolly show.

It's been a terrific few weeks for our manager. The completely unexpected British championship title and a successful tour of Australia, despite missing some key players, has vindicated Billy's no-nonsense approach, his tactical awareness and, of course, his choice of Catholic captain. The final victory against Western Australia in Perth is the cherry on the top.

'I think it has been a good success this trip, don't you?' he asks me in a quiet moment back at the Perth hotel.

'I couldn't agree more,' I answer.

'It gives me a chance to get to know the players who are new to the squad, and it gives you the opportunity to exert your own influence on the team,' he continues. 'I think we're on the right lines. I like the attitude and the spirit of the lads, don't you?' I find myself agreeing with Billy's every sentence.

I am ready to go home now, though, and so are the players. Bingham retires to bed, reminding me to get everyone ready to leave for the airport after breakfast in the morning. I'm not sure it's my job to get Billy Hamilton out of bed but I don't argue. I can see what the manager is building here. The World Cup in Spain may not be such a pipe dream after all.

By late 1980 we are three games down with three points on the board and two away games played. It's not a brilliant start to qualification, but not desperate either. In our group of fellow World Cup aspirants, Scotland and Portugal are level with us on points but both have a game in hand, which, as it turns out, they will both win.

We have four months before our next game, in March 1981, which we will play against Scotland at Hampden Park: four long months to brood over the dropped points. It's funny how little time I spent thinking about our 3–0 victory over Sweden in October. It's always the 'what might-have-beens' that capture the attention. If only we had done this instead of that.

Four months isn't so bad for the players, as we have plenty of club games to concentrate our minds. However, spare a thought for Billy Bingham. The only thing he has plenty of is time – time to ruminate, time to do everything except look forward to an upcoming game. There is no upcoming game. Not for four months anyway.

When late March 1981 finally arrives, we have all had far too long to ponder. The Scotland game is upon us and we simply cannot afford to get beaten. If Scotland are victorious, our chances of going to Spain are practically nil. We will not have sufficient fixtures to remedy the deficit. I am injured on the Saturday playing against Arsenal. I travel with the squad to Scotland but I know I won't recover in time for Wednesday evening. Billy knows it too and, on Tuesday, he tells me to forget any notion of playing. He needs fit players in the team and he's not prepared to risk lads who might have to come off early.

Late afternoon, the day before the game, Billy spots me talking to a couple of the players and beckons me over to join him at his table. I think he just wants to have a chat, most likely about Scotland tomorrow. He asks me what my thoughts are. 'We just cannot get beaten,' I say. He knows that already, but I think that having it reinforced aloud unnerves him. I'll get exactly that same unsettling jolt many times later in my managerial career at Celtic when I ask John Robertson a question I already know the answer to.

'What do you think Jock Stein might be planning?' Bingham asks.

'Well, Scotland are at home. They know that if they beat us, that knocks us for six. They can virtually limp to Spain in their final few games.'

'In normal circumstances I would agree with you. But I think that even Jock Stein might be a bit more circumspect than he would have been in his Celtic days,' Billy responds. 'Anyway, we have got to shore up midfield tomorrow. Can't let them go through us easily.' I nod my head in agreement.

'Have you yourself ever thought of management?' Billy asks, changing the subject, probably not wanting to fret too much about the impending game before it's really time to do so.

'Not really,' I reply, intrigued. 'Maybe I should give it a little more thought now that I've turned twenty-nine.'

'You should, you know. I think you could do well at it. You're a good communicator, which I think is vitally important, you know the game, and you have some presence about you. Of course, luck at crucial times is an imponderable, but you should give it some thought. Oh, by the way, I was also right about Garry Birtles,' he adds, as a reminder of our first-ever conversation. As he rises, he says, 'What time's dinner again?', as if I am the one calling the shots. It's an enlightening few minutes from our manager, and a welcome boost to my confidence.

Billy's instinct that Jock Stein might play it gingerly proves correct. When Scotland line up, we see that Kenny Burns, my ex-teammate at Nottingham Forest, will vacate his normal position at centre half and play in a totally unfamiliar holding centre midfield role. As expected, Scotland have much of the early possession and Northern Ireland survive some anxious moments.

Early on, Chris Nicholl clears the ball off the goal line to keep it scoreless. I find watching a tie of such importance from the sidelines is brutal. I am powerless and can do nothing else but fret, worry, frown or shout encouragement to my teammates. I cannot make a pass, make a tackle, run with the ball or shoot for goal: all that is left to my teammates on the field. But I live all these moments with them and by half-time feel as if I have played the forty-five minutes myself. As the players leave the field at the interval, we are still level with Scotland.

So far, so good.

The second half is much like the first, with us being resolute and determined. However, our attacks have a little more bite and accuracy. With twenty minutes to go, we break through and score, Billy Hamilton heading the ball into the Scottish net. Incredibly, we are in front at Hampden Park with time running out for the Scotsmen.

Can we actually win the game? Sadly not. Scotland increase intensity and we concede an equalizer. But still, the point we have is precious and we protect it to the end of the game. When the referee ends proceedings, we are still in the competition.

Three of the last four games are at Windsor Park, with the next being the most important of all, Portugal. But with Belfast being torn apart with bombings and shootings, will our opponents even want to come to Northern Ireland? To their credit, Portugal come to Belfast. It's late April 1981. Bobby Sands has been on hunger strike in Long Kesh for almost sixty days and rioting and bombing are daily occurrences.

We have two days to prepare for the match. As usual, Billy Bingham's sessions are intense. There is no time for long, leisurely warm-ups. We have to be ready come kick-off time on Wednesday and every second of our preparation is key.

The Scotland game last month was a mustn't-lose match. Wednesday against the Portuguese is a must-win. A draw is simply no good to us.

The dressing room is as tense as I've known it, relieved in part by some funny wisecracks from Arsenal defender Sammy Nelson. Bingham makes last reminders about our set pieces and there is the final roar of togetherness as the sounding bell denotes time to play.

Chances for us in the first half are few, but Portugal seem content to sit in and counter-attack. Bingham reminds us at half-time that only victory will suffice, but he's only verbalizing what we all know. It's all in these last forty-five minutes. As tension rises on the field, so it does on the terraces. Bottles thrown onto the pitch close to the Portuguese goalkeeper force the referee to stop play, approach Bingham and issue a warning.

There are more bottles thrown, and another warning. The rest of the game is in real jeopardy. Abandonment of the match looks probable more than possible. Concentration is broken. We need to refocus, if the referee even allows the play to continue. He does.

The antics have disturbed Portugal. We get a free kick, float the ball back into their penalty area, a Portuguese defender heads clear. Terry Cochrane, our pint-size winger, races to retrieve, delivers an inviting cross and Gerry Armstrong – who else? – guides the ball into the net.

It is the moment we've been waiting for.

However, more missiles are thrown onto the pitch. Bingham has had enough. He races to the Kop end and, in a fit of anger, remonstrates with the supporters and pleads for sanity. We need this game to finish properly, not to be abandoned. The whole campaign is on the line. Please stop this immediately and do not jeopardize the game.

His shouts and gesticulations have the desired effect. There are no more incidents. Portugal throw everything at us in the dying embers of the tie, but we hold on.

We are definitely back in the race for Spain. But, on witnessing the scenes at Windsor Park, England refuse to travel to play a British championship game there and Wales follow suit. We are disappointed but probably not surprised, given the volatile situation still existing in Northern Ireland.

Our next World Cup qualifier is in Stockholm against Sweden in early June 1981. Preparation for a game in June is fraught with difficulties, particularly against a country whose own home football season is in full flow. The game should never have been fixed for now, a full month after the British season has finished. But those details will be forgotten in due course. What will be remembered is how pitifully we play.

After the euphoria of the Portuguese result, this is a complete let-down. We seem to be devoid of energy, drive and – most of all – passion. The game drifts and we drift with it. Sweden are leading 1–0. It's a difficult time for me, the captain, and I know I should be better than this. I should be able to rouse the players, stress the magnitude of the game, the significance of at least a point to put on the table, but I can hardly even rouse myself.

Back in Northern Ireland, the *Belfast Telegraph* football reporter Malcolm Brodie savages our performance, calling it perhaps the worst he's ever witnessed in all his time covering the

Northern Ireland internationals. He's been covering this patch for a long time, but this particular group of players seems to bring the worst out of his scribblings.

The dressing room is a depressing place to be when you have lost a big game. We are all down, and Bingham is subdued too, with every reason. The enormity of the defeat does not sink in immediately – that will come in spades later on – but he realizes the significance of the result. And for me at least, this desolate dressing room becomes a sanctuary of sorts. I do not want to go outside and face the world. I want to stay here until the supporters go home, until the lights are all turned off and there is not a sound to be heard. Maybe then I'll take off my football gear, shower, change back into civilian clothes and walk into the night.

Very few players decide to venture from the hotel that Stockholm evening. We are distraught. There are no sing-songs from Gerry Armstrong. Nothing. A group sit round a table in the foyer, zombified. I'm in this gathering. Maybe as the captain I'm expected to make some forlorn rallying call, but right now I'm finding that difficult. But then something inside tells me that all is not lost.

The game against Sweden was poor. We have been lousy and they deserved to win. But honestly, I think that is because we have overlooked Sweden's strengths and capabilities. Like jurors sitting in a room having been sent out by the judge to consider the facts of the case, someone has to speak first.

'Sweden will beat Portugal in a couple of weeks,' I say with some defiance. 'They will be really confident after this result and they will surprise the Portuguese. I honestly believe they will win the game.'

Pat Jennings is not so sure. If there are two Northern Ireland players in the last twenty years who deserve to play in a World Cup, it's Pat and George Best. I'm sure he feels that this result has put paid to his chances of ever participating in one. But I haven't said what I've said as some sort of false pick-me-up. I genuinely think the Swedes will win. My view does not in any way dull the pain, but I cling onto that hope for the next fortnight. And it turns out I'm right.

Sweden beat Portugal 3–0. Even I do not expect Sweden to win so convincingly, but they take both points with aplomb. Goal difference may come into the equation in the final reckoning, so it's a brilliant result for us in every respect.

It's amazing how excited you can get about a result over which you have no control. Sweden have done us an almighty service and have put themselves back into the race for that second spot behind Scotland who, barring disaster, look Spain-bound next year in June.

As for ourselves, only two wins in the last two games will suffice and, despite their two losses, the Iberian men still have their World Cup destiny in their own hands. But we can only do what we have to; we must concentrate on ourselves.

It's mid-October 1981 and we face Scotland at Windsor Park, Belfast. Again, we need to win. They are virtually assured of their passage to Spain next summer, so we hope that will give us the edge.

We play with the desire, passion and energy that had been missing in Stockholm, but we cannot get that elusive goal. The second half is one-way traffic towards the Scotland six-yard box. It's relentless pressure against a very talented team, and there are goalmouth incidents aplenty. It's frenetic, tenacious football and it's everything that we are about. But exasperatingly, we cannot score. Scotland hold out and they are in Spain.

We should have won. We played with heart and desire. But once again we have come up short. This was another chance, another chance lost, again. Portugal play Sweden later tonight but lightning is not likely to strike twice, especially in Lisbon.

We are back at the Culloden Hotel. There is a phone call at reception for me. Alan Green, a young sports journalist, is on the other line. I hear the news in a way that I'm sure a lottery ticket holder must feel when a cursory glance at the numbers forces a more studied examination. Sweden have scored in the very last minute in Lisbon to beat Portugal 2–1.

'It's true? Can I tell the players? Definite? Absolutely definite?'

I rush to tell the lads in the lounge. They ask the same questions that I've just asked myself. The roar in the lounge is so loud it forces couples on other tables to spill their drinks. We apologize, and buy them copious rounds thereafter. If we can beat Israel at Windsor Park next month, we are most likely through. What a night we have.

There is much talk about George Best. Billy Bingham names him in his provisional squad. Best is playing in America, and if the clips of goals he's scoring are anything to go by, he's in sparkling form. He's also thirty-five years old so age is not really on his side. But he is George Best. I know I speak for all the players when I say we would welcome him into our group with open arms. Maybe a twenty- or twenty-five-minute spell with the superstar on the field might be enough to win the game. How we long for a Best at twenty-five years old. Any anxiety before matches – wondering about where goals might originate – would dissipate. All we would have to do is stay strong defensively and this wizard would weave a magic path to victory. But it turns out he won't be gracing us at any age. For whatever reason, when the squad is cut further, George's name has been removed.

Before the crucial game, there is more good news for us. Portugal's collapse is as rapid as it is astounding. They lose 4–1 in Israel. Our fate is now completely in our own hands. Even if we draw, we will be in good stead. But now there is nothing else but victory on our minds. I do a fitness test on my hamstring on the Monday morning. Billy is dubious but wants to wait another day. I face the same test again. I desperately want to play and captain this group of players when we walk out to the thunderous welcome we will get from the expected crowd. And I want to be captain when that final whistle blows and we have made it to Spain. But in the test I don't feel great. The match is too big, too important to take a chance, particularly with a hamstring strain. The supporters are packed into Windsor Park. Almost 40,000 people.

Complacency is a word that never has to be used when Northern Ireland play a football match, for the simple reason that 90 per cent of the time we will be the underdogs. And, despite our supposed advantages this evening, we are not counting our chickens. But then Armstrong scores, and the cheers reverberate around the stadium. It is enough to frighten any visiting team and the conquest is ours. The celebrations at the final whistle are unforgettable. I may have been on the sideline today, but I will captain this band of brothers in Spain. Billy Bingham is in seventh heaven, if indeed there are six others.

World Cup fever abounds. I've watched these tournaments on television, both in black and white as a youngster and then in glorious Technicolor as a budding young adolescent footballer. I remember every country that took part in England in 1966. I may even, if jolted, remember every score. Then there's 1970 and Brazil's finest team, maybe even the best international team ever to play. Northern Ireland will not be afforded that type of accolade but, now that we've qualified, we vow to make a splash. And to have a bit of fun along the way. We form a players' pool. All the payments made by media, TV and radio outlets to interview us pertaining to the World Cup are to be collected in this pool. We hire an agent to look after it for us. Well, that's what England are doing, so why not us?

We even decide to make a record.

Dana, who won the Eurovision Song Contest as a teenager way back in 1970 with 'All Kinds of Everything', wants to do the song. And we all want Dana to do it. So that's settled. We meet in London. There are quite a few of the players present at the recording, all hoping, myself included, to at least be part of the backing track, if not joint lead singer with Dana herself. We have a very amusing day in the studio, even though – when the editing is complete and the record is released – the backing vocals don't sound exactly like ours.

Our players' fee pool is never going to be the size of England's, despite the best efforts of those players constantly asked to do the interviews. We have a bit of pre-World Cup difficulty with the Irish Football Association around bonuses. I am one of a three-man committee for the players – the two others being Chris Nicholl and Sammy Nelson – who will negotiate with the IFA on these incentives.

Throughout the qualification games we never discussed anything about remuneration with our governing football association. Playing for Northern Ireland is the reward, not the appearance money, if indeed there is any at all.

But we have now qualified for a World Cup, and some financial appreciation should be considered going forward. There is some intransigence on the IFA front. They say we shouldn't be paid any more than Scotland, which seems fair enough. They are using Scotland's bonus system as their template, but they haven't read it properly. I know because I phone John Robertson, part of Scotland's squad now acclimatizing for Spain in the heat of the Portuguese summer. He reads a copy of the incentives to me. There's a second part to it which the IFA have missed. He tells me that they won't get paid a penny if they don't make it to the quarter-finals but if they do, then the bonus is 'worthwhile'. We players agree that the quarter-finals of the World Cup is what we will aim for.

The IFA are surprised to find out there is a second page to the Scottish FA's agreement with the players, but having promised to abide by the Scottish FA's reimbursements, they cannot back down. It's a kind of a victory for us, but honestly, deep down we don't care about the incentives. We just want to be contenders in the most distinguished and exciting competition of them all.

We are holed up in Brighton for pre-World Cup training. Scotland are in Portugal and heaven knows where England are. We get lucky with the weather and enjoy day after day of sun at

Sussex University sports complex. The intense training sessions with Bingham give us all the preparation we need.

Finally, the day arrives. We head to Valencia where we will be stationed for the group stage of the competition. It will be the hottest summer in Spain for over thirty years. Two from four will qualify for the quarter-finals. We are grouped with Honduras, Yugoslavia and the host nation Spain. Our first two matches, Yugoslavia and Honduras, will be played in Zaragoza, so we will fly on the morning of both games from Valencia. It's nine o'clock in the evening but the heat and humidity refuse to abate.

Match one: 17 June. Within minutes of the whistle blowing, I'm having to pull my lips apart with my fingers, so stifling are the conditions. Yugoslavia are a talented team. They have cruised to Spain and were many people's choice to go a long way in the tournament. I have played this game so many times in my head since the draw was made, I should know what to do and when to do it. But it isn't at all like I imagined it. By half-time, I haven't beaten those three Yugoslav defenders and slotted home our opening goal.

The opposition are finding the heat rather oppressive too and, thankfully, they slow the game down when in possession, allowing us time to retreat and regain our shape. But we are well drilled and, despite the occasional scare, which is always going to occur sometime, we force a scoreless draw. At least we are off the mark in points, if not in goals. We haven't scored tonight but we have found a proper player. Norman Whiteside, on taking the field, becomes the youngest player ever to play in the World Cup finals, beating Pelé's record set in 1958. Norman is strong, aggressive, with a brilliant left foot, and he can not only hold the ball up but he can ward off encroaching defenders with his sturdy frame. He has made the headlines this evening.

Bingham is genuinely happy with the point and we will return to Zaragoza in a few days' time to try to beat our Central American opponents, Honduras. Billy allows us some time off to sit around the pool, but only for an hour. After time is up, if we don't

1. Here's me as a boy, about to go to Holy Communion in Kilrea.

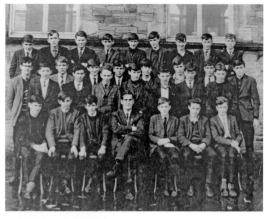

2. At St Columb's College, Derry. I am in the first row, second from the right, looking quite pleased with myself.

3. Reunited with the Distillery lads, who won the Irish Cup in 1971, some years after the fact.

4. (*left*) Looking fresh-faced as a new Nottingham Forest player in 1971.

5. (*below*) Scoring on my full international debut against Portugal in 1973. The match was a World Cup qualifier, played in Coventry due to the Troubles.

6. (*bottom*) The All-Ireland team in 1973. Due to protestations we had to play as Shamrock Rovers XI. The game was against Brazil, then the world champions. We lost 4–3.

7. Brian Clough celebrating victory over Tottenham Hotspur in an FA Cup third-round replay at White Hart Lane, his first game in charge of Nottingham Forest. Few players would remain to lift the European Cup four years later.

8. The Nottingham Forest team in 1978.

9. Here's me rifling in a shot against Birmingham City, on the way to winning the league that year.

10. Clough and Peter Taylor lifting the League Championship trophy for winning the top division.

11. Enjoying our second consecutive League Cup victory in 1979, against Southampton.

12. We were all given a tankard. I'm here on the right with Frank Clark (*left*) and John Robertson (*centre*).

13. Interplay with Garry Birtles in 1979 against local rivals Coventry.

14. Celebrating victory over Cologne with Ian Bowyer in the second leg of the European Cup semi-final in 1979.

15. Winning the European Cup in 1980.

16. In action against Spain at the 1982 World Cup, which we won 1–0.

17. The Northern Ireland team that played against Austria in one of two quarter-final games.

move we will be chased indoors like naughty schoolboys by his assistant Martin Harvey, a genuinely nice man with manners to match. No player wants Martin to be offended, so we always do as he tells us.

Our hotel in Valencia is comfortable despite the heat and we are well treated by the staff. In turn, we are well behaved and focused. But we are somewhat cocooned in the hotel, so getting to know what is happening back home presents a bit of a problem. The journalists following the Northern Ireland story fill us in with little snippets of what the media is saying about us. Jimmy Greaves, a magnificent footballer and wonderfully funny pundit for ITV, has poked a little fun in our direction. Apparently, when asked if Northern Ireland can get out of the group stages and go further in the competition, Jimmy answers, as only he can, by saying that the only thing Northern Ireland should bring with them is an overnight toilet bag and a toothbrush.

Had it been any other pundit we might have been maddened but we all think it's a hilarious take on our chances of success.

Back to Zaragoza and the temperature is still oppressive as a much smaller crowd arrives to watch us face Honduras. When the draw is made, Honduras looks a possible win. But their 1–1 draw against Spain made people sit up and take notice, and our match duly proves to be exceptionally difficult. Bingham takes me off with about fifteen minutes to go. It's the first time I'm really angry with him. He has seen me do some stretching a few minutes before the substitution. Yes, I am cramping up somewhat, but I still hope to shake it off.

I want to stay on the field and see the game through, even if we do only draw. The manager is seeing a different picture, or at least he's drawing a different conclusion from my stretching. There is a thought that crosses my mind. If there is a criticism about the performance this evening then the removal of the captain with fifteen minutes to go may shift the blame to me.

We draw the game 1–1, having scored first. We haven't been brilliant this evening and the draw, although probably the right result, leaves us having to beat Spain on their own ground, in front of their own fans, to reach the quarter-final of the World Cup. It's a tall order.

Bingham actually apologizes to me on the way home for substituting me and tells me to 'get ready for the game of your life'. I accept the apology wholeheartedly. The *Belfast Telegraph* reporter Malcolm Brodie tries to make more of the substitution, apparently raising a possible relationship breakdown between Billy and myself, but we all know Malcolm by now and park it to the side.

The night before the Spanish match, a group of us are sitting in the very large foyer of the hotel, chatting idly. What's happening back home? Are any members of family coming out to the game tomorrow? What about tickets for them? All of this is a prelude to what we really want to discuss: tomorrow's match. We all have the same big concern: the influence of the fanatical Spanish crowd on the referee. They have already had two penalties in their games to date. There is a creeping desperation about their performances which can be used to our advantage, but only if the referee is strong.

We all know that frustration on the terraces can seep through to the players so quickly that it becomes a burden too heavy to carry. And if we can turn the crowd against their own players, we may be able to take advantage. But for that strategy to succeed, we must defend resolutely ourselves, keep opposition chances to a minimum and be ready to counter-attack with purpose. One thing we know for certain. We must score. We are doomed if we don't. But with Whiteside, Hamilton and Armstrong all in splendid form, we think we will manage at least one goal. And who knows, that may well be enough.

The night of 25 June 1982 is very warm once again, but the two matches in Zaragoza have allowed some semblance of acclimatization to seep into our bodies. I don't know why but my nerves have been stored away in some far-flung cupboard and I feel remarkably calm, in contrast to the febrile atmosphere enveloping the Luis Casanova Stadium. Kick-off is seconds away. I look behind me. Jennings, Jimmy Nicholl, Chris Nicholl, John McClelland, Mal Donaghy. To my side, David McCreery and Sammy McIlroy. And in front, the dependable Whiteside, Hamilton and Armstrong. I couldn't be in better hands.

The Spaniards start strongly and we are driven back. It is all the incentive needed to keep the crowd at fever pitch. Their attacks are quick and incisive, unlike their two previous games, and they get the response from the fans that they are looking for. We have to do more to prevent this onslaught. We must ensure we cover for each other, a trademark of our game, and weather the storm. And we start to come into the game ourselves. But the referee is wilting. Spanish tackles are going unpunished. We knew last night what might happen and we need to stay strong.

The proposal that FIFA had of putting a Paraguayan referee in change of this game when he had never refereed two European teams before and his mother tongue is Spanish seemed lunacy when upheld. It is likewise proving almost farcical in practice.

Half-time and we are still alive. Bingham composes himself before speaking. 'Superb, boys,' he starts. 'We can win this game! We will get a chance, maybe more, and when it comes we have to be clinical.' We all think that this can happen. And it does. Within ten minutes of the second half, Gerry Armstrong fires in one of the most talked-about goals in Northern Ireland's football history from just inside the penalty area. As he does, we brace ourselves for the Spanish backlash.

There are just over twenty minutes to go. The ball has gone out of play for a throw-in but it's hard to tell which team it's for. Suddenly there is a commotion in that very corner of the pitch. Héctor Ortiz, the referee, attracted by the linesman's flag, rushes over to the incident and within seconds reaches for his pocket to hoist a red card into the night air. Unbelievably, he sends Mal Donaghy off the field.

Ortiz himself has seen nothing but seems determined to

allow Spain their best opportunity to pull this World Cup match out of the fire, or the 'bubbling volcano' as later described by the press. We are inexplicably down to ten men.

Stunned momentarily by Gerry's goal, the crowd regain their fervour, and Mal's sending off has intensified the frenzy within the stadium. The onslaught on our goal is unrelenting and the Spanish players now need little excuse to hurl themselves to the ground at the slightest of contacts. Anxious moments abound, but are averted with a Jennings save or a towering header away by Nicholl and McClelland. We are holding firm but time is crawling. 'How long left?' I shout to the bench, but cannot hear the reply, so loud is the noise echoing round the arena.

The spirit and willpower of the team has grown exponentially since Bingham took over two years earlier. It is being tested to the limit, but reigns supreme. We must see this game through to the end. Victory will have us drinking with the gods tonight. Another dangerous Spanish attack repelled, and the ball booted clear.

It must be over now?

Ortiz puts his hand to his mouth and almost reluctantly, it seems, whistles the end of the game. We have won. We have defied the odds and beaten Spain, the host nation, in their very own stadium. I can't believe it. Bingham is on the field, as well he should be. Players are hugging each other like long-lost friends reacquainted. It is an evening that will stay forever in our memories.

We will take our place in the quarter-finals of this wonderful World Cup in a few days' time.

But that can wait until tomorrow. Tonight, Valencia belongs to Northern Ireland. These are the moments you live for. This group of players have emulated Peter Doherty's brilliant 1958 World Cup team. Bertie Peacock, now assisting Billy Bingham here in Spain with us, was a brilliant player for that very squad. This must take him back to those golden days.

We have a short bus ride back to the hotel. Some Northern

Ireland fans are already there, and it looks like a long night ahead of us. The result and its impact have travelled far and wide these last few hours.

At close to half past one in the morning, Billy Bingham calls our group together. He says he has a bit of bad news for us. What could possibly be bad news for us on a night like this?

'The IFA didn't think we would qualify for the quarter-finals, and they've booked our flights home tomorrow to London. At the minute they're frantically looking around for a hotel for us in Madrid,' he says.

It is hard to make up a story like that, but we realize from Billy's face that he's not joking. Personally, I could not care less. Hotel or no hotel, I want to captain the team and try to reach the semi-finals of this glorious World Cup. In the end, some lousy hotel not far from the airport is found for us. Still, it could be worse and it does have a roof, so we're fine.

The 1982 World Cup is an oddity in that it has two group stages, a result of expanding the tournament to twenty-four teams. Twelve teams qualify from the first group stage rather than the usual eight. So, in order to get them down to four, we are put in four groups of three teams in the quarter-finals. Each team will play two games, with the winning team in each group progressing to the semis. The format is not repeated ever again, although I'm excited by the prospect of two further matches.

First up are Austria. In the Vicente Calderón Stadium, home to Atlético Madrid. It's an afternoon kick-off on 1 July 1982 and the heat is unrelenting. We fight like demons, entering half-time in the lead. We should win the game but end up drawing 2–2, with Billy Hamilton getting both goals. To win the round of quarter-finals we now have to beat France, who beat Austria themselves. They now only need a draw against us to go through.

Rest becomes the most vital element of our preparations. My job as captain is to get the players to believe that we can beat France. I don't want to hear any talk about going home now. It's been a great tournament but we are not done yet. It's probably nothing, but I don't want rumours circulating that families are being missed. I don't want that getting into players' heads. There will be plenty of time to see our families when we are finally done with this competition. I strongly believe we can beat Michel Platini's team.

We are back again at the Vicente Calderón Stadium for the showdown with France. We are resolutely strong, and if we score first in these hot conditions, we will be hard to break down. And the blazing heat of a Madrid mid-afternoon might actually be in our favour.

This is a brilliant French team that brims with individual talent: Platini, Jean Tigana, Alain Giresse. These are all names that will be remembered for many years in every corner of France. But I'm still sure we can prevail. The first goal is everything today. And after twenty-five minutes, I score it.

I receive the ball playing a one-two with Armstrong and flash a left-footed shot past their goalkeeper and into the net. We are in the lead. My teammates are celebrating with me.

But no one has spotted that the linesman's flag is in the air. He has waved my goal offside. It just cannot be, I think. It's almost impossible for it to be offside! But the linesman has decided it.

Television pictures at the time show that I'm at least one clear yard onside. But in 1982, that's beside the point. It takes the wind out of our sails and less than two minutes later, Giresse scores for France. I am heartbroken.

We chase the game in the second half, leaving a lot of gaps, and France take advantage. We are well beaten in the end. But I know in my heart that if my goal had stood – as it should have done – we would be in the semi-final of the World Cup. I meet a couple of the French players some years later, and although they don't admit that we would have won, they do acknowledge that my disallowed goal was a turning point of the game.

And so our World Cup journey comes to an end.

A multitalented French team go on to face West Germany in

the semi-final of the World Cup in one of the most sensational games in World Cup history. They lose on penalties. Brazil, the best team in the competition, lose to Italy, who eventually go on to win the 1982 World Cup.

We will go home to a rousing reception in Belfast and – for the rest of my life – I will ponder what might have been.

7

NUMBERED DAYS

Despite the incredible World Cup in 1982, the heroics of Forest's 1980 European Cup final are the zenith of my playing career. Such incredible heights could not have been scaled without the genius of Clough and Taylor, and the defiant team spirit they fostered. But the mercurial management team that achieved the impossible soon serves us less well when we are no longer the plucky underdogs.

Forest's East Stand, built in 1980 to house many more supporters, has, according to the newspaper reports, cost much more than expected. And whether because of that or a growing complacency, few new signings are made over the summer following our second European victory. Money is tight and deep European Cup runs will become essential to the club's coffers. So when we are knocked out of the European Cup early in the 1980/81 season by CSKA Sofia of Bulgaria in the first round, Clough and Taylor are furious.

A further loss to Birmingham City in November 1980 sets off a haranguing match between myself and the management team. Their words suggest that I alone am responsible for the result, and Taylor has the last word on the subject. These squabbles seem to be happening a little too often for my liking. And sure enough, I'm on the bench for the next game against Tottenham Hotspur. But then, with injuries to the squad, I get the opportunity, at last, to play centre midfield. It's a position that I have craved for my whole Forest career.

If I'm to stay in the centre of the pitch, Forest must win. Too often in the past when results don't go to plan, the manager has looked in my direction. But sadly, despite good play from myself, our performances are average. So when everyone returns to fitness, I'm shunted to the right wing for an away game at Ipswich. We lose and I do not play well. By Tuesday, I'm already beginning to resign myself to the weekend's natural denouement.

I've swallowed some 'bravery tablets' and decide that if I'm made substitute for the game away to Stoke on Saturday – the team sheet will go up on the board on Friday morning – I will not accept it. This will be the final straw in a relationship that has been declining for some time. I'm going to knock on Clough's door and tell him that I'm not going to turn up for Saturday's game. By Thursday evening I am totally fixed on this plan of action. My wife does not agree, but I'm prepared to do it. Friday morning comes, I arrive for training at the City Ground. The team sheet is up and my intuition is correct – I'm substitute for the game.

Only my wife is aware of what I may do, but in my mind there's no going back. I tell John Robertson my plan and he's dead against it. I tell him I've had enough of it all. I knock on the manager's door and my lower lip quivers as the door opens.

'What do you want?' is the manager's question. I do not ask for an explanation as to why I've been dropped. I just tell him, 'I'm not turning up tomorrow, I've had enough.'

Taylor is also with the manager and looks flustered. 'What do you mean you're not turning up? It's your bloody job.'

As he says those words he moves towards me, but I'm already on the retreat and I repeat myself, 'I'm not turning up tomorrow.' I leave the door open and head quickly to my car, half expecting a roar from the manager to come back to his room. If he does shout I don't hear it. I don't hear anything other than the sound of the car engine as I drive out through the gates. At home, I get empathy, sympathy, and an almighty rollicking in equal measure, before the phone rings. It's Robbo. 'What happened?'

'I did it, I told them I wasn't turning up.'

'You're daft, squire, but good luck anyway,' says the talented winger, and the phone rings off.

Saturday morning comes round all too quickly. It's 9.30. The bus is due to leave the City Ground at 10 a.m. It will, as normal, collect the manager on the outskirts of Derby, and then head to Uttoxeter for a pre-match meal. That's the usual plan if we are playing a team not too far away in that direction.

The phone rings at home. It's Robbo.

'Squire, I've got some good news and some bad news for you,' he says, almost baiting me. Before I can ask more, he says, 'The good news is that the game is off, frozen pitch. The bad news is that the manager travelled over to the City Ground this morning to see if you turned up.'

The die is cast. Saturday and Sunday go so fast and Monday morning comes round all too quickly. I drive through the gates and head for the dressing room, half expecting a call to go to the manager's office. Carol must be reading my mind because she's waiting at the door. I'm summoned immediately.

I knock lightly but the door is ajar, as if my attendance is expected. I'm trying to be calm but inwardly I'm shaking like a leaf. Clough and Taylor are together, as they were on Friday. It's as if they never went home for the weekend. Those sixty-six hours have taken sixty-six seconds to flash by. The barrage begins.

'You're a fucking disgrace,' bawls the manager.

Taylor interrupts, his anger equalling Clough's. 'Just who do you think you are?'

And he moves his face to within twelve inches of mine. He would love to plant his fist on me, but pulls away at the last second. However, his action has the desired effect. 'If it was up to me, you would never play for this club again,' he roars, possibly not exactly sure what the sacking rules are.

'I told you I wasn't turning up,' I blurt.

'Fuck off out of here and don't come back to this club until I say so,' says the manager.

I don't respond. I turn and walk out, fuming. A fine for the fortnight wages duly follows and I sit at home, wondering what will happen next.

My slow drift away from Clough and Taylor started some time previously, before we won our second European Cup. The Nottingham Forest bus was travelling back from Elland Road in January 1980. Clough and Taylor were seated together at the front, deep in excited conversation. Forest had absolutely trounced Leeds United in the FA Cup and once again Clough had come up big against his old club. The league championship and the European Cup at the City Ground in successive seasons were surely enough to assuage the hurt of those forty-four days in charge of Leeds back in 1974. But a League Cup semi-final victory and now another hammering in the FA Cup on their own patch were the ultimate dagger into the heart of the club that had dismissed him so readily.

The players were in buoyant mood and the card school was in full swing. I wasn't involved, of course. I had been left out of the team so it was difficult to join in any type of celebration at all. I didn't feel part of the victory.

However, my day was about to unexpectedly get worse. I caught Taylor's eyes as he glanced over his shoulder up the bus. Yes, it was me he was looking at. He gestured for me to join him at the front. Clough moved away to the adjoining seat. I sat down beside the assistant manager who never beat about the bush.

'Coventry City want to buy you and we have accepted their offer. I want you to meet Gordon Milne tomorrow afternoon at his house. Here's his phone number. Call him when you get home this evening.'

That was it. No sugar-coating anything. Not even some patronizing nonsense about being a loyal servant to the club for the past eight or nine years. I said nothing, although I wanted to. I took the piece of paper and, rising from the seat, I looked over to Clough, who ignored me completely. I walked back up the bus like a man who had just been given a long prison sentence. The players could tell that something was up and asked me what had happened. I took a moment or two to compose myself.

'They want me to go to Coventry. I have to see their manager tomorrow about the move.' There seemed to be genuine concern from my teammates, but Burns got a laugh when he said, 'Who'll take your place in the card school, squire?' Even I thought it was quite funny coming from him.

At home, I told Geraldine the news. She knew my heart was not in the move at all. But she pointed out that if Clough and Taylor didn't want me then there was nothing to lose by seeing the Coventry manager. I phoned Gordon Milne. 'Peter Taylor gave me your number and told me to call you tonight.'

'Yes, son, we want to sign you,' he said, getting straight to the point. 'Can you get over to my house tomorrow afternoon, say half past two?'

I wrote down his address and the following day Geraldine and I were ringing his doorbell at exactly the time he had requested. Gordon's wife answered and ushered us into the living room. The biggest Christmas tree I had ever seen in any house seemed to be growing from the carpet. Trying to break the ice I asked who had the dangerous task of putting the fairy on the very top of the tree.

Gordon's wife made the obligatory tea and sandwiches, and with the small talk about families over, Gordon and I retreated to another room off the kitchen to hold talks.

He was a very well-spoken man, probably in his early forties. He had been a fine footballer in his day, making many appearances for the legendary Bill Shankly's Liverpool. Now he had put together a decent squad who had enjoyed two great seasons but were finding it a little tougher this time round. I didn't want to leave Forest, but I realized that I might not have any alternative. I believed I could make Coventry a better, more consistent team, but I doubted very much if they would be contesting major trophies. Gordon was a very persuasive talker, outlining his plans for the club going forward and where and how he saw me fitting into these aspirations. Centre midfield, he mentioned, which immediately got my attention.

'Sounds like you don't need to sell players then?' I asked.

'Well, actually, your deal is a swap deal. We are selling Mick Ferguson in part-exchange for you.'

'Part-exchange? What part am I?'

'Well, Mick is valued at £750,000 and you are valued at £250,000, so we get you and half a million pounds.'

'That's a brilliant deal for Coventry,' I said, trying to bolster my ego.

'We think so as well,' replied Gordon.

I had no agent to negotiate for me and had been at Forest for almost a decade. For a number of seasons since 1975, I had signed one-year contracts, thinking that things would be better financially the following season. We had won the First Division championship, the European Cup, two League Cups, the Super Cup, but financially life more or less remained the same. I had never had one penny signing-on fee in my entire Forest career, and I felt woefully ill-equipped to argue a case for myself.

Gordon sensed my unease. He reached for a pen and some notepaper to put into writing what I was finding extremely difficult to articulate aloud. Whatever was being discussed between us had to be approved by Jimmy Hill, who Gordon now phoned. I listened while Gordon relayed the figures but I couldn't hear what Jimmy was saying in reply. A few minutes later Gordon put the phone down and said that everything seemed to be in order. I had asked for what I was on at Forest – £500 per week.

'Clough and Taylor have asked to see Mick Ferguson at the City Ground tomorrow evening,' said Gordon. 'I'll bring along my secretary and we'll complete the forms over there.' By the forms he meant my yet-to-be-signed contract with Coventry. I shook his hand, said that I'd see him tomorrow evening, collected Geraldine from the living room and drove back home, in total disbelief at what I had just done. My Nottingham Forest days seemed to be over.

Monday morning at training felt very strange.

The lads were naturally in great spirits, and why shouldn't they have been? We'd just had a big victory over Leeds and could look forward to the fourth round of the FA Cup draw. I told the players of my trip to Gordon Milne's house and that I was signing tonight for Coventry and Mick Ferguson was coming to Forest. They wished me luck. Taylor pulled me aside at the end to confirm a time to meet at the City Ground. Six o'clock.

Gordon Milne and his secretary arrived just before me. They must have been very keen. Taylor had invited them into his own room, adjacent to the manager's office. But Clough had not arrived yet. This, in itself, was not a major surprise. Clough and Taylor liked to keep opposition managers waiting around, whether for a post-match chat, or a potential transfer. But it was quite possible Clough was just late. Ferguson and his wife arrived in expectation of meeting the mercurial manager himself and putting pen to paper as quickly as possible. Now Taylor had to deal with the whole situation himself, with Milne and his secretary in his room, Ferguson and his wife in another room, and me in the corridor watching all this unfold with more than a curious eye.

Taylor looked ill at ease. 'Brian will be here shortly,' he reassured Gordon Milne. I could hear because Peter had opened the corridor door to make the situation a little more convivial and a little less tense.

Brian finally arrived at half past six. He ignored Gordon Milne and put his head in the other door. He addressed Mrs Ferguson. 'Young lass, have you eaten yet, because I'm starving. I would like to take you up the road for some pasta, if you don't mind joining me.' Her husband did not get an invitation. This was bizarre, I thought. He was signing Mick not his wife. Mrs Ferguson, a little taken aback, but not wanting to seem bad mannered, hesitatingly acceded to Clough's request. Taylor looked like a fish out of water. He would have to engage in more small talk with Gordon Milne, who looked more than a little perplexed at what he had just overheard.

I talked to Milne for some time. He asked me if this was common practice for the manager during a transfer. I replied that I hadn't been transferred by him before so I didn't know.

Taylor took Mick into his room. Taylor was a funny man, but this wasn't his forte. After a strong 'hello' and 'you're exactly what we need at this football club', he would run out of things to say to someone he didn't really know. One thing was certain: he wouldn't want to apologize to Gordon Milne for Clough's immediate disappearance with the player's wife, having already been half an hour late.

I spent the next hour or so with Gordon Milne. He expanded on his plans for the club but he didn't need to sell it to me any more. My head had already left the City Ground when in Gordon's Warwickshire house. My heart was gradually following it to Highfield Road that evening.

Milne's secretary produced four contracts. All had to be signed and witnessed, of course, but there were no details. Nothing that I had talked about the day before was included. I was assured that there was nothing untoward going on. Once Ferguson and Clough agreed, then everything else would follow and all the details would be put into the contracts immediately.

But we were still waiting for the manager to come back from the trattoria at Trent Bridge. Then, finally, the door opened. In walked the manager. 'Hello Gordon. Sorry about that but I was starving.' 'Hello son,' he said to me. 'Hello boss,' I retorted. At last, we could get on with proceedings. Mr and Mrs Ferguson were reunited in the corridor and Clough and Taylor retired to Clough's room. Just the two of them.

There was a knock on our door. Mick wanted to have a word with Gordon Milne. I excused myself for a few moments and waited in the corridor. Mick vacated the room in a matter of seconds. Gordon Milne unhesitatingly told me that Taylor had sent Mick in to get more money from Coventry himself, after four years of service there. Considering this had nothing to do with Clough or Taylor, it seemed a little strange. Having said that, the whole evening had been rather odd.

Gordon dismissed the idea out of hand. Ten minutes later, there was another knock on the door. It was Mick again, with the same request. Taylor had sent him back in again, insisting Mick had some right to make his demands. The request was refused once again by Gordon, who was not only bemused by Taylor's insisting on Mick getting money from Coventry, but pretty angry that he had been continually ignored by Clough and Taylor himself.

This time Mick wanted to have a word with me. In the corridor he told me what was going on. He didn't actually want any money from Coventry. He never had. This was Taylor's idea. He just wanted to sign for Nottingham Forest, and whatever deal was put to him by Clough he would accept. He asked whether I had any idea what was going on. But I genuinely didn't. Perhaps Clough and Taylor were purposely dragging out the saga until they were ready to do the deal. But why?

It was half ten and the musical chairs were still going on. Gordon, the secretary and I were still in Taylor's room. Taylor and Clough were in Clough's room. Mr and Mrs Ferguson were somewhere in between.

I'd had enough. I reached for a pen and signed all four blue blank contracts, and said to Gordon, 'I trust you to put in the figures that we agreed on yesterday. You will have to sort out the rest with Taylor and Mick and yourself. I'm leaving but will be at Highfield Road tomorrow.' Gordon was surprised, and so was the secretary, but they all too readily agreed. I signed the forms and became a Coventry City player.

I walked out of Taylor's office and went the few paces to Clough's room, knocked on the door and opened it. 'I'm going home now. I've just signed for Coventry.' Both Clough and Taylor stared straight at me.

'You've done what?' Clough bellowed.

'I've signed the contracts next door. I'm not waiting any longer this evening.'

'You've done no such thing,' shouted Clough, quite irate now. 'You be on the bus tomorrow morning for Gravesend.' The first team were going to Gravesend to play a game and open some new floodlights there. Apparently that included me.

I was actually delighted to hear the news. Something had happened for them to change their minds about the whole swap deal. I still don't know to this day what it was. But I went back in to see Gordon to tell him that at least my part of the deal was off.

Back in February 1981, I am still in the doghouse. Day follows day. Night follows night. Finally the phone rings. Carol is on the line. There is a reserve game at the City Ground this evening, she tells me, and the manager says I must play in it. Maybe it's the end of my expulsion but I'm not betting on it. I play in the game, score, and we win. But the manager doesn't put his head into the dressing room. Instead, I'm told not to come into training tomorrow and to stay at home again until called. A few more days go by and I'm still at home. Forest play an FA Cup tie but I am not involved at all.

In some ways, I regret what I've done but I have moments when I feel I'm absolutely right to have taken that stance. My days at Forest are undoubtedly numbered. But they would have been anyway, regardless of my actions. The papers say that last season's League Cup winners Wolves have made enquiries about my availability. And Norwich might be interested, but they are in the relegation zone just now. Wolves and Norwich. Seven months ago I was a European Cup winner. Now I'll probably not be at the club much longer. I miss going into training. I miss being involved with the players. John occasionally calls to say that not much is going on, which serves to make me feel better temporarily. But then the ache starts again.

A few days later, Carol phones once more. Have I got my passport in the house? I should bring it into the ground tomorrow morning to be collected with the others. I'm on the trip to Tokyo. We have a game against Nacional of Uruguay for the

World Club championship. It's in Japan's capital city during the week. I am delighted.

Clough and Taylor completely ignore me when I get on the bus to travel to the airport. Just now that matters little. I'm back with the lads again, at least for a while. The flight is long, very long, broken off at Anchorage for refuelling. We get off the plane – we are in economy seats at the back, so by the time we get into the seating area there's a bit of a commotion with the other passengers. Unbeknown to just about all of us, the rock band Queen are on the same flight but naturally travelling first class. They have already been spirited into the premier lounge and the rest of us can only stare at the closed doors in envy. We do have a large stuffed polar bear with us in a glass case to occupy our attention in our seated area, but we would all prefer to have a glimpse of the band members of Queen, if truth be known.

Trevor Francis, using all the power that the first million-pound player can muster, sidles his way up to the doorman and asks to have a message passed to Brian May. It works. Trevor gets in to see them. No one else does. Brian may well have an interest in football. I don't know. The second stage of the journey – Anchorage to Tokyo – is taken up with how Trevor's conversation with the band actually went. Trevor has to admit that Freddie said very little, and that at first he thought Trevor was the drinks server coming to take their order. I doubt that Freddie is very up-to-date with Nottingham Forest's league position. And there are a finite number of times that you can tell the lead singer that 'Bohemian Rhapsody' is a brilliant song.

By the time we touch down in Tokyo, we are completely zonked out. The club doctor has already told us to stay as closely as possible to British time. Bed is not yet on the agenda. As we make our way towards the main airport building we see legions of young fans waving, obviously at the airport to greet us. This must be a big game for them, we are thinking. Yes, a World Club match to decide the best team in the universe should, of course, be big news, but this enthusiastic greeting is a little more than we are expecting. Naturally we wave back to the crowd in acknow-ledgement.

And then, it dawns on us. We are not the intended target of the applause, Queen are. The fans have absolutely no idea who we are. Of course, when the luggage has been collected and we are on the bus to the hotel, those of us who waved to the crowd are ribbed by the others without mercy.

We are walking the streets of Tokyo at three o'clock in the morning. It's a vibrant city, with an incredible history, more neon than any big Western city, less than forty years on from the Second World War. We visit the stadium the day before the game. We have had no time to do any training, so we venture a walk round the running track. The pitch itself is terrible, devoid of grass, like a well-worn schoolyard. Clough and Taylor are viewing this from up in the stand. Suddenly I hear an almighty shout: 'O'Neill!' – not 'Martin', not 'Martin O'Neill', but 'O'Neill' – 'Get your bloody hands out of your pockets!'

I do so immediately. And so do the five or six other players who have also had their hands in their pockets. But they are not called to account. Regardless, Clough puts me into the starting line-up the following day for the big game. There is actually a very large attendance at the match but, in truth, we are treating the whole affair like a glorified friendly. That's not to say we don't want to win, but remarkably the disappointment at losing doesn't seem to linger as long as usual. We lose by the only goal of the game and their goal-scorer wins a brand-new car for being named man of the match.

As we make our way back home from Tokyo, I reflect on having played in the World Club championship match, suppos-edly the pinnacle of a footballer's club career. The winners of the European Cup against the South American champions. But the game has merely ticked a box. Perhaps it was the state of the pitch, flat and grassless, or perhaps it was just the atmosphere. I believe the Liverpool players feel exactly the same as us next year when they too lose the play-off game to South American opposition.

Saturday's FA Cup tie against Bristol City is the only thing occupying my mind now that my incarceration has come to an end. But I am afraid I've jumped the gun. The manager sends word up the plane that I am still persona non grata, and that I am to stay at home until he sees fit to bring me back into the fold. Seemingly my status doesn't apply to trips to Tokyo, only back in England.

Forest beat Bristol City in the cup tie on Saturday 14 February and John Robertson scores the winning goal from the penalty spot at about the same moment my wife and I are having a cup of tea and a sandwich in a Bingham café.

Monday morning brings better news. My 'sentence' is up and I'm allowed to join the players again for training. Ironically, the postponed Stoke City match is rearranged for this Wednesday and, with perfect Clough acerbity I am made substitute for the game against them. This time I turn up.

I get my chance in the second half. I feel like my career is just starting again. Even if it is only twenty-five minutes, I throw off the proverbial shackles and play with complete freedom. Maybe it's because I know Norwich City want me badly and actually it's no bad thing to be wanted.

The Stoke City game ends. We win. I have played an important role in our victory, and even the manager endorses my own thoughts with a fervent, if blunt, 'Well done you.'

The following day I receive a phone call from Ken Brown, the Norwich manager. The two clubs apparently have agreed a fee – £250,000. Norwich desperately want to do the deal. They are playing against Birmingham City on Friday night at St Andrews. I say to Ken that I'll come to the game and make up my mind afterwards. Ken promptly dissuades me from this notion. Perhaps watching them play is not such a good idea, he's thinking. I may not want to come if they get beaten.

On Friday morning, our own team sheet goes up. I'm playing tomorrow against Arsenal at the City Ground. My cameo role at the Victoria Ground on Wednesday evening has done the trick. In the evening, Birmingham City trounce Norwich City 4–0. My brother Owen phones me to say, 'That's a relegation result if ever there was one,' in an attempt to stop me even thinking about going to Carrow Road. I have to admit that Norwich's desperate run, six consecutive defeats in the league, would make anyone think twice about going there.

On Saturday 21 February, at 7.45 a.m., the phone rings. Who could be calling this early, on a match day of all days? I answer, prepared to be more than a little rude to the caller. It's Ken Brown.

'Martin, sorry to ring so early but I've got our chairman, Sir Arthur South beside me. He wants to talk to you,' and he hands the phone over to Norwich City's head honcho.

'Martin, Arthur South here.' His voice is gravelly but extremely clear. 'Apologies about ringing you so early but we desperately want you at Carrow Road. You are just what we need to get us out of this trouble we find ourselves in. From myself, Ken and the board of directors, we want you badly at the club. I can't emphasize this enough.'

I reply, 'Thank you very much for taking the time to phone me personally. I appreciate it greatly. But can I say something to you, and it's nothing to do with last night's result. I'm playing today against Arsenal and if the manager wants me to stay at Forest and says so after the game, I will stay. Is that OK? If he doesn't want me, then I'll come to you.'

'That couldn't be clearer. Ken has heard every word and he just wants to say something.' With that Sir Arthur hands the phone back to Ken.

'I heard that, Martin. Just don't play too well today,' he says, in a manner totally belonging to Ken, as I will find out down the line.

The phone call ends.

I do not want this to be my last-ever game for Nottingham Forest. I don't think that was my real intention the day I charged into Clough's office, when he made me sub against Stoke City. But then again, maybe it was, I don't know for sure now. Would I do it again under similar circumstances? Probably. Well then, that's my answer.

I get a tremendous ovation from the Forest supporters as I take the field. I sometimes think that the manager resents my popularity, like it's undermining him in some way. Sometimes it happens that the fans take to a player and have some sort of empathy with him, even if it collides with the view of the one they know they cannot do without. He shouldn't worry. He's the king of the castle here. Today the acclaim I receive reverberates, not just at the Trent End but all throughout the stadium, and I respond big-time. I score twice in the game and we beat Arsenal 3–1.

In the dressing room we await the arrival of the manager, who has been talking to someone in the corridor. On entering he picks up a plastic cup of tea, takes a sip, leaves it back on the tray, points to me and says, 'Brilliant. You and I should fall out more often if you're going to play like that.'

I accept the compliment with a nod. The praise I've been yearning for finally comes my way, even if it is somewhat backhanded. Better late than never. And, with that, he turns and walks out the door and heads for his office retreat. But as I look around the dressing room, I realize possibly for the first time that things at the City Ground are not quite the same any more. Larry Lloyd is leaving to become player-manager at Wigan Athletic. That's a big blow for us. A couple of youngsters, Stuart Gray and Colin Walsh, have both played this afternoon. Gary Mills and Bryn Gunn have also started and, although both have European Cup medals in the cabinets at home, they are still very young. Change, subtle or otherwise is afoot.

As usual I am the last to get dressed. I walk through the players' entrance door, only to be besieged by the waiting press.

'Is there any update on your future?' I am asked, 'will those goals and your performance change anything?'

I'm about to answer that I would be happy to stay at the club but suddenly we are joined by John Sadler, the top soccer writer from *The Sun* newspaper. He interrupts proceedings. 'I've just come from Brian Clough's office and he says that nothing has changed. They want you to go to Norwich.'

'Is that true?' one of the press guys asks.

'One hundred per cent,' answers Sadler, and he should know, he's the manager's big friend.

'What do you think of that news?' I'm asked.

I am bitterly disappointed but try to hide it. 'Well, there's not much I can do about it, is there?'

I collect my wife and we go home. This time it really is over. Nottingham Forest are no longer my club.

At home I call Ken Brown and tell him I'm coming to Carrow Road. He thinks that I'm going to prevent relegation. There are eleven games left, twenty-two points to play for. European qualification form is needed if the drop is to be avoided. This means about fifteen points are needed out of those eleven games. Nothing about their recent form, confirmed on Friday night's mauling at Birmingham, suggests anything other than relegation. What the hell I am thinking?

Over the weekend, Brian Clough and I agree to meet on Monday evening, but this will not be a Coventry City re-enactment, when I stayed at Forest at the eleventh hour. I arrive at the City Ground about seven o'clock. It's dark outside and has been for several hours. The manager beckons me into his office. It looks like he hasn't gone home today; he's still in his tracksuit.

'Do you want a beer, son?' he asks.

'No boss, thank you all the same.'

He relaxes into an armchair and asks me to take a seat close by.

'We've had great days here, haven't we?' he says with some resignation, almost as if he will not be able to replicate them, at least not soon. I certainly won't.

During the next few minutes of conversation, he mentions

memorable moments where I have played a significant part, but then he starts to drift off and reminisce more generally. I get the impression I could be anyone as long as I'm listening to him. He sinks further into the seat, drink in his hand, with his mind anywhere but here. Perhaps that day in Munich, the first European Cup. Maybe even that afternoon at Highfield Road when the coveted First Division championship was secured. Knowing him, he may even be contemplating the afternoon when he heard the news that Bolton had lost at home to Wolves, which all but secured his passage into the First Division. Had that result not gone the right way, none of the big successes would have followed.

Then he awakens from his reverie.

'You've been a big part of that success, son,' he said.

'Thank you very much, boss,' I answer.

Then why are you letting me go, I think to myself. I don't say it aloud. Don't spoil these last few moments with the man who has changed your life.

And from somewhere within my body, I find some of the simplest but hardest words to say to him. 'I'm really sorry to be going, boss. But I want to say something. All the success we've had over the last number of seasons would never have happened if you hadn't come to the club.'

I stop short at saying he's the most charismatic manager in the game, but he probably knows that anyway. He shakes my hand in some form of acknowledgement at what I've just said.

'I believe your young Mrs is pregnant, son. I've only met her a couple of times but she's a charming young lady, and good looking too. Look after her young man and . . . good luck.'

'Thank you again, boss.'

With that, I walk out of the very office where I signed my first contract with Nottingham Forest in October 1971, where the great Dave Mackay said that I was a top-class player, where Allan Brown said I caused him too much trouble, and where I told Brian Clough only a few weeks ago that I didn't want to play for him again.

Well, it doesn't matter any more now. I have a medical tomorrow afternoon at Carrow Road and, all being well, I will don a Norwich City shirt against Brighton on Saturday. On the short journey back home to Bingham I switch on the radio.

Unbelievably Joe Dolce's 'Shaddap Your Face' is still keeping Ultravox's 'Vienna' off the number one spot in the charts. Whoever said life was fair?

8

ENDGAME

With the best will in the world, Norwich City will not be contesting European Cup finals in successive seasons, most likely will not win the league title in the foreseeable future, and recent results suggest strongly that relegation is the most likely scenario. Yet they are still prepared to pay me better wages than Forest. However, there's another world outside my own bubble. It's late February 1981, and news of the engagement of thirty-two-year-old Prince Charles to a nineteen-year-old girl called Diana Spencer is dominating the front pages.

'Welcome to Carrow Road, Martin. We are all delighted you're here.'

The voice is recognizable, the speaker less so. Sir Arthur South greets me with a powerful handshake and escorts me into the Carrow Road boardroom. The blue contracts are neatly spread out on his desk and, if my medical goes as planned, I'll be a Norwich City player within two hours. But I sign the forms right away, anyway. Ken Brown is in the office, too, and beams a contented smile. The club have agreed to a clause in the contract that if they are relegated, I can leave at the end of the season if another First Division club is prepared to pay £275,000 for me. Norwich therefore would not lose out financially in the deal.

I said to Ken that I would take responsibility for matters going forward on the pitch but that I couldn't be blamed for Norwich's run of twenty-two points from their thirty-one league games beforehand. Ken ushers me down to the medical room to see Tim

Sheppard, the club's physiotherapist, and follows me as if he and not Tim is going to do the examination. I think it's just to check that I am fit to play against Brighton on Saturday. After a cursory inspection, Tim assures Ken that unless the X-rays and the full examination throw up any major problems, I'll be good to go. 'When I heard that you had scored two goals against the Arsenal on Saturday, I must admit I thought you would definitely be staying at Forest,' says Ken. Tim pushes and pulls my knee, listening for any clicks that might denote some cartilage damage.

'For a while I thought so myself,' is my response to Ken's comments, 'but it's all worked out for the best,' I add. Whether I believe what I'm saying or not is another matter.

'See you at Trowse – the training ground – in the morning. Tim will show you how to get there,' are Ken's parting words. I have X-rays at the hospital and undergo further tests by Tim – there's some wear and tear after ten years in the professional game, but I still pass the medical.

Tonight I'm staying at Sprowston Manor Hotel, which will be my abode for the final few weeks of the season. Sprowston Manor is a very grand building but in need of a little refurbishment. However, the hotel staff can't be more pleasant. Despite the unfamiliar surroundings, and the uncharted waters in front of me, the goals against Arsenal last week have given me a big personal confidence boost. I also remind myself that I scored a great goal against a number of these Norwich players at Carrow Road the season we won the league, running from the halfway line, beating a couple of defenders before slotting the ball into the corner of the net.

I arrive at Trowse long before the players turn up; it's not far from Carrow Road itself. I'm introduced to Mel Machin, the first-team coach. Mel and Ken are the proverbial chalk and cheese. You feel you know all about Ken in three minutes. You might need three months to find out what Mel is thinking. But as it transpires, he's a terrific coach. Ken is quietly spoken with an outgoing personality, always trying to find the lighter side of life.

He seems to be continually smiling, possibly in an attempt to ignore the precarious position the club finds itself in. Mel smiles when he chooses, although quite often he chooses not to, unless, as he says, 'There is something to smile about.'

A few seasons back Mel scored a hat-trick at the City Ground against Forest when still playing for Norwich City. I remind Mel about it but, in truth, he doesn't need my help to remember his one and only hat-trick in league football.

One by one the players are introduced to me by Ken as they arrive. Some I recognize immediately because of playing against them, others I don't know at all. 'Welcome to the madhouse. Fallen out with Clough again?' are Joe Royle's first words to me.

'Why you? It can't just be for the money, can it?' he says with a sardonic smile. Joe Royle is a big character in the game. Bursting on to the scene as a sixteen-year-old kid at Everton, he has experienced just about everything in football. A constant back injury has plagued the latter part of his career, and he says if he had been a horse he would have been shot long ago! But he has an effervescent enthusiasm for football that is totally infectious, and he has fallen for this club in a big way since his arrival. There's a healthy respect for him within the dressing room that is clearly evident from my first day at Trowse. He may not be able to play every minute of every game, but it's clear that he is needed in the camp. 'We are on a bit of a bad run, to put it mildly,' he says, going on to add in typical Joe Royle macabre humour, 'but nothing that an earthquake in Diss putting paid to the rest of the season won't cure.'

'Why have you struggled?' I ask.

'No confidence, not scoring, and letting in a lot of soft goals. Other than that we are pretty good,' he laughs.

'Meet our midfield maestro,' Joe calls as he grabs Mick McGuire's arm to get his attention, 'and the best-looking player in the team,' he adds, 'although that wouldn't be too difficult with this motley crew.' I shake hands with Mick. I don't know him personally, but I do know all about him as a player. He broke into

Coventry City's first team at a very young age. He is an excellent midfielder, a really good passer of the ball, with control and vision to match. He takes responsibility on the pitch and has loads of courage. He has been a regular member of a team which, up until this season, has held its own very comfortably in the top flight.

Brighton face us today. Our home dressing-room door leads directly onto the road running parallel to the main stand. If one of the windows is open, then any passer-by on a match day could listen to any conversation taking place inside the dressing room, whether it be interesting or not. You can easily get this feeling that this door is actually a 'stage door' and that you are an actor changing costumes in the wings. One minute you are on the outside in civvies and the next minute you are in full Canary regalia.

The Norwich City supporters give me a very encouraging welcome as I take the field. At least for them, a new face means new hope. I've had little time to settle into the team. We practised some set pieces yesterday morning, and I have a fair idea of where I should be standing when the opposition takes a free kick, but no one has mentioned the code word for racing out together and catching the opposition offside when we are defending free kicks.

Ten minutes into the game, Brighton get an opportunity. I take up my defensive position and find myself marking Michael Robinson, a young forward starting to make a name for himself in the First Division. There is a loud call from our captain, Graham Paddon to 'get tight'. These two words are passed down the line to each one of us in turn. Naturally I obey them to the letter, and get even closer to Robinson as the ball is about to leave the free-kick taker's foot, trying to prevent him making any inroads into our penalty box.

No one has told me that 'get tight' actually means the opposite, and our players race out en masse the split second the ball is about to be delivered to catch Brighton offside.

I stand my ground, however, preventing Robinson from

escaping my grip, but in so doing I leave at least four other Brighton players onside, giving them a big opportunity to take the lead. Thankfully, the Brighton player blazes the ball over the bar and I am reprieved.

A few apologies from my new teammates follow, as they realize that no one has told me the code word. It's not the start I'm looking for. Parts of the game pass me by as we try to establish some sort of foothold. Despite the string of bad results, we possess some excellent talent in the team. McGuire wants the ball all the time, even taking it when the odds of losing it and incurring the wrath of the home supporters are pretty high.

He, Paddon, and our little winger Mark Barham are now starting to dictate affairs, and then McGuire lashes a pile-driver into the Brighton net and Norwich are ahead. A deflected goal gives us a 2–0 lead at half-time. In the dressing room, a beaming Ken Brown, having realized that I was not told beforehand about the offside code word, apologizes to me. A manager apologizing to me? I haven't encountered that in a long time. I think Jimmy McAlinden might have done so in my Distillery days, but then again maybe not.

I could get used to this style of management, I think to myself. And I admire the fact that a team like Norwich City have a plan to combat dangerous free kicks being loaded into the penalty area. At Nottingham Forest we relied on Lloyd, Burns or Bowyer to come and head the ball clear from danger. Regardless, it's a buoyant home dressing room at 3.47 p.m. today.

Communal encouragement, so hollow-sounding in previous weeks, suddenly seems genuine as we strut out for the second half. At least that's what Mick McGuire tells me at the end of the game. Midway through the second half, we force a corner. Mark Barham swings the ball into the near post, a touch on and I meet it with my head to score and put the game beyond Brighton's reach. It's a surreal moment as I score a club goal for a team other than Nottingham Forest. There may be different fans, different players, different shirt, different ground, but a First Division goal still brings forth the same euphoric feeling. Momentarily my ten years at Forest are banished into the shade.

The players' spirits have been lifted by our 3–1 win, and life looks a little rosier. In the dressing room I ask someone for the other results in the First Division, with Forest's game uppermost in my thoughts. 'Forest drew away at Leicester', comes the reply. I don't want Forest to win, particularly since I have just left, but Leicester City are fellow strugglers with Norwich, so I don't want them to win either. A point each seems a fair enough result then.

We do not have another game for a fortnight due to FA Cup matches next week. Norwich are already out of that competition, so the manager gives me a few days off to gather both my belongings and my thoughts together and bring them down next Wednesday to Sprowston Manor.

What an extraordinary five weeks it has been. And by this victory, Norwich City retain hope that relegation can be avoided.

A few weeks later I am at the City Ground.

But for the first time in ten years I'm not in a red shirt. I would like to be in better physical condition. Last week, against Arsenal at Carrow Road, I sustained an injury to my shin that has not responded well to treatment. X-rays are curious. It seems there is a possibility of a stress fracture but it is very unclear. I want to play today, I need to play today. I want to show Brian Clough and Peter Taylor that they have made a terrible mistake.

I get a brilliant reception from the Forest fans but Norwich lose the game and I'm on the periphery. My shin aches more and more as the game progresses. Not having trained all week hasn't helped either, and I'm a broken figure walking off the pitch as the referee's whistle ends the match. By the time I've shaken hands with my friend John Robertson, Clough has already made his way down the tunnel. I hadn't expected him to wait for me, hug and clap me off the pitch, but I might have imagined more moving endings to the game. In reality it's just another game in the annals of the club's history. A few familiar Forest supporters wait patiently outside to pass on their very best wishes for my future and hope that my new club can stay in the First Division, but that's it really. There is no exalted fanfare. No fuss. No 'life's not the same here without you'. Nottingham Forest will have new heroes to cheer until they too become expendable. That's the game and that's life.

On the Thursday morning before Norwich City's home game against Manchester City, I train with the squad. My shin is feeling a great deal better. Ken has been monitoring my progress all week and Tim assures him that Saturday will see a different player than last week, and so it proves. We beat Manchester City 2–0. I play well in the game, the team play exceptionally strongly, and it begins a four-game winning streak that turns forgotten hope into fervent anticipation that we can avoid the drop.

We win at Goodison Park. We follow that win with a magnificent performance and victory over Tottenham Hotspur at White Hart Lane, and then beat our local rivals and big favourites Ipswich Town to get all eight points and allow us to believe that if we take a win and a draw from our last two matches, Manchester United away at Old Trafford and Leicester City at home on the final day of the season, relegation will be avoided. United at Old Trafford is a tough ask and we lose 1–0, although we perhaps should have drawn the match. It's down to the last game.

We feel we can beat Leicester City at Carrow Road. Our opponents are already relegated and have nothing to play for. Sunderland are away to Liverpool, who are preparing for a European Cup final against Real Madrid in Paris. If Liverpool beat Sunderland – as they should – and we beat Leicester City, then we will stay up and Sunderland will be relegated. There is everything to play for, but we are still dependent on the results elsewhere going our way. It arouses all sorts of emotions as we keep telling ourselves that we can only control what's in front of us and, if we do that, things will work out for us at Anfield.

And so to the game. A sunny wind blows over Carrow Road. Our opponents play with a freedom that nothing-to-play-for teams seem to find, especially at the end of the season. Had Leicester City played like this over the course of the season, they might be plying their trade in the First Division rather than being relegated weeks ago. Jim Melrose, their young centre forward, scores the opening goal. Jim will play an important role for me later on in life, but today he's the brat who's causing our defence too many problems, and within a few minutes he does it again. We are 2–0 down with less than twenty minutes played. But all hope is not lost as Mick McGuire pulls a goal back for us with a tremendous header. We go in at half-time just one goal behind. But news is not good at Anfield. Sunderland are leading by a goal to nil. That certainly wasn't in the script, but we are hoping that Liverpool can put matters right in the second half. Justin Fashanu equalizes and we have half an hour to find the winning goal. But by pressing forward for that elusive winner, we leave gaps that Leicester exploit, and Melrose scores his third goal of the afternoon. We now have a mountain to climb. We need two goals. For a moment there is a stirring within the terraces and we players dream to think that Liverpool have scored twice to lead Sunderland, but it isn't true. Liverpool haven't even scored once. And even if they do, we still have to find two goals ourselves in ten minutes. We are unable to do so.

When the final whistle blows, Norwich City are relegated.

Defeat in any game is hard to take. Defeat in this game – with relegation consequences – is unbearably difficult to stomach. Those four successive victories against big clubs are rendered meaningless. Sunderland have won at Anfield, but that's the only consolation we can draw upon. Even if we had beaten Leicester City it wouldn't have mattered. We would have been relegated anyway. But not to even have the satisfaction of winning our final game in front of the Carrow Road fans is a sickening feeling. I've been at the club for eleven games, six of which we have won. In the previous thirty-one league games, Norwich have managed to win only seven times.

I love the club and I would no doubt have stayed if relegation had been staved off. Maybe if I had signed a week earlier, we might have beaten Birmingham City that Friday night. Who knows? But retrospective what-if-ery unfortunately features too regularly in my thinking.

There is much to ponder on the way home. Geraldine is due to give birth to our first child in just over two months' time. Norwich City have an end-of-season tour in Florida arranged for next week. Today no one is in the mood to even think about it. Gloom hangs over Carrow Road. It's hard to find the energy even to take your boots off. The reaction in the dressing room is typical of a defeated and beaten-up team. Expletives fly in all directions. There are a few accusations, recriminations and some finger-pointing, but actually not much: Norwich City is not that type of club. I want the manager to let rip, get something off his chest. But he's not that type of character either. It's left to Mel Machin to dig a few of us out. I have witnessed Clough berating us for dropping points in the games we should have won. God knows what he would have done if relegation was on the agenda.

The trip to Florida is low-key, hard to enjoy. Exactly twelve months ago I was preparing for a European Cup final in the Bernabéu Stadium. Now, next season, I will be playing Second Division football. Norwich will probably have to sell players, so it may well suit the club if I leave, considering my wages in contrast to those of others at the club. And young Justin Fashanu is attracting a lot of First Division interest with his goal of the season against Liverpool, propelling him into the limelight. I leave Florida a few days before the tour ends, as the Northern Ireland team demand my attention.

John Bond, manager of Manchester City, wants to sign me, and is willing to pay Norwich City the £275,000 required to release me. He will give me the same wages that I'm currently on at Norwich City but that's it. Take it or leave it, no signing-on money. I take it.

Manchester City reached last season's FA Cup final only to

lose to Tottenham Hotspur in a replay, the Argentinian Ricky Villa scoring a memorable goal to seal victory for the north London club. Bond himself took over the reins at Maine Road halfway through last season when Manchester City sacked Malcolm Allison. It looks as if he's steadied the ship and the squad has a good combination of youth and experience at its disposal.

I meet Bond and his assistant John Benson at Maine Road and sign the forms. I tell him my wife and I are going to Northern Ireland where our first child is going to be born, but I will be there for the opening day of preseason training. In Northern Ireland, Geraldine and I stay at her sister Vera's house in Dunloy, about seven or eight miles from Kilrea, where we were both raised. Vera is a midwife and Geraldine is in very good hands. Aisling, our daughter, is born and all is good with the world. I decide to join some old school friends in a Gaelic football kick-about one evening. I pull my calf muscle, only days away from going to Manchester for preseason training.

I phone the Manchester City physiotherapist who wants to see me as soon as possible. This I do. He has a look and decides that it's not too bad. He believes I should be able to start with everyone else in a few days' time. I'm not completely convinced but I take his word for it. I have only ever done preseason training at Nottingham Forest and all teams have different approaches.

The idea is to get players as fit as possible for the opening game of the season and continue to build that fitness throughout the coming months. No one looks forward to the preseason, not even those players who can run for ever. In my first couple of years at Forest I noticed that those lads who could belt round Wollaton Park Lake in sub-Olympic times were usually the ones who never made the grade. Brian Clough's preseason, although not easy at all, was much less onerous than others I had experienced, yet a league title, two European Cups, a couple of League Cups and a Super Cup might suggest he was getting something right.

Manchester City's preseason under John Bond is torturous. I

cannot find any other word to describe it. I have never really excelled in long-distance running, certainly not up there with Garry Birtles or John McGovern. Shorter distances definitely suit me better, ideally ones where I can see the finishing line in front of me. Off we go on a long-distance run: I think it's from Manchester to Glasgow and back within an hour, but I might have got that wrong. Within minutes, Nicky Reid and Tommy Caton, two young players who have done well so far last season, are out of sight, and even Tommy Hutchinson, a brilliant footballer a few years my senior, is a distant figure on the horizon. And my calf is killing me, absolutely killing me.

John Bond has posted himself on a hill with a stopwatch in his hand, naturally timing all those who reach his vantage point. I can hardly see the hill, never mind Bond himself, and by the time I get there it's almost time for tomorrow's session to begin. This is not a good start. I tell him about my calf but he believes that if the physiotherapist has given me the OK to go I should be doing better. And it may be true. Joe Corrigan, the goalkeeper, finished a long time ago. Now that really is bad news from my viewpoint.

The manager naturally is not happy with me, but decides that I should miss the afternoon session and get some ice on my calf. I'm not making a great impression with the players, but Tommy Booth does offer words of encouragement and tells me I shouldn't worry too much about early preseason since I'm the only one in the squad with a European Cup medal.

At Manchester City there is an initiation for new players. No, not singing a verse of some corny song, but rather to receive a punch of welcome from Joe Corrigan, England's third-choice goalkeeper behind Peter Shilton and Ray Clemence. Joe is very, very strong. We have just played Bideford in Devon in a preseason friendly and we are climbing aboard the team bus to travel to Glasgow to play Rangers in two days' time. Spirits are good despite the long journey ahead. Tommy Hutchinson shouts over to Joe.

'Hey Joe, you haven't given Martin his welcome to the club yet.'

Joe steps over, smiles, and lets rip a snorter of a right hand that would have shaken Muhammad Ali. His fist hits my chest and I am knocked back over three seats and land in a heap somewhere in another galaxy.

Joe then looks at his fist, realizes that the friendly welcoming punch is perhaps too forceful and leans over to apologize. I cannot get a breath even to force an expletive out, so sore are my ribs. Joe apologizes every service station along the route, but a calf injury and now most likely some cracked ribs is not the start I am looking for. John Bond actually starts me in the game at Ibrox on the Monday night but hauls me off at half-time, telling me that I haven't had a kick of the ball. I would like to answer him back but find it too sore to speak. I look past Bond to see big Joe looking guilty as he proffers an apology with a waved hand.

Despite my woes, John Bond later asks me about Trevor Francis.

'Brilliant,' I tell him. 'And he's exactly the type of player the Maine Road fans are longing for.'

'What about his injury?' he asks.

'He was over that a long time ago. He is as fast as he ever was and, in fact, may even be quicker if that's possible,' I tell him.

'I sometimes believe that when players leave Brian Clough, that's the end of them. They cannot produce the goods any more.'

Although I realize that I haven't got off to the best start I do say to him, 'Well, you've signed me, and now you're thinking about signing Trevor. Seems to go against your theory a bit. If you can get Trevor that will be brilliant.'

Thankfully, preseason comes to an end and the real football begins. We are actually doing fine as a team, although I could be doing much better as an individual. John Bond disregards his own instincts and signs Trevor Francis, who hits it off straight away with the Kippax Stand fans. If we get a bad result, the manager not only wants to criticize us in the dressing room, which is absolutely right, but reiterates his chunterings to the press guys outside, almost word for word. On any given week, nobody in the team is any good or – conversely – they are the best players in the land.

The new year of 1982 is soon upon us. In fairness to John Bond, it seems clear that Manchester City are not in a good financial position. He has a lot of juggling to do to bring in revenue and having to balance that with trying to win football games. Some payments on a transfer involving Kevin Reeves have not been handed over to Norwich City. It is clear they need a cash injection and I am the answer.

Norwich City want me back at Carrow Road. Life in the Second Division since relegation last summer has not been a stroll in the park. In fact it's been one long struggle for them, and by January they find themselves languishing in the bottom half of the league table. John Benson, Manchester City's assistant manager, summons me to tell me that they and Norwich have agreed a price for me and that the manager wants me to leave Maine Road as soon as possible. He phones Ken Brown, puts him on to me and leaves the room. Ken is remarkably cheerful, considering where Norwich are positioned just now in the Second Division. Ken feels that my return will galvanize the club for the second half of the season and that promotion can still be achieved.

The transfer fee would be reasonable because Man City owe Norwich not only for Kevin Reeves, but also for me, back in July. 'There's only one little snag, Martin,' Ken adds, almost as an aside.

'Because of relegation, no one here is on more than £400 a week. So we cannot pay you any more than that. I'm afraid that's where we are. What about it, then?'

'So you want me to virtually halve my wages, to come to you, to see if we can get promotion from, let's face it, a pretty poor position just now?'

'That's about it, Martin. I cannot do any more.'

'Any more? Sounds like you can't do any less, Ken.'

I hear that old familiar laugh on the other end of the telephone. I like Ken, but I'm not sure I like him *that* much.

'I'll speak to you later, Ken, if that's all right.'

'Absolutely Martin, please come, we need you and we need you now.'

At least I know where I stand with John Bond. He's prepared to let me go. I need to be playing regular football, with the World Cup in Spain in June coming up. I am the captain of the team and World Cups do not come round too often for small nations like Northern Ireland. I do not want to miss that competition having helped them to get there.

I phone Ken the next day. I will come to Norwich for £400 per week, the same as everyone else. But if we get promotion, and that's a big if, I want to be put back to £700 per week again. Only if we get promotion. Ken agrees.

So, I'm back at Carrow Road for a midweek game against Sheffield Wednesday. I am a new man. I am reborn. I respond to the Norwich crowd's boisterous welcome for me by scoring a goal. I honestly don't think I've ever celebrated so defiantly. And I'm back with only one thing in mind: promotion.

Sheffield Wednesday beat us 3–2 this evening but I'm not perturbed. We can get there by the season's end. After tonight, there are nineteen games to go. I believe my return has lifted the spirits of the team. Mick McGuire comes into his own again and there is definite improvement in the younger players. Subconsciously, I feel that for the first time I'm beginning to look at football not just from the playing side. Management has never really crossed my mind but maybe, just maybe, recent developments have broadened my horizon.

Of the nineteen games left, we win fourteen. With three points for a victory, for the first time, promotion is achieved on the last day of the season at Hillsborough. I play superbly in this run-in and I go to the World Cup knowing that I am in splendid condition physically and mentally.

The campaign in Spain is a phenomenal success for Northern

Ireland. And as captain of the team I come back to preseason training at Norwich as proud as I can possibly be. However, the summer break has been very short, and I am actually quite tired after all the emotional and physical euphoria has died down.

Mel Machin, the head coach, takes little notice of my fatigue when devising our preseason agenda. Long-distance running is again the order of the day. Stamina-building is fair enough for those players who have summered in Majorca with beer cans to keep them company, but I'm thirty years old and I have been running up and down at Sussex University sports complex for weeks as I trained for the World Cup, as well as playing against France, Austria, Yugoslavia, Honduras and Spain in the sweltering heat.

I also see no sign of my wages being put back to what they should be now.

I wait a little but decide to act. I know there's an evening board meeting at Carrow Road, chaired by Sir Arthur South. I knock on the door and am invited in by a surprised but welcoming chairman. I ask about my contract. Sir Arthur isn't aware of our agreement. He admits that Norwich City would not be playing against Liverpool or Manchester United this coming season had I not come to Carrow Road in January, but there is nothing in writing to support my claim that I have been promised increased wages. The best he can do is put it right at the start of the following season if the club are still in the First Division by then.

I am not best pleased with the outcome nor the manager, but that's life. We don't start off too cleverly in the league, but we steady ourselves and pull off some big results during the course of the season.

We are at Portman Road, Ipswich, two days after Christmas for our derby game. The atmosphere is absolutely fantastic. Ipswich are favourites to beat us but we do not succumb. The game ebbs and flows, punctuated by some terrific goals. It is 2–2 with a minute to go. Norwich get a free kick outside the Ipswich penalty box. I want to take it, and so I immediately grab hold of the ball, like a young lad who hasn't been picked for a team, snatching the ball away so no one else can play. I set the ball down, step back, run up, and with the outside of my right foot bend it round the wall and into the corner of the Ipswich net. An incredible feeling of joy comes over me and within seconds the final whistle sounds. The fans are in dreamland and so am I.

This result turns the season in terms of confidence, and later we will go on an excellent unbeaten run, including victory – and a goal from me – at Anfield against Liverpool.

But as the 1982/83 season ends, my grumblings over perceived wrongs come to the surface again. I actually want to stay at Carrow Road, but suddenly Ken doesn't seem as friendly to me as before, which surprises and disappoints me. Well, it disappoints me, anyway. It is maybe not so surprising, given that I burst in on a board meeting last summer demanding my contract be put right.

Howard Wilkinson, manager of Notts County, who are in the big league, wants me to go to Meadow Lane. Ken Bates, chairman of Chelsea, wants me to go to Stamford Bridge. Chelsea are in the Second Division but look poised for promotion. I travel to London. Ken couldn't be more charming. However, I own a house in Nottingham and maybe I want to go back there and live.

I meet Howard in London at the sprawling Thameside apartment of Jack Dunnett, the Notts County chairman and Labour MP. Howard lays out his plans for the club and I am impressed. As a Forest player for over ten years, there are a few issues that might need resolving before going to Notts County, but they are not insurmountable. Howard has been very persuasive. But deep down I actually want to stay at Norwich City. I love the club, I get on well with the players – or at least I think I do – and I have still a lot to offer, especially to the younger lads now doing well in the first team. Come on Ken and Mel, reach out to me, I think. But they don't.

I agree to go to Notts County. But within two days Howard leaves Meadow Lane to become manager of Sheffield Wednesday. That puts a spanner in the works. Then, out of the blue, Larry Lloyd, my former teammate at Forest, is given the task to replace Howard. Larry calls to tell me that he would still want to take me to the club and that Mr Dunnett still wants to do the deal. I'm coming, I say to Larry.

August 1983: we travel to Filbert Street and absolutely hammer Leicester City 4–0. It's a great start to my career with Notts County and I play exceptionally well. Trevor Christie scores a hat-trick and a little winger called John Chiedozie, bought from Tottenham Hotspur, is unplayable today. We follow this up with a midweek win at Meadow Lane against Birmingham City and it looks like we are in business. Seamus McDonagh, our goalkeeper, arrived at the club a few days before me and we forge a friendship that will last for years. He has an important role to play for me later on in life, but just now he's a fellow player and a good conversationalist, with encyclopaedic knowledge of all things America.

We fall to earth on a Saturday afternoon in early September when Ipswich come to town and in unseasonable stormy weather beat us convincingly. It's not just a blip and it starts a poor run, with cracks appearing all over the place.

I personally find the move back to Nottingham more difficult than I imagined it would be. Obviously results on the field dictate how I'm feeling, but occasionally when I'm not concentrating, on my way into training, the car will automatically go to the right at the Trent Bridge lights, and sometimes before I know it I'm on Radcliffe Road leading to the City Ground.

Larry Lloyd is also finding being head coach difficult. I do not want to have too many discussions with him as I'm a player and he's the boss, but he seems not to be his own man, and if Lloyd is anything in life, he is his own man. I imagine there is a lot of interference from Jimmy Sirrel, the general manager, who has a long history at the club, and Jack Dunnett, the legendary chairman. Larry hints this is exactly the case, but he has to get on with it.

Lloyd's exasperation in office hours naturally spills over to the training field, and cajoling players into doing their job becomes frustrating for him. We train at the University Grounds, a few miles from Meadow Lane. It can be a soulless place even in good weather. Larry is taking the main session. We are going through some set-piece routines. Larry feels that there has been a reluctance from some players to want to head the ball when under pressure in games, and he wants this rectified as soon as possible. The exercise is not going well and Larry is frustrated with what seems to him to be a lack of enthusiasm. He watches on for a while but it's still the same. Half-hearted attempts. Larry is not only frustrated, he's getting irate. He stops proceedings right there.

He is going to lead by example this morning.

'Hey,' he shouts over to the corner kicker. 'Hang it up next time.' Larry steps back and says, 'Tell you what, I'll attack the ball myself, and you lot defend it. OK, let's go!'

The ball comes into the penalty box. Larry steps back a yard or so then arcs his run and, towering above three defenders, heads it into the net. He doesn't say a word other than to order another delivery like the last one. He does exactly the same with the second cross.

'Again,' he shouts.

And does exactly the same a third time. It was the Lloyd I remember. Arrogant, conceited, and with a point well made.

'Now then. It's simple. If you really want to head the ball, nothing will stop you. If you don't want to head it, everything will stop you. So next time it comes into the box, head it, please.'

Maybe that's why Larry Lloyd has two European Cup medals.

We put aside our wretched league form and set off on a good FA Cup run. A quarter-final tie at Meadow Lane against Everton is our reward. Unfortunately, in a scrappy game we lose to a scrappy goal, and Everton go on to win the whole tournament at Wembley. Our league form continues to falter and relegation becomes inevitable.

It's a miserable year for me on the pitch, but there is some great news off it for Geraldine and me. Our second daughter Alana is born at the end of May 1984 in the same hospital as Aisling, back home in Northern Ireland. Like her sister, she is a beautiful child and we count our blessings. But I think both of us feel that we should not have returned to Nottingham.

Notts County is a very fine football club but I have spent so much of my life on the other side of the Trent that I don't want to be reminded of past glories that will never return. Following relegation, Larry Lloyd loses his job and is replaced by Richie Barker. I feel for Larry. Of all the players gathered round Clough's table in those heady days, I felt that Larry was the one cut out for management.

Fortunes do not improve under Barker. Early February 1985, we are at Meadow Lane playing against Shrewsbury. I go in for a challenge to try to win the ball, when suddenly I feel the most excruciating pain in my knee. I just cannot get up. I know immediately that this is not a three- or four-week injury. It's only a minute or two before half-time and a stretcher is called to carry me off the field. I am laid onto the physiotherapist's table and I can hear the sound of the players' boots as they stomp past the room at the interval. A couple of them put their heads round the door to enquire how I am, then Barker walks in. The physiotherapist speaks for me by saying I'm no good to continue. Barker shrugs and exits.

I know my injury is serious, but I don't think this will be my last-ever game of professional football. It is. My contract is up in June but it will be at least seven or eight months before I'm playing again, maybe longer. Three weeks later, I am summoned to Jack Dunnett's office. With my crutches I struggle a little to open the door, but eventually I limp over to his desk and sit down slowly. He gets straight to the point.

'As you know, your contract is up at the end of June. We will not be renewing. But I'm quite sure you will have no trouble finding another club. Of course if you haven't done so by the end of June, we will pay you the extra month's salary until the end of July.'

I tell him there is not a prayer I'll be fit by July, but Mr Dunnett is in no mood to listen to expendables like me.

PART TWO

MANAGER

9

MANAGING EXPECTATIONS

As I run for the ball, I know it's all over for me. Despite months of rehabilitation, my knee buckles.

I'm helped off the pitch and carried into the dressing room. The physiotherapist has been called back to the dugout. I can hear the crowd noise outside but I'm not part of the game any more. Five short years ago I was young, strong, extremely fit and clutching a European Cup medal while parading around the Bernabéu Stadium. Now, in 1985, I'm lying on a treatment table with no one in attendance, at a testimonial match in Cambridge – one in which I shouldn't have played.

Nobody asks whether I'm all right. People have other things to do, more important things that concern them. I have ceased to matter. For the first time, it hits me: I'm done with playing this game of football.

The players come into the dressing room at half-time but I am ready to go home. I decline the offer of crutches because I don't know when I'll be able to return them. Cambridge and Nottingham are not exactly neighbouring cities. By the time the second half is ten minutes old, I'm driving painfully and uncomfortably back to Nottingham. I'm thirty-three years old; I have a wife, two small children and no money.

Several months later my old friend Sammy Nelson, a Northern Ireland colleague who is now in the world of finance, throws me a lifeline by organizing an interview with the manager of the

Nottingham branch of the pensions company he works for. I somehow get the job and I join the workforce. I need to earn.

One day, I'm coming out of a shop in Nottingham city centre and who should be walking by but Peter Taylor. Initially I try to avoid him – I don't want to be quizzed about where I am in my life and where my future might lie – but he's having none of it. He wants to talk. We have not spoken since I left Nottingham Forest more than five years ago.

'Hey, you,' he says in the friendliest manner possible. 'What are you doing with yourself?' I don't get a chance to reply; Peter often doesn't wait for an answer to his own questions. 'I thought you'd go into management,' he continues. 'I always felt you would be cut out for it. You disappoint me. Thought you would want to do it. And you've had the two best influences you could ever hope to have in me and Brian.'

Peter is now retired from the game. His infamous falling out with Brian Clough a few years ago is still unresolved. He has an avuncular approach with me today and it's hard to argue with his conclusion; I only wish he had been as friendly in my playing days. In fact, I would also love to tell him that he and Brian should bury the hatchet and speak to each other. But I don't have the nerve, and anyway, there are a lot of people I'm not speaking to myself these days.

I will never see Peter again and he will pass away four years later, but his legacy with Brian Clough will live on. And in a lesser way, his words to me will live on too. By the time I'm back home I've given his suggestion a lot of thought and it combines in my head with Billy Bingham's earlier musings on the same matter. I make up my mind that I will apply for jobs. Because of my knee injury I cannot play any more, so a player-manager's role – in vogue for lower-league clubs in recent years – is a non-starter. But surely my top-flight career will at least afford me an interview somewhere, and I'll take it from there.

Every managerial casualty in the new season allows me to write my letters to club chairmen. No one is biting my hand off.

Then, in January 1987, Second Division Bradford City sack their manager and I apply for the role, with not too much confidence of a reply. But a letter arrives at the house – I have been granted an interview. I get very excited, mainly because I've got a response at last. On a snowy January morning I set off for Bradford.

I wait about an hour in the foyer before being called. I'm escorted to the interview room on the first or second floor, where I knock and wait for the call to enter. There are six people sitting around a table. I'm welcomed by the chairman, Stafford Heginbotham, who does the probing. There is a man sitting to his right-hand side, the vice-chairman Jack Tordoff, who also asks a few questions. After a shaky start, I do OK – well, better than OK, but I'm not the judge. They thank me for my time and say they'll be in touch one way or the other.

A day goes by without news. A second day passes in the same manner. Then, on the third day, I get the call. It's Mr Tordoff. They want me back for a second round. He tells me that of all those interviewed, I'm the only one asked back. That's a positive start.

Mr Tordoff likes me. But he reveals that all those interviewed a few days ago had excellent references from very good managers, which I lacked. Could I, he asks, get a glowing reference from Brian Clough? If so, it would help me immensely in the second stage. I say yes, although I'm reluctant to do so, not having spoken to Clough in a long time. But needs must. I phone down to Nottingham Forest. The manager is over at Derby County's training ground, watching a game. I'll get him there.

I head over to meet him. He sees me coming from a good distance and looks a little surprised. He asks me what he can do for me and I tell him the story of Bradford City. He says he'll do a reference with pleasure and that if I don't get the job after his recommendation, he'll eat his hat. I thank him and head back home. Soon I'm back at Bradford, in the same hotel and the same room.

Terry Dolan, the caretaker manager, is doing well and is probably now in pole position for the job. Nevertheless, I impress at the interview and I believe I have a good chance. Mr Heginbotham asks me if I could work with Terry, with me being the manager. I don't know Terry well and I tell the panel that it might be difficult for both of us. In the end, I don't get the job. Terry Dolan becomes permanent manager of Bradford City and their position improves. I never do ask Brian Clough if his flat cap was eaten.

Early the same summer, there's a knock on my door at home. A man introduces himself: he is Kevin Greene, a director of Grantham Town. Would I have any interest in managing the club? Although Grantham is only twenty miles from where I live in Nottingham, I don't even know what league they are in.

'Beazer Homes Midland Division,' Kevin says.

'How many leagues below the Football League?'

'Three,' he answers. 'We train two nights a week and then a Saturday game.'

Two things are going through my mind. First, Kevin is very persuasive. He and the board have big plans for the club. Second, Peter Taylor's words are still ringing in my ears. Kevin wants me to meet the chairman, Mr Balfe, and the rest of the board. They too are very persuasive.

And so I'm now a football manager.

I have a three-week coaching clinic in America that I was invited to some time ago and as a consequence, I miss much of Grantham's preseason. Early results are not great and I don't yet know the strengths and weaknesses of the team. But I soon spot a young lad playing in an Inter County game at Grantham. We sign him from Lincoln United. And Gary Crosby wins the next seven games for us with scintillating performances.

I tell the coaching staff at Nottingham Forest about him. They are put off – why should they believe a nineteen-year-old lad, recently playing for Lincoln United, deserves a place for First Division Nottingham Forest?

'Because I say so,' I tell them, a bit too arrogantly.

Clough grants him a trial, Gary impresses, he signs for Forest and has a terrific career with them. The transfer fee doesn't do us any harm, either.

I really enjoy all aspects of managing the club: organizing the training sessions, picking the teams, motivating the players, and of course the matches themselves. We go close to promotion, failing by the thinnest of margins, and we are almost as close the following year too. Shortly after that, I leave to manage Shepshed United. Geographically closer to Nottingham, it means I can have more preparation time for training sessions after finishing work. They are of similar standing to Grantham, only in a different regional league; but I only spend a few months there, as my relationship with the owner quickly sours. I decide that I do not want to work with him and so we part company. I'll continue with some radio punditry work, sporadic as it may be, and see what life brings in the future. I do hear from Shepshed's owner again some years later. It's a congratulatory letter to me on Leicester City winning the League Cup in 1997.

It's early 1990 and I am covering an FA Cup tie between Norwich City and Liverpool at Carrow Road for BBC Radio. It's half-time and after a few comments about events so far, I nip off to the toilet. I bump into Alan Parry, the TV commentator, who is also having a comfort break. It's a chance meeting because he is only at the game to watch Liverpool, his favourite team; he is not working himself today.

I have met Alan a few times at sporting functions over the last few years. He is mightily good company, a brilliant raconteur and a terrific commentator. As befits a Scouser he is extremely opinionated on all subjects and, with a pint in his hand, as stubborn as the proverbial mule. Despite not being a churchgoer he is very fond of talking about religion, its merits and drawbacks – the merits usually mean Reverend Ian Paisley and the drawbacks may well centre on Roman soil. However, he argues so coherently and so passionately that one could be forgiven for changing religion after half an hour in his company.

'I thought you might have applied for the Wycombe job,' he says, referring to Wycombe Wanderers, the Vauxhall Conference club in Buckinghamshire, of which he is a director.

The reason he thinks this is that I applied for the post a couple of years ago. I had travelled down from Nottingham one sunny Sunday morning for the board interview, held at Loakes Park on the edge of High Wycombe town centre. Brian Lee was then the chairman of the club – he had also been a very successful manager there, but now he was running things from a chairman's viewpoint. There were a number of directors there that morning but Brian did most of the talking. Wycombe Wanderers were a very famous amateur club and tradition was their very essence. Blazered men on match days, good hospitality shown to visiting directors and a kindred spirit within its gates. I loved all of this, and said so at the interview. However, I felt they wanted someone with more local experience and some knowledge of the Vauxhall Conference itself. I was manager of Grantham Town at the time, a few leagues below the conference, so I knew what non-league football was all about, but I still didn't get the job.

'I didn't know it was even available,' I answer truthfully to Alan.

'Yes. We were beaten by the Metropolitan Police in the FA Trophy a few weeks ago and the manager left,' says Alan. 'The board are actually interviewing some people today. I can put a call into the chairman, if you have any interest? But bear in mind they may even have decided by now. I'll call immediately after the game.'

'No harm done, I suppose,' I agree, somewhat reluctantly. 'They can only say no.' They turned me down only two years ago, I'm thinking; so even if I do get an interview this time, why would they go for me? I'm not at any club right now and I dread being turned down twice for the same job, some two years apart.

After the game, I make the three-hour journey back to Nottingham without seeing Alan again. There is a call later. It is from the current Wycombe Wanderers chairman, Ivor Beeks. His predecessor, Brian Lee, has been asked to supervise the building of a new stadium for the club, with the move taking place this summer. Ivor is sorry to tell me that just this very afternoon – probably while Alan Parry was telling me about the job – they offered the manager's role to Kenny Swain, ex-Aston Villa full-back and current assistant manager to Dario Gradi at Crewe Alexandra. Kenny will confirm this as a formality this very night.

I thank him for taking the time to call me personally and put the phone down. Alan calls a few moments later with words of consolation.

'Nothing to worry about,' I reply. 'If I hadn't met you at Carrow Road I wouldn't even have known the job was available.'

But then, later on, the phone rings again – and once more it is Ivor Beeks on the line. Kenny Swain has changed his mind and wants to stay with Crewe Alexandra. Ivor asks whether I can come in for an interview tomorrow evening at his hotel close to Loakes Park. I agree.

I get to junction four of the M40 and descend Marlow Hill in darkness, save for the street lamps intermittently placed either side of the road. I recognize the steep descent, naturally, but cannot immediately place Loakes Park behind the general hospital. At the bottom of the hill are a couple of small, confusing roundabouts, which I negotiate at the second attempt before steering my car towards Ivor's small but well-maintained hotel. Ivor is already waiting for me. I introduce myself, although I'm hoping I'm the only one he's interviewing tonight. He tells me we've already met. He was one of the directors round the table when Brian Lee interviewed me the first time, but he stayed in the background and didn't ask any questions.

During the course of the next hour there seems to be a good chemistry between us. Ivor is a self-made man, extremely success-ful in the building trade. He has a strong work ethic and doesn't suffer fools but there is a warmth to his character that draws you towards him. I think he also likes me, although laughter at some of my jokes doesn't necessarily equate to love at first sight.

The manager's post will be full-time. Although the players only train two nights per week, usually Tuesdays and Thursdays, part of the manager's contract is to coach in schools around Buckinghamshire during the day. Frankly this isn't something I particularly relish, but if it means managing in the Vauxhall Conference – the winners of which go into the Football League – then I'm prepared to do it. Ivor seems happy with my commitment but wants to 'sleep on it' before making his mind up.

He calls the next day and offers me the job. I thank him for the opportunity and tell him I'll do well for him. He tells me that his one major ambition as chairman of Wycombe Wanderers is to win the FA Trophy at Wembley, the non-league equivalent of the FA Cup. Getting into the Football League would be nice as well, he adds with a smile.

He wants me to have a look at the new stadium being constructed on the outskirts of the town so that I can add my thoughts on, for instance, how the dressing rooms and the manager's office might be situated. I'm genuinely excited about the road ahead. Whatever happens now, my chance meeting with Alan Parry at Carrow Road has changed the course of my life forever.

High Wycombe is the most inapt place name in England: the town centre lies in the valley of the River Wye, at the bottom of some very steep hills. I'm convinced Edmund Hillary must have practised here before scaling Mount Everest in 1953. If your car is heading down Marlow Hill into town with faulty brakes, you may find yourself in a bit of trouble.

For all that, the Buckinghamshire town is replete with history. A Roman villa dating back almost 2,000 years was discovered after excavations in the Rye Mill. A short distance from this, Ivor Beeks has built a small apartment complex. I will forsake our home in Nottingham, move my wife and two young daughters from their school and take up residence in one of these two-bedroom flats early in 1990, with a plan to live there for perhaps three months. We will still be there almost three years later.

This Buckinghamshire town, an overnight stop for the carriages travelling from London to Oxford in bygone days, will come to define me as a manager. It has taken me far too long to realize that the world does not owe me a living because I once played football at the highest level and won a bag full of medals.

Up until now, I thought of playing football as a privilege; I never saw it as a living. But perhaps I ought to have done. Had I considered it a living, I wouldn't have given in to Brian Clough's first proposed contract with me back in 1975. I wouldn't have left Manchester City to go back to Norwich on half my salary. I can't change the past, but I can affect the future. I no longer have the luxury of thinking that way.

This football management game I find myself in just has to succeed. I do not have any other alternative. Whatever this job in this town demands – commitment, perseverance, long nights in the car watching football matches outside office hours – I have to be prepared to do it. And I am. During my short time in management I have already begun to form a nascent management philosophy in my head, and at Wycombe it will start to become more concrete.

Sometimes I must be steadfast. Take timekeeping, for instance. Players late for training because of their other work commitments just won't hold with me. They will be breaking their own semi-professional contract with the club and should be fined accordingly. And they must be seen to be fined, in full view of the other players.

But then, I must also rely on my gut instincts: my ability to coach and man-manage the players. Their response to me will be the making or breaking of me. Naturally, I have picked up ideas and methods from managers I worked with when I was a player. But essentially it will be my way of doing this job, my own character, that will determine whether I succeed or fail.

I hold my first training session on a Thursday evening, on a small playing area behind the main stand at Loakes Park. I ask the players what happened against the Metropolitan Police in the FA Trophy. Glyn Creaser, the captain, tells me they played badly on the day and deserved nothing from the game. Even from this one training session I can tell that Creaser is not just the captain but the leader of this group. He used to play for Barnet, the best team in the conference. Worrying rumours are circulating that Barry Fry, their manager, wants Creaser back. Fry is the king of the non-league and a very good manager. Not only does he know all the best players, he invariably gets what he wants. But even at this early stage, I know I want Creaser to remain at Loakes Park, and after we've had a conversation or two he decides to stay. Not only is this a relief, but it marks the beginning of a turnaround in Wycombe's fortunes.

The last few months of the season are not wasted. John Reardon, foisted on me as an assistant manager, has been part of the furniture here at Loakes Park for a long time. I am wary of assistant managers who retain their jobs when the manager gets sacked, so I'm more than a little unsure of him to begin with. He senses this, but says nothing for some days. Then he comes to me and says, 'I know what you're thinking. I know you don't know me at all; I've been here a long time, but that doesn't mean I'm indispensable. If you want me to leave, just let me know and I'll go. I want to help you and the club but I'll understand if it's not what you want.'

His words seem so genuine that I say, 'Let's see how we get along, John. I'm sure we'll be fine together and anyway, you know the conference well. I might just need to rely on you until I get to know the players.' When I eventually leave Wycombe Wanderers John Reardon is, thankfully, still at the club.

My first game as manager of Wycombe Wanderers is in February and will be at Merthyr Tydfil, Wales – coincidentally also the opponents in my first-ever game in charge of Grantham Town a few years back, some leagues below the Vauxhall Conference. Merthyr have seamlessly risen through the ranks since then and are now poised to break into the Football League. I will travel on Saturday morning by car and meet the team bus at Aust Services on the way towards Merthyr.

It's noon on Saturday and the team bus duly comes into view. I watch from a distance as the passengers alight. Club officials first . . . then more club officials . . . then, incredibly, even more club officials. I start to think there must be another bus coming behind with the players. It reminds me of a scene in *Butch Cassidy and the Sundance Kid* when the two outlaw heroes, brilliantly portrayed by Paul Newman and Robert Redford, watch from a distance as a train carriage opens and about fifteen horses with lawmen already mounted jump out of the carriage, one after the other. The confused cinemagoer wonders how they all could have fitted in.

I cannot see a film director at Aust Services shouting *Action!* to those on board the Wycombe Wanderers team coach, but just when it seems the bus has finally been emptied, out come the players – accompanied by a young woman, whose name I soon discover is Ruth. Everyone chats in such a carefree fashion that one could be forgiven for thinking a picnic awaits them. I am starting to get an inkling of why they lost to the Metropolitan Police.

'What's your job?' I ask Ruth as we take our seats at the tables set aside for the group.

'I sell lottery tickets.'

'On the bus?'

'Yes.'

'How long does that take? And why on the bus?' I don't think she's taking too kindly to my questioning.

'I'm allowed on the bus and I've been doing it for some time now.'

'OK,' I say, not wanting to make a big fuss with the game only a couple of hours away. Leaving my car parked at the service station, I join everyone on the TARDIS-like bus for the rest of the journey to Merthyr, lucky to find a seat. Ruth rejoins the players at the back. I sneak a glance over my shoulder. She is actually sitting on one of the players' laps. I need to sort out a few things, I'm thinking, if my dream for Wycombe Wanderers is to become a reality.

I have been left a talented group of players – they just don't know how to win consistently. I tell them that if it's fun they want from playing football, there are about fifty matches taking place every Sunday morning on the Rye Mill playing fields and they can ask for a game down there. To win more frequently, they will need a stronger mindset and a more determined approach to every game than is presently on display. This is my focus: to ensure players know their roles and what is expected of them, both in training and on match days. Enjoyment comes from winning.

The last few months of the season are taken up with reinforcing these principles, best shown with a brilliant victory at Darlington in April. Our new stadium is also being prepared for the start of August, so there is a more refreshing intensity to our play in anticipation.

'We need to do something for the last-ever game at Loakes Park,' announces vice-chairman Graham Peart.

'What are you thinking?' I ask.

'Well, you've got contacts in the game. Why not have a group of ex-players play the present team? How well do you know George Best? Do you think he might play?'

'I don't think George would even know where High Wycombe is, never mind Loakes Park. But I can ask,' I answer.

I get George's number and call him. We haven't spoken for close on fifteen years, so I'm not sure what he'll say.

'I'll be there, Martin,' he says. 'Just remind me about a week or ten days before the game.'

'Thank you very much, George. Can we tell the press that you'll be there?'

'Go ahead.'

I'm able to attract some other very notable names to play in the game. Mark Lawrenson, a brilliant defender for Liverpool and a European Cup winner who is now managing Peterborough United, promises to come; so does my old colleague John Robertson. Gerry Armstrong and John McClelland from my Northern Ireland days, Alan McDonald, Danny Wilson and ex-Everton goalkeeper Seamus McDonagh are all happy to give up their time to come to Loakes Park too.

As requested, I phone George about ten days before the game. He's definitely coming, he says – but until he actually arrives, I won't be sure. So I phone again the night before. No answer. I try once more. No answer. Panic sets in. There is no doubt that the people coming tomorrow will be anticipating George's appearance. He is the star attraction. An hour goes by. My phone rings. It's George.

'Sorry I missed your call. I was out jogging for twenty minutes. What time did you say you wanted me there?'

The final game at Loakes Park draws over 4,000 people to the stadium, double our average attendance for Vauxhall Conference games. George Best does not disappoint. He arrives to great fanfare and is escorted from the car park to the dressing room, signing autographs and programmes along the way. I am delighted to see him and, in all honesty, somewhat relieved.

The famous old ground is bathed in sunshine as the teams take the field. George, a little heavier than in his prime, is gloriously cheered when in possession of the ball and he responds with a couple of mazy dribbles, a throwback to his electric days at Old Trafford. He even chips in with a goal of his own. Of course, much reverence is paid to the wayward genius by the opposition. No one wants to spoil George's day. Indeed, I have already told young Matty Crossley – one of my Wycombe Wanderers players, and a die-hard Manchester United fan himself – that he can mark George Best, but not to tackle him. Matty is only too pleased to oblige.

The plan is for George to come off the field with about twenty minutes to go and milk the applause of the crowd. This scene is just about to be enacted when a streaker seizes his own opportunity to steal the show, racing onto the pitch. He even has the temerity to shake hands with the departing Best before being escorted from the field, a cap delicately placed to hide his modesty. Alan Parry and that wonderful actor, Warren Clarke, take the field to round off proceedings, and soon the referee whistles the end of the match. The famous old stadium with its sloping pitch has housed its final game.

It's a wonderful day, made even more magical by the presence of George himself. He has been a big hit both on and off the field. When eventually he is allowed some time for himself in the corner of the boardroom, he beckons me over to join him. We sit quietly for a few moments, reminiscing about days gone past and what the future might hold for both of us. I cannot help thinking about those few days in Scarborough almost two decades ago, but I stop short of mentioning them. He may not even remember anyway.

We are joined by the directors of the club, all wishing to have their moment or two with this footballing rock star. George seems genuinely delighted at the attention and favour shown to him by all of us this afternoon. He accepts Alan Parry's offer to be the first speaker at the new stadium in autumn time, when the monthly dinner evenings restart.

The sun is casting long shadows over Loakes Park when George decides to leave, signing a last few autographs for people still waiting out in the car park. Wishing me the very best of luck, he climbs into the passenger seat of a car driven by his partner. Through the gates they go.

I have been at Wycombe Wanderers Football Club for only ninety days, yet somehow I feel a real connection to its ninety-five-year-old home. I sit a little while longer with Parry and some of the directors. My two young daughters are out playing on the sloped pitch. I wish that this old stadium could be refurbished, the pitch levelled, and that football could still be played here for another ninety-five years; but it's not to be. Adams Park will house the new season's fixtures and will, in time, acquire a story of its own. Of course, there is much excitement in the town over this move.

I come up with one idea to inject some history into Adams Park from the beginning. Wycombe Wanderers' first-team shirt is pale blue, like Manchester City. But in the past they have worn a dark-and-light-blue quartered shirt, the colours of Oxford and Cambridge. We have shirts like this especially made for the occasion of Loakes Park's final game. I love the kit and believe that we should return to this shirt, made famous by the club's great teams of the past. I want the quartered shirts to be our colours going forward. Ivor Beeks agrees, and so it is done: Wycombe Wanderers will be back wearing those magnificent colours for many a long day going forward.

I have shown the chairman that at least I can attract big names for the ultimate game at Loakes Park, but I'm acutely aware that winning football matches is what I will be judged on. Reflecting on my three-month tenure at the club, I find myself looking forward to a new beginning in a brand-new stadium.

Brian Clough brings Nottingham Forest to officially open Adams Park in the summer of 1990. The appearance of Stuart Pearce and Des Walker, fresh from their World Cup exploits with England in Italy a few weeks ago, helps to swell the crowd and everything passes smoothly. I meet Brian for a few moments after the game; he is impressed with the new stadium and wishes me good luck.

With optimism high, we start the season with a flurry of goals. Garry Smith scores the first-ever competitive goal at our new home in a 4–1 win over Welling. Our form stays constant for the next few months. In December we are drawn against Peterborough United in the second round of the FA Cup, sparking sufficient interest from the media to bring John Motson and his BBC crew to cover the game. Three or four inches of snow falls so quickly that the game is called off, and John's broadcast from the centre circle in the blizzard, clothed in his iconic sheep-skin coat, becomes folklore.

The league is strongly contested with Barnet showing the way but we are making real headway in Ivor Beeks's favourite compe-tition, the FA Trophy. By the time we reach the quarter-final stage in March, however, we have many injuries. We need re-inforcements and Ivor is willing to help. I think he too sees the twin towers of Wembley beckoning.

Mark West, a small lad with an excellent first touch and our most natural finisher, has a niggling injury problem. He is willing to start the quarter-final with Northwich Victoria but doesn't know how long he will last. I'm prepared to take a risk on him, especially as I know that no long-term injury will result, at least according to our first-rate physiotherapist, David Jones. If West can help us get in front then the risk will have been worth it. If not, I'll accept the consequences.

I connect with Brian Clough over his reserve-team left back Stuart Cash. He needs to be playing competitive football somewhere. After a little discussion, we come to a beneficial arrangement for all three parties. I've also spotted a robust centre forward, a professional footballer with Lincoln City who is out on loan to Boston United. He's exactly what I require, both in terms of potency and complementary skills to Mark West. Keith Scott will terminate his loan at Boston and agree to come to Wycombe Wanderers. I agree terms with Lincoln City with a view to buying him at the end of the season. I believe both additions will give us a better chance of winning the FA Trophy.

We beat Northwich Victoria and face Altrincham in the semi-final. They are an industrious team who are chasing Barnet all the way to the Vauxhall Conference title. The first leg is home at Adams Park. Altrincham score before people have finished their Bovril – not a good sign, when away goals play such a crucial role in deciding ties – but we have learned a resilience that has stood us in great stead over the season.

Although we are not at our best, we manage to turn the game around, and a late winning goal gives us something to hold onto for our return journey north.

Wycombe fans arrive at Altrincham Stadium in their droves, commanding the whole area behind one of the goals. They have not deserted us just when we need them the most, and the sea of blue-quartered shirts will give the players the inner resolve they need to repel Altrincham. In the dressing room before the match I witness a steely determination written all over the players' faces.

We are vigorous and Glyn Creaser, our captain, is a colossus, heading everything that comes into the penalty area. At half-time, it's still 0–0 in a tight game. Forty-five minutes of willpower and fortitude are required to ensure our trip to Wembley. Altrincham cannot breach us and we score two late goals ourselves to clinch victory. A pitch invasion by our fans follows the final whistle, and Wembley celebrations begin. It will be the club's first appearance there since 1957.

Our average attendance this season at Adams Park is just under 3,000, yet we sell 17,000 tickets for Wembley in the first week of sale. Eventually almost 27,000 Wycombe Wanderers fans will parade up Wembley way to support the club, a phenomenal turnout for the town. Kidderminster Harriers, our opponents, will bring almost 10,000 with them themselves, making a record attendance for an FA Trophy final. Kidderminster are a well-balanced team: many of their players will go on to have solid careers in the Football League, and in Graham Allner they have a tactically astute manager in charge. But we ourselves have an array of talent and Wembley is as good a place as any to showcase such skills.

I find it difficult to think of anything else on the days leading up to the match, such is the excitement in this Buckinghamshire town. Football fever has not only gripped High Wycombe, it's also engrossed my own household. New outfits for my young daughters are in order and conversations between my wife and me draw nervous conclusions about what may lie ahead.

Preparation for Wembley is as thorough as possible for the team. We spend a few days and nights at Burnham Beeches Hotel, situated some miles from High Wycombe. England will use this very same hotel during the 1996 European Championship. It's imperative that the players feel like full-time professional footballers and adopt that mindset. Most of the lads have to ask for time off from work for these few days, but their commitment to the task is total. Little training routines the day before the game become rather competitive and I have to intervene. While I'm pleased there is fighting spirit, I want to save that for the game.

As the bus pulls away from the drive of the white Regency building on Saturday, the hotel staff are lined up just outside reception to wave and wish us good luck. On the journey there is quiet and casual conversation among the players, but I am nervous. I was always nervous before games as a player, and now that I'm a manager the same is true. It cannot be any other way with me and I don't want it to be, either. If I'm not a little tense, I'm not totally focused. The key is not to display this to the players. And I don't.

I remind the team what it will take to win this trophy today. Our plan of attack is to have our two wide players, Steve Guppy and Dave Carroll, in possession of the ball as often as possible, as the Wembley pitch will offer plenty of space down the flanks. But I also have two terrific midfield players in action today. Simon Stapleton and Keith Ryan have been powerhouses all season long. Strong and athletic, they give the team energy and dynamism, and they can really play. They both have that other ingredient that distinguishes them – courage. What I do know is that we are a far better team when they are playing together. I am buoyed by the fact that the dressing room is teeming with character and one thing is certain: nothing in terms of commitment and determination will be left on the Wembley pitch. We are ready.

The walk from the dressing room to the centre circle never ceases to stir emotions. And when I get to the top of the incline, it seems like the whole of the town of High Wycombe is here to support the Wanderers, flag-waving and banner-bearing.

As play begins, the two teams are evenly matched. We've been able to keep secret the fact that John Granville, our goalkeeper, is playing with a broken thumb. How will he cope mentally? Will he need another painkilling injection at half-time? What about the first save he has to make? Or when he has to come through a crowd of players and fist the ball clear? Thankfully he is not seriously tested, and we take the lead through Keith Scott and hold it until half-time. Granville has come through so far and feels more comfortable with things now that we're halfway through the game.

On the hour mark, Kidderminster equalize when a shot slips from John's grasp and finds the back of the net. It's a blow, a major blow, but not fatal. We have to withstand some pressure but we stay resolute – and then comes the moment I have been playing over in my mind for weeks. Scott's athleticism brushes off a challenge on the wing, he whips over a cross, and West, racing in to meet it, flies through the air and heads the ball into the Kidderminster net.

It is a sensational goal, a fitting denouement to any Wembley cup final. Surely that will be sufficient to win the trophy. Granville pulls off a critical save towards the end and the referee soon blows for full-time. We fling our arms aloft: the trophy belongs to Wycombe Wanderers. Ivor Beeks has had his dream fulfilled, perhaps more quickly than he had imagined.

The feelings of elation and pride within me mirror those I experienced when winning trophies at Nottingham Forest as a player. But if I try to analyse it, there's something different about winning a cup as the manager. It's that feeling that you've been the architect of victory. You have created an environment in which players can thrive and display their talents, and success suggests that the formula has worked. The cynic in me would point out that if the manager takes the flak when things go badly, he should at least take some of the plaudits when life is good, as it is today.

The players are applauded vociferously as they go up the thirty-nine steps to collect their medals. I am able to bring my two daughters onto the hallowed turf of Wembley. As they race across the pitch, flags tightly grasped in their little hands, I don't think they are aware that they are following exactly the same path George Best took when scoring that wonderful goal against Benfica in the 1968 European Cup final.

Ivor has organized a party for the team back at Adams Park. The players are naturally in great spirits and Ivor is still hugging the trophy at eleven thirty that evening. I remark to Alan Parry that our serendipitous encounter at Carrow Road has worked out.

We finish the season in a very creditable fifth place and our trophy win at Wembley gives me a stronger profile. Football League clubs start to take notice. Bristol Rovers approach Ivor Beeks for permission to speak to me. Gerry Francis has left to take over at QPR, where he was once an extremely successful midfielder, and Geoff Dunford, the chairman of Bristol Rovers, wants me as his replacement. Ivor tells me about Mr Dunford's interest and he does seem like someone I could work with. However, I don't want to leave Adams Park, as I have unfinished business. My burning ambition is to guide Wycombe Wanderers into the Football League. Isn't that why I have come here in the first place? Ivor doesn't want me to leave, regardless of any compensation Wycombe might receive for me, and he's delighted I'm staying.

It's an accepted view in the 1990s that a manager should learn his trade in the lower leagues before taking on one of the bigger jobs. I've never agreed with this because if you fail at a lower level, the chances are that you will not get an opportunity to manage further up the football pyramid; in fact, you might never get another chance to manage again. Coaching in the lower leagues is fraught with difficulty, featuring limited time with part-time players, implementing your training methods on only two nights a week and with a general lack of resources. It is a dangerous chessboard on which to plot a fledgling managerial career.

The news about Bristol Rovers' interest in taking me to Twerton Park, their temporary home at Bath, becomes public. The local reporter for the *Bucks Free Press*, a young journalist with a dogged determination to get a story, seems to camp outside Adams Park on a daily basis. While I think Peter Lansley can be a nuisance, I admire his tenacity. 'I must press you for an answer, Mr O'Neill,' is his opening gambit in each new encounter, picking up from the previous day's interview. This persistence will stand him in great stead as he goes on to write for the national broadsheets.

The 1991/92 season proves as memorable as the one before, if for different reasons. John Granville leaves the club and I sign Paul Hyde from Hayes, who will become a cornerstone of the team during the next few seasons. Another target is a young defender who has just been released from Brentford and I don't ask any questions – I just sign him. I cannot pay him a full-time salary, but he believes this move will give him the opportunity to eventually become a professional footballer again. Jason Cousins will make an indelible mark in the history of Wycombe Wanderers with his footballing ability, bravery and will to win. He and Dave Carroll, who himself has skills that wouldn't look out of place in the top division, will form a flourishing right-hand-side partnership.

Colchester, unable to exploit their full-time advantage last season with Barry Fry's Barnet proving too strong, are keeping their full-time status in all-out attack on the league. In truth their inherent advantages should see them win this league at a canter. That's our challenge this season, yet we are determined to go toe to toe with them, buoyed by our FA Trophy victory.

A fight it proves to be: both Colchester and Wycombe Wanderers end the season with ninety-four points, twenty-one points clear of the third best team and with a Conference record haul. After forty-two games, we lose out on Football League status on goal difference. It is a herculean effort by a squad I have come to hold in the highest possible esteem. However, the points record is little consolation. I am still devastated weeks later. When I speak to the players, I want to know if they still have that desire to go again next season. They do. And as for me, I have an even stronger resolve to bring Wycombe up.

The next season, we are greeted by good news: no club will have an advantage like Colchester United have had these last two seasons. There will be no full-time team in the Conference League this coming season, so it's a level playing field. The appetite for promotion has been whetted and it will be an unforgettable season.

We get off to a flying start, but soon injuries catch up with us and we drop some points in the process, giving encouragement to the other clubs. An FA Cup second-round match against West Bromwich Albion, managed by the legendary Ossie Ardiles, sees Sky coming to Adams Park. Despite the game being broadcast live on television at Sunday lunchtime, a capacity crowd of 7,000 people pack the stadium to see a brilliant non-league performance against the Midlanders. We come from 2–0 down to draw 2–2. In the replay, we should maybe win but eventually lose by a single goal. Wycombe are beginning to get on the footballing map.

But then disaster strikes. In early 1993, captain Glyn Creaser has a freak accident at work and will miss the rest of the season. It's a body blow for the team and the fans, but particularly for the player himself, who has been a tower of strength in recent years. We buckle down and drive on regardless. I add a couple of players to help with the tough run-in.

Our neighbours and arch-enemies Slough Town are making inroads into our lead at the top. We play them in a midweek match at Adams Park. A new attendance record only tells half the story: those who cannot get in take themselves up the elevated hillside behind the Woodlands Terrace. The whole scene evokes a throwback classic football photograph of the 1950s, with people finding all manner of ways to watch the game even on this coldest of nights. Drama, excitement and anxiety abound.

We take the lead through Scott, then play almost all of the second half with ten men after Andy Kerr, our centre half, gets his marching orders. Hyde pulls off a couple of great saves to keep Slough at bay and we hold on for what will be a magnificent victory, as well as a decisive step towards winning the Vauxhall Conference. A few games later, we clinch the title.

We're also gunning for the FA Trophy once more. Our semifinal opponents are Sutton United, who were in the headlines themselves a few seasons ago when they beat Coventry City in the FA Cup. They come to Adams Park and deservedly beat us 3–2 in the first leg. Gander Green Lane is absolutely packed to the rafters for the second leg. The atmosphere in our dressing room reminds me so much of that day at Altrincham; I know we are going to win the game and overcome the deficit from the first leg.

Matt Crossley, towering above everyone, sets us on our way with his header. By the end of the afternoon we have scored four goals. If I could choose just one match from my days at Wycombe Wanderers to epitomize everything I wanted to bring to the club, today would rank very high on the list. We will be going to Wembley again. The players had better get shopping for new suits and I'd better get shopping for some more new outfits for my daughters.

As the FA Trophy final approaches, I am brimming with confidence, even though we have always found Runcorn difficult opponents. Confident, yes – arrogant, certainly not. I want to win the Double. The football team I am managing deserves it. The players have been simply magnificent. Their determination to put aside last season's ninety-four-point disappointment, to regroup and start all over again, has been rewarded with promotion to the Football League. Now we need to crown our achievement at Wembley. And we do. On a bright May afternoon in 1993, Wycombe Wanderers, in beating Runcorn 5–1, complete the Double. We have proven ourselves one of the best teams in Vauxhall Conference history.

In sharp contrast, Nottingham Forest have been relegated and Brian Clough has departed the City Ground. He is now virtually unrecognizable as the fresh-faced powerhouse who stormed into my life almost twenty years ago. Relegation with a vigorous Clough in charge would have been unthinkable, but on TV at the end of Nottingham Forest's final Premier League game of the season he looks worn out. It is extremely sad to see that pained expression on the face of one of the brightest minds in football history.

Fred Reacher, the Nottingham Forest chairman, is at Wembley to watch our match. He speaks to me in one of the stadium's anterooms, asking if I would be interested in becoming the new manager of his club.

I have achieved the goal that brought me to High Wycombe in the first place: the Wanderers will be a Football League team. Ivor can celebrate with not one but two FA Trophies, although in fairness he has bigger ambitions for the club while he is chairman. He will understand if I leave, but wants me to stay to oversee its transition from part-time club to fully-fledged professional entity. A decision awaits me.

I visit the City Ground and sit with Fred in his office. I have known him for a long time – he was a committee member when I was a player – and we've always got on well, but today is different. Our conversations on previous occasions would have been small talk; now we are discussing the possibility of me managing his football club.

According to straw polls I am the popular choice to take over the reins, but I soon detect that Fred is not convinced of my credentials. He still sees me as that young curly-haired footballer he watched from the directors' box for a decade. In his eyes, I'm not a fully-fledged football manager with a different mentality, maybe even different views than I might have held as a player. He asks me if I could work with Frank Clark. I ask in return who would be the manager, the person making the decisions. 'You would,' he replies, not entirely convincingly.

I've known Frank Clark for a long time too, and I have great regard for him. He is also vastly more experienced in football management than I am – I actually haven't managed one game yet in the Football League – and if I look purely at that statistic, I can understand Fred's concerns. Frank, used to making his own big decisions, may not even agree to this possible arrangement. Finally, there is another significant element to all of this: following Brian Clough will not be easy. Yes, the circumstances are mitigated by the team's relegation, but perhaps Fred is right: perhaps experience is what's needed at Forest just now.

I reach a decision. I have taken Wycombe Wanderers into the Football League and I would like to be in charge of their first-ever historic game come August. Ivor will also be depending on me with the club going full-time professionally.

I return to Wycombe to let Ivor know I want to stay. 'I've helped wind up the clock,' I tell him, 'so I might as well hear it chime.'

I want to strike a balance between bringing a more professional approach to the football team, and retaining that Corinthian spirit found within the gates of this very special club. For Wycombe Wanderers to survive in the Football League it must become a full-time professional club. If it stays part-time with training sessions only two nights a week, it will soon find itself back in the Vauxhall Conference.

There is a general, but not universal, acceptance of this. My secretary, the redoubtable John Goldsworthy, is not in favour of a full-time team – at least not initially. Things are happening too fast, he thinks. I can understand his feelings but the players, almost to a man, want to become professional footballers at the club. They are prepared to give up their day jobs, which combined with their part-time professional wages would be greater than any salary the club can offer them at the moment, yet they still have the desire to turn professional. These players deserve a fair shot at the Football League.

The fixture list comes out and our first-ever game in the league is away to Carlisle United. On the day, we take almost 2,000 fans to witness the historic occasion. It is difficult not to be moved by the scenes inside Brunton Park: a sea of light-and-dark-blue-quartered shirts mingled with matching flags crammed behind the goal makes for not just a splendid scene, but a stirring call to arms. If our fans are ready, surely we must be as well.

It is a proud moment for me. After 105 years in existence, Wycombe Wanderers will play their first-ever Football League game. However, the game itself proves to be tough. The players can hardly get a breath, so fast is the pace of Carlisle's play. Almost inevitably, we fall a goal behind. We just have to hang on until we come to terms with this new league we find ourselves in.

An equalizer just before half-time is the tonic, courtesy of an own goal by a Carlisle player. They all count. Even better, in the second half Steve Guppy scores to put us into the lead and wheels away in celebration. A late equalizer spoils the day for me and the players, but judging from the jubilant arm-waving by our fans it has not spoiled the occasion for them. We are up and running in the Football League. In the dressing room afterwards, I ask the players their views on the experience.

Keith Ryan and Simon Stapleton, both superb athletes, say that the opening quarter was tough-going, but when they acclimatized to the pace of the game they felt really good. This is comforting news for me. A midweek cup win at Leyton Orient gives us a big boost of confidence to set the scene for our first Football League game at Adams Park. Keith Scott becomes the first-ever player to score there in the Football League as we beat Chester to complete a thrilling week.

Highlights and low moments abound in the season. To offset the loss of Glyn Creaser I buy a centre back, Terry Evans from Brentford. He is a giant of a man who has fallen out with his manager at Griffin Park. Terry has an indifferent start to his

Wycombe career but he pulls it together and becomes a colossus for the club in the months ahead. One of the great nights in the club's history happens when we overturn a 3–0 deficit against top-tier Coventry City in the League Cup to take the game into extra time at Adams Park. We are actually 4–0 ahead in the second leg before they score two goals that will be enough to take them through to the next round. The result garners headlines the following morning and for a while at least I bask in the publicity the club receives.

When Wycombe were in the Vauxhall Conference we never had a permanent training ground, and often found ourselves practising two nights a week on artificial turf. Now that we are in the Football League and training every day, we need new facilities. I find a new training area for the team a few miles outside the town. The complex is run by a wonderful gentleman and his dear wife who cannot do enough for the players and me. Every morning is a joy to be there, regardless of the weather conditions. And Friday is treat day, when the tea after training is accompanied by jam doughnuts and all things savoury. I don't know whether Roy Keane or Paul Scholes eat these types of buns on a late Friday morning before the next day's game, but it's having a morale-boosting effect on my team in South Buckinghamshire.

In October 1993 the financial director, Graham Peart, announces that the club has declared a profit for the previous year in the Vauxhall Conference. The number of season tickets sold has doubled owing to the success of the team on the field.

Within a few weeks Keith Scott is sold to the Premier League club Swindon Town for £300,000, which is ten times the price we paid Lincoln City for him two years ago. I'm sorry to see him leave but delighted that he will get the opportunity to play top-flight football. His departure leaves a rather large void, but as a replacement I sign Simon Garner from West Bromwich Albion. Cigarette-smoking Simon is one of the league's great characters. A brilliant goal-scorer for his beloved Blackburn Rovers, he is now in the autumn of his career but retains the agility that made him a penalty-box specialist. He settles in immediately at the club and scores important goals in the second half of the season.

We win against Preston North End at Deepdale, Hakan Hayrettin scoring a last-minute screamer to win 3–2. Far from stabilizing our position in the league, we press on for promotion, with the players now unafraid of any team; and after a long season, we reach the play-offs. Creaser is thankfully fit again, a timely return to compensate for the injury to Terry Evans. Back at Carlisle again for the semi-final, Garner proves his worth and wins the game and we do enough at home as well to get to Wembley. Preston await us there.

In April, three Wanderers players are chosen for the Professional Footballers' Association's Division Three Team of the Year: Steve Guppy, Terry Evans and Jason Cousins take the honours, with Wycombe the only club to have three representatives. Now, at Wembley, a season that has been full of promise may be transformed into an unforgettable one – it will all be down to ninety minutes of football. We have a big problem before the game, though. Paul Hyde, who has been magnificent in goal since signing, is ill. He's not been well for several days and feels very weak. Paul will do everything he can to play this game but, as he hasn't been able to train all week, at twenty-four hours until kick-off it's not looking good. Nevertheless, he desperately wants to play and he goes into the biggest game of his career with our hopes and aspirations resting on his shoulders.

I have never seen a team so prepared to win. Preston's history doesn't bother them. Nor does the fact that this is their first year in the Football League. We start brilliantly in the game and we should be three goals ahead in the first twenty minutes. Instead, we go behind when Preston score from a long throw-in. But we equalize quickly afterwards through Steve Thompson, who is proving today what a terrific player he is with a virtuoso performance. Preston score again before half-time to lead 2–1. I am calm in the dressing room. I tell them that they have been so good, they must not allow their heads to drop.

It will come right for us in the second half. Within a minute of the restart we equalize. Garner controls a ball in the Preston penalty area and lashes a left-footed shot into the net. Then Dave Carroll puts us ahead with a move that Barcelona would have been proud to produce. The same lad scores a magnificent solo goal to make it 4–2. It's our victory. This is an amazing feat: Wycombe Wanderers have been promoted for two successive years and, thrillingly, will now compete in the Second Division.

We break for summer before preseason to prepare us for life in a new league. Even if we have ambitions to do well, the calibre of club in this division is a step up again from last season – and only one team will be automatically promoted. We are up against Birmingham City, Brentford, Huddersfield, Hull City, Swansea, Brighton, Bournemouth, Plymouth, Cardiff and other well-established Football League teams. Ivor wants me to sign a new deal after our Wembley triumph and there's no place I'd rather be. I move my wife and family into a house in nearby Beaconsfield, mortgage myself to the hilt and get ready to go again.

I sign Cyrille Regis, who proves to be an excellent acquisition, and when he teams up with Simon Garner I have the oldest strike force in England. We have another excellent season in 1994/95, our first year in the Second Division, but the problem with being successful for a prolonged period is that a hiccup is viewed as a catastrophe. We finish sixth but the reconstruction of the Football League means that only one team is automatically promoted and the play-offs only go down as far as fifth position – so we are left to rue a few dropped points towards the end of the season.

By the late spring of 1995, Ivor and I are in a petty stand-off which has lasted since March. He has been incredibly supportive over the years but was vexed with our lifeless performance at Bootham Crescent, when we could only draw 0–0 with York City. Normally a point away from home, particularly at York, is a good result, but we needed to win and we didn't play well enough on the evening to warrant victory.

He came into the dressing room and allowed his irritation to spill over, with strong criticism of my team. I had already had my say to the players and I was not in the room when Ivor delivered his diatribe. By the time I came back, he had returned to the club's boardroom. I got to hear about Ivor's disgruntlement from the players. I didn't think they needed to be told twice about the evening's performance, so I headed off to the boardroom to confront him. I should have waited until I had calmed down and conversed with him the following day, but I didn't, and our dispute has now continued until the end of the season.

When the news reaches us that struggling Norwich City wish to talk to me about becoming their new manager, Ivor and I agree that perhaps a move to Carrow Road suits all parties. Had we made the play-offs, I know that everything would have been fine again. Those two extra points at Bootham Crescent would have been very helpful indeed.

It's a real shame that my days at Wycombe Wanderers end by falling out with the man who gave me the chance to manage the club and for whom I still have the utmost regard. Ivor and I have shared many great moments during the past few years but we can both be stubborn, and our combined stubbornness has forced an impasse that lasts far longer than it should. Fortunately, we run into each other by chance in a restaurant some years later. A reunion is unavoidable. Our friendship, renewed that evening, will remain firmly intact from then onwards, and I have much to thank him for.

Norwich City have been relegated from the Premier League. Their manager at present is Gary Megson, who took over from John Deehan towards the end of the season. Megson was unable to halt the club's slide into the First Division but many people in Norfolk feel that Robert Chase, chairman of the club and a big admirer of Gary's, will give him the opportunity to steer

Norwich back into the Premier League. That possibility is not well received by the fans and according to some polls held in the city, they would prefer me to become their new manager instead.

I arrive at Norwich City's training ground, where I am to meet Mr Chase. A new facility on the outskirts of the city is in place. Lots and lots of newly mown football pitches surround the main building. It would be difficult not to enjoy coming to work in this environment. Gary Megson is the first person I meet. He's just come out of the shower room and looks a little surprised to see me. I get the impression that he either doesn't know I'm in talks to become the new manager, or that Mr Chase has only told him moments ago. Either way he's not happy.

Mr Chase and I sit down to discuss the disappointment of last season and formulate a plan to rectify the situation – without Gary Megson, I have to add. If I do take the job I will be bringing Paul Franklin, my coach at Wycombe Wanderers, and Steve Walford, who has been working with the youth set-up at Adams Park. He will essentially handle the reserve team but also oversee the youth development until I get the first-team squad up and running. I think Robert Chase is hoping that I can find a place for Gary in my set-up, but other than that, he gives me little indication of how he wants things done.

Norwich have some talented footballers in their midst, making the collapse last season all the more surprising. Ian Crook is an excellent midfielder, Darren Eadie is a brilliant young winger, and there are a few others who will play prominent roles in my career in the not-too-distant future. But it seems there's the potential for more. Robert asks if I would be able to spend £5 million before the end of June. Considering there are not that many days left before then, I tell him it might be a challenge.

I'm led to believe that the deadline is something to do with the tax year; it doesn't make a great deal of sense to me, but I do not know the running of Norwich City FC and Mr Chase does. Either way, I'm pleased to hear that even if 30 June passes, there will be a sizeable kitty available to help Norwich ascend immediately back into the Premier League. Wycombe Wanderers deal in much smaller currency than the figures now before me and I decide it is time to move on. I uproot the family and head to Norwich. It's July 1995.

Within days the players arrive for preseason training and I form the immediate impression that some of these lads feel they should be starting the new season in the Premier League. Being relegated doesn't really hit home on the day it happens. It's only when the fixtures for the new season emerge and you stare at them, realizing that you will not be going to Old Trafford, Anfield or Stamford Bridge. Instead our opening fixture is away to Luton Town at Kenilworth Road, and Oldham Athletic and Port Vale will be early visitors to Carrow Road. Despite the fact that most of the group seem scarred by their precipitous collapse in the second half of last season, there is still a belief that they can, if a good start is engineered, go straight back up again. That is heartening to hear.

A couple of preseason games in Northern Ireland are organized. This is my chance to work with the players in the mornings and sit with them in the evenings. I have some fun at the expense of Mike Milligan, a robust midfielder signed last season from Oldham Athletic, where he had been a big success. Mike is a chirpy, likeable lad, unafraid to voice his opinion on any subject. He is the centre of attention when quizzing me on something. I mention to him that with a name like Milligan, he must be a Catholic. He says he is. 'Do you go to church?' I ask.

'Yes, I do,' he quickly replies.

'Well, the next time you go, why don't you kneel down and pray for some ability?'

It gets the loudest laugh of the evening, but Milligan takes it in the spirit it is meant and laughs it off. A possible rethink of strategy, tactics and training methods passes through my mind as the opening game of the season approaches but for the most part, the players seem to enjoy the schedules and exercises put before them.

30 June passed some time ago, and Robert Chase doesn't mention the £5 million any more. In truth, I do not quiz him too strongly; I want to see how we can adapt to this division first. He and I have devised a points target – or rather, Robert has devised it and I've gone along with it. It will be revised after every five games, and the target is ten points from the first five matches. Two points per game will gain automatic promotion at the end of the season. Simple, really.

On the day of our opening match at Kenilworth Road I give a debut to young full-back Danny Mills, who plays admirably despite giving away a penalty early in the second half to allow Luton Town an equalizer. Jon Newsome heads two goals and Neil Adams scores a brilliant goal to give us a 3–1 victory. Carrow Road is decked with colour for my first home game the following week. However, an enthusiastic welcome from an eager crowd does not guarantee a win, and our scoreless draw against Sunderland feels like coming down to earth after last week at Luton. I add Matthew Rush from West Ham United for £350,000 to the squad, but unfortunately he sustains a serious injury on his debut.

The requisite ten points are on the board after five games. So far, so good. But now I feel that the team needs strengthening. I've identified Dean Windass of Hull City as a goal-scoring midfielder that we need. He played brilliantly last season against Wycombe Wanderers at Adams Park and I've been monitoring his progress ever since. Windass will cost around £500,000 if it goes through. Together with Matthew Rush, I will have spent less than £1 million; so, going by the conversation I had with Robert when I signed, that shouldn't be a problem.

I discuss the possible transfer with Robert. Would he be prepared to pay the fee to Hull City for the lad? Robert tells me he will deal with this 'chairman to chairman', which is not how I operated with Ivor. Of course, I'm not going to do anything without Robert's permission, but having been given the go-ahead I would normally expect to speak manager to manager about any possible transfer.

A day becomes a week, and a week becomes a couple of weeks. I ask the chairman a number of times what has transpired in his negotiations with Hull City. Has he made a bid? If so, what was Hull's reaction? How much do they want for Windass? Robert isn't happy with my questioning, and any slip-up on our points in the next five games will give him retaliatory ammunition.

By November 1995, I'm sure Dean Windass is sitting in his Humberside house blissfully unaware that he is the subject of a heated debate between myself and Robert Chase. I decide to phone Terry Dolan, the Hull City manager, hoping he can enlighten me about what's going on. When he picks up his phone he tells me that his chairman did receive a call, but he has heard nothing back from Norwich. I give this news to Robert, who is not happy that I've called Terry Dolan at all.

I'm not particularly happy myself, and not at all sure what game the chairman is playing. Having started by wanting me to spend £5 million before 30 June, it doesn't make a great deal of sense that he's now not even following up on our interest in a Hull City player. I decide to raise the matter in the next board meeting, to which I'm always invited to discuss current club football matches.

In the interim, Mark McGhee resigns at Leicester City to become the new manager of Wolverhampton Wanderers. Martin George, Leicester's chairman, once offered me the job of manager some seasons ago, but on that occasion I drove to his Northamptonshire house to tell him that I would be staying at Wycombe. That seems to have made some kind of impression on him, because he now calls me to ask how I'm getting on at Norwich. I say it's not that fantastic with the chairman, and that I hope to discover more at our coming board meeting. He asks me to keep him informed about any developments.

On a dark, damp December night, the board convenes.

Robert Chase welcomes me to the meeting and asks what has happened in the last two games – which have yielded one point – and how I plan to address the situation. When I get my chance to speak, I decide that I'm going to have my 'day in court'. I remind him that just before the draw and loss, we had four consecutive wins, and that we are still well positioned to mount a serious challenge for promotion. I then ask him why he has not followed up on the proposed Dean Windass transfer. Mr Chase does not get a chance to answer this. Instead one of the board members abruptly interrupts, remonstrating with me that I have no business whatsoever addressing the chairman in such a manner. The others chime in, upbraiding me. Within minutes, shouting fills the room.

Regardless of Martin George's interest in me, I'm not sure that I've done my chances of staying at Carrow Road much good after this evening. Within ten minutes of the meeting beginning I'm asked to leave, as the football business has come to an end. Other issues, such as a plan to widen the car parking area behind the River End goal, are now to be discussed. I'm not needed for my input. But there is a fairly decent chance that whether the car park is widened or not, my car won't be in it.

I come back to our city centre flat and tell Geraldine what has just happened at the board meeting. She can never be quite sure how the arguments I have and the decisions I make are going to impact her life, or the lives of our daughters. One outburst could lead to another home, possibly even another school.

I phone Martin George, too, to tell him what has transpired. He says that he might have some issues to resolve, but he hopes to work them out. He'll let me know very soon. In truth, I don't feel too good about the boardroom incident. Would I have been as bold if I hadn't thought Martin George was in the background? Who knows? I keep telling myself that my arguments with Robert started long before Mark McGhee resigned at Leicester City and I found out weeks ago that Mr Jones, the vice-chairman of Norwich, was the champion of my being at Carrow Road in the first place. Still, I do have a history of argumentative discussions, and not just in my own house. Much to ponder in the hours ahead, with Christmas close at hand.

By Sunday morning, I have made a decision. Just after ten o'clock, I am parked outside a hotel near Melton Mowbray. I take a couple of deep breaths and try to control my nerves, but it's not really working. For the hundredth time, I rehearse the words I'm going to deliver to Robert Chase in the next four minutes. They will be brief: 'Mr Chase, I am resigning as manager of the football club with immediate effect.' I repeat this sentence two more times under my breath during the walk to the hotel lounge, where I know he will be.

I also brandish a handwritten letter enclosed in a white envelope – the formal resignation letter that must accompany my sentence. I see Robert rising from his cushioned seat as he catches me entering the lounge. He is holding court with three other directors. He is surprised to see me. I deliver both my utterance and my letter simultaneously, turn on my heel and walk away. He must be shocked, because he offers no reply. Once I get outside, I race off down the broad hotel driveway like a bank robber fleeing a botched heist. I am no longer the manager of Norwich City FC.

The Norwich City game will be broadcast live on television this afternoon, but I will not be in charge. Ironically, they are playing Leicester City at Filbert Street. I travel to my brother's house in Nottingham to watch the game and he is somewhat surprised to see me. As the pre-match interviews take place, the news of my resignation has obviously broken. Mike Walker at Filbert Street, in a punditry role for Anglia TV, looks totally bemused. I later discover that he was going to be unmasked as the next manager of Leicester City in the next twenty-four hours.

It's a difficult game for me to watch. Norwich take a 2–0 lead but Leicester stage a comeback to win 3–2, and with this victory they swap places with Norwich in the league table. Two days later I travel up to Leicester, as snow is beginning to fall and turning the rooftops white. I feel very sorry that I've had to leave decent players with good attitudes: Crook, Milligan, Adams and Robert Fleck, to name a few.

But what has been done cannot be undone, and only time will tell whether the choice I've made is right.

10

THE FOXES OF FILBERT STREET

There is angst and frustration among the Leicester supporters. It is late 1995 and another manager has departed. Brian Little left to go to Aston Villa not long ago, and now Mark McGhee has just departed for Wolves. It's cold, with Christmas around the corner. Snow sprinkles the ground. The mood of the players is palpably uneasy. Do they really want a manager who has left after less than six months in charge of a rival club? Not especially. Are they pining for the loss of their manager? Absolutely. But it's me who they've got.

McGhee has left the team in eighth position in the league, but his parting words are that the squad is 'good enough to win the division by a stretch'. I am not yet convinced. Norwich were actually in front of Leicester when I left; not by much, I admit, but they were still in front.

Upheaval is rife. I meet Barrie Pierpoint, the Leicester chief executive, for the first time just outside the boardroom. He is with Roy Parker, one of the directors. They welcome me graciously, both wishing me well at the club, and add that if there is anything they can do to help I need only ask. I am not yet aware that I'm only at the club because Martin George, the chairman, insisted on me over the board's choice, Mike Walker.

I make my way to my office. On the way I see Martin, who is talking to press officer Paul Mace. I mention that I've just met Pierpoint and Parker. 'They were both very welcoming,' I add.

Martin rolls his eyes, looks at Paul, winks and turns his attention back to me.

'Let's hope your first impression of my colleagues remains constant,' he says acerbically. 'Just to let you know, if Barrie had been allowed to vote yesterday morning you wouldn't be at the club now,' he adds. Apparently Barrie, not being a director of the club, is excluded from voting on the new manager. I begin to wonder what I have let myself in for.

We have an abundance of centre backs at the club but Steve Walsh, the captain, is the best. Friday morning, just after training, there is a knock on my door. Walsh wants to have a word. He has just trained well with the squad minutes earlier, walked off when the session ended, and showered. He's the captain, so I expect him to ask for a few extra tickets for the players' families or friends at Grimsby tomorrow. No. He says he's struggling to be fit.

'You just finished training twenty minutes ago,' I say, somewhat confused.

'I know, but my thigh is killing me. I can hardly walk.'

I'm devastated by this turn of events. I call in Alan Smith, senior physiotherapist. Alan calms things somewhat. 'Let's see how you are in the morning, Walshy, but travel up with the lads this evening and check things again tonight.'

Walsh, a little hesitant, leaves the room, in forced agreement with Alan.

'What's happened there?' I ask.

'Don't worry, gaffer. He'll be OK. He does this every Friday before games. It's a ready-made excuse if he doesn't play well, an inbuilt defence mechanism and all that.'

'He'll be OK?' I ask, not quite reassured.

'He's fine. And he'll start – and finish – the game.'

Walsh does indeed play the following day at Blundell Park. The game ends in a 2–2 draw and we come from behind to get an equalizer. There is some consolation in this but, in truth, we haven't played well. Boxing Day will be our next game, at home to Ipswich Town.

Most football pitches at this time of year are not in good shape. The winter prevents grass from growing and depending on how cold the weather is, the playing surface is either muddy or riveted with frost. We have flimsy tarpaulin sheets laid over the pitch to prevent the incoming cold. It's supposed to protect the surface from anything down to −5°C, but on Boxing Day morning we can see that it clearly hasn't worked. The tarpaulin sheets are removed like a tight Elastoplast being peeled away from a festering wound. The remaining grass on the pitch sticks to the tarpaulin and when everything is laid bare for the referee to see, there is not a blade of green left – not even near the corner flags. It is completely brown, and frosted brown at that, resembling rutted tarmac. The protection has not only failed, it has ruined the pitch for the rest of the season.

The referee calls the game off immediately. This will prove costly over the coming months, but for now it's just a postponed Boxing Day match. Barrie Pierpoint is disappointed, since the restaurant has sold out all eighty covers for the day. To my consternation, this is bemoaned in the boardroom for the whole morning. What other football club can sell out its restaurant on Boxing Day? Who can rival Leicester City for such hospitality? Well, I think to myself, just about every other club in the land that has a home fixture on Boxing Day and an eating area within the ground. Still, eighty covers are eighty covers, and the food goes to waste.

We draw at Millwall a few days later, so my first match in front of the home supporters at Filbert Street is an FA Cup third-round game against Manchester City – a division, and a class, above us. We scramble a 0–0 draw, with Manchester City players complaining about the state of the pitch and some of our more discerning fans complaining about the football.

January falls into February and we are lurching, like a boat stuck on the rocks. Fridays are always the same: Walsh comes into my office to tell me he's 'in bits', but plays the following day. By now, almost forty days into my tenure, we still haven't had a win. 'Infamy, infamy, they've all got it in for me,' shouts Kenneth Williams as he runs out of the forum in *Carry On Cleo*. This scene goes through my head right now as I get a knock at my door.

It's not Friday, so it cannot be Steve Walsh. No, it's Steve Corica, our Australian midfielder: a quiet lad by nature, both on and off the field. He was bought by Leicester City at the start of the season and must have played exceptionally well in August and September. He is very popular with the fans, but I haven't yet seen why. He's a runner with the ball – which, incidentally, I love in attacking midfielders – but so far, in the games under me, he has failed to produce.

'I would like to leave the club,' he says, before I even ask him to take a seat.

'Why?'

'I'm not enjoying my football any more.'

'Why do you think that is?' I ask again.

'I miss the previous manager. I really respect the guy and I would like to go to Wolves to join him there.'

'Does he want you?' I ask, suspiciously.

'I believe he would, since he brought me to Leicester City.'

'That doesn't necessarily follow,' I point out, 'unless of course you know for sure that he wants you. Have you spoken to him recently?'

'No, not really, but I have so much respect for him,' Corica says again.

'I know. You told me that a minute ago. Would you not try to see if it could work here? You're very popular with the crowd and they wouldn't be happy to see you leave. Anyway, I haven't had any offers from any club, let alone Wolves, for you. But in fairness, nobody knows you want to leave – at least until now.'

'I've made up my mind. I want to go to Wolves,' he reiterates, in a voice devoid of emotion.

I reluctantly say that if that's what he wants to do, he needs to get Mark to give me a call. Then, if it's true, I'll put it to the board and find out their view on it all. The sooner he phones Mark, the sooner the ball will be rolling, I suppose. With that, the little Australian turns, opens the door and disappears up the corridor.

The crowd love him; and yet he not only wants to go, but go to Wolves. It would be anathema to our own fans. They are not overly fond of me, results, of course, dictating all sentiment. But I'm not sure Corica is quite as good as the Leicester fans seem to think, and that repeated remark about really respecting Mark rankles with me, implying he doesn't feel similarly about me. Right now, this view may well pervade the dressing room.

I need to win a match, sooner rather than later. But it's not happening. Martin George, the chairman, is beginning to wonder what he's done in taking me on. He is supportive but tells me that there are boardroom rumblings and murmurings, which he is finding more difficult to control. I am in a spot.

Who is that bright spark who wrote that your first hundred days in a job determine your success or failure? I don't remember reading the chapter on not even reaching that milestone. My first forty days seem like forty years. The replay at Maine Road, Manchester doesn't help. We get mauled. Georgi Kinkladze is on sparkling form, too much for us. The result is not unexpected, as City are a league above us and going strongly themselves, but our performance leaves a lot to be desired and moments of self-doubt start to creep in.

In the following home match at Filbert Street, an incandescent fan behind me continually shouts 'Get Lewis on! Get Lewis on!' I don't want to look round. Neil Lewis is a young left back converted from left wing. He is quick and has a decent left foot, but he cannot defend. I know this from the innumerable training sessions I've had in the weeks I've been manager. Mike Whitlow is playing left back at the moment. He is bigger and stronger than Lewis, but not as quick. Right now, I think he's more dependable. The 'Get Lewis on!' shouts have gathered momentum over recent home games, and are now getting much more traction from a large number of know-it-alls behind the dugout.

Lewis is substitute, and Whitlow is not good today. But I cannot allow Lewis onto the pitch. His surrogate dad behind me will have won, and I will have no option but to continue with him until the season ends – or my time as manager ends, which might be much more close at hand. I cannot buy a win.

Whitlow is injured for our next home game and I finally start Lewis in the match. At least 'Popeye' behind me will be satisfied. But with fifteen minutes gone Lewis slips, allowing the winger to cut inside and fire a left-foot shot that whizzes inches past the post.

What happens next is unbelievable. From just over my right shoulder, the same face that has for weeks been screaming for Lewis's appearance roars more loudly than ever, 'Get Lewis off! Get Lewis off!'

It will stay with me for eternity.

A few days later, we're at Molineux and there will be no way back for me if we lose. Mark McGhee's Wolverhampton Wanderers, with Steve Corica in midfield, lie in waiting. Steve has got his wish, joining his mentor in the West Midlands. We have still to taste victory since my arrival in December. It's now mid-February 1996.

The skies open up as the teams take the field and the game is played in torrential rain. Mark is getting some stick from our travelling supporters and for a while I feel some respite. Young Emile Heskey comes up big tonight and we win a marvellous football game, made even more special for me when Corica is hauled off with twenty minutes to go. He passes close by as he trudges off.

I move closer to him than a normal official would allow and bellow a few profanities in his direction. He never looks anywhere else but down at the ground, but he has heard me all right. I think most of Molineux's main stand have as well.

Is this the start of the revival? We have played excellently tonight on Molineux's wet but well-kept pitch and the travelling support leave the ground in good spirits. Mark, in his press conference, replies to the question of his being booed by the Leicester fans by saying that he understood their reaction, and that he didn't even mind Leicester winning. 'They need it more than we do just now,' he comments. Mark is absolutely right.

But the season is far from over and there will be many twists and turns before the end of May. Just now, my reprieve is to be short-lived. The following month, the dam bursts and all hell breaks loose.

It's March and today's match is a big deal: it's a big day for me and my managership of Leicester City. We are playing Sheffield United at Filbert Street. It's a home game for the football club but anything but a home game for me. Our supporters, restive for some weeks, are agitated to breaking point, and if the result doesn't go well this afternoon, things could turn rather ugly.

I am beginning not to enjoy the last mile into Filbert Street on match days. About 400 yards from the stadium, there is an old brown brick building resembling a textile factory which almost juts into a small roundabout. A sign daubed in large white painted letters, about four floors up, easily catches the eye. It has been there for a number of weeks but this afternoon it seems larger than ever: 'O'Neill out, O'Neill out'. A repetition in case anyone could possibly misread its intention.

Everyone sees it: the fan who painted it, those going to the game, and for good measure, the opposition team, who will peer at it from their bus windows as they pull up outside the ground. They will be buoyed by the fact that the home fans don't want the manager at the club. Particularly today, the sign evinces a feeling of foreboding.

The transfer window passed some forty-eight hours ago. It was the last chance to strengthen the team before the shortened run-in. The supporters are completely underwhelmed. I have signed Julian Watts, another centre back, for £210,000 from

Sheffield Wednesday, and a young lad from Chelsea Reserves, Muzzy Izzet. I know all about Muzzy. I have seen him every second Monday night at Kingstonian's ground in London, where Chelsea Reserves play. He is a proper footballer despite his appearance. A heavy shower of rain might show him in a very uncomfortable light, so thin is he. His legs look as if they will not hold him up for the whole of the day, never mind the rough-and-tumble of a football match. But he has fabulous ball control and an ability to dribble past opponents and a courage to match that ability. He has signed on loan until the end of the season.

Late Thursday afternoon, a few hours before transfer deadline, I had another target in my sights. Chris Allen from Oxford United and his agent were in my office. Martin George walked past and looked in on proceedings. He didn't look happy. He signalled that he wanted a word in private, so I left the room and walked the fifteen or so paces to his office further down the corridor. I told him that I wanted to sign Allen, a speedy winger and a decent crosser of the ball. Martin knew his players and he knew Allen's qualities, but he didn't want to sign him. The £210,000 for Julian Watts and Izzet on loan until the end of the season were quite enough business for transfer deadline.

'We need him, Chairman,' I pleaded. 'I'm in negotiations with his agent just now. In fact, I've just made him an offer and they've gone out to their car to consider it.'

'You have no right to do that without my permission,' Martin countered, and of course he was right. But since I hadn't been able to get hold of him all day, I'd taken matters into my own hands. According to the local press it was make or break, and I needed to bolster the team. A few new faces might help to quell the crowd, buy me a little time to turn things around and get into the play-offs. I knew – and so did Martin George – that only promotion would suffice. But he still wouldn't do the deal.

I said, rather rudely, that if the agent accepted the offer I had given him, Martin would have to go into the room himself to tell him the deal was off.

'I won't be doing anything of the sort,' he retorted angrily. And I realized it wasn't going to happen.

I walked out of the chairman's office and made my way back up the corridor, joining Allen and his agent. They were looking for something extra in the contract, which gave me the opportunity to bail out. 'You've got ten seconds to accept what's on offer,' I said. 'If not, the deal's off.'

I was worried to death that in those ten seconds they would say yes. But I took the risk and as I reached ten, I said: 'The deal's off, you've had your chance.'

They were speechless. I asked them to leave the office immediately, not giving them an opportunity to say anything. I walked back to Martin's office and said to him, 'You got your way, they've gone.'

I left his room believing that I could blame the chairman if things went badly in today's forthcoming game; but it was a passing comfort. Reality would set in soon enough. And just to top it all off, Martin told me that he would not be at Filbert Street on Saturday. I would have to face the music alone.

Three o'clock comes round quicker than I would like. Just over 13,000 people bothered to turn up last week when we beat Millwall 2–1, but today is different, with 16,000 fans whose grace and forgiveness will be in short supply this afternoon; that's a given. I have to win to keep hopes alive.

I look around the dressing room. Walsh might help us keep a clean sheet, although since we've only kept two of those in fifteen league games during my tenure, that might be a pipe dream. The irony is that those two clean sheets were against the two teams, Sunderland and Derby, who will canter to automatic promotion at the end of the season. Heskey and Steve Claridge are playing. Neil Lennon is suspended – a big blow. I signed him from Crewe a couple of weeks ago for £750,000 and his influence on Leicester City over the next couple of years will be immeasurable. He will play a significant role in my managerial career.

I've fallen out with Garry Parker in a dressing-room incident.

As a result, he's not playing. I've totally misread Parker. Right now, I think he's a barrack-room lawyer with one aim, and that's to turn the dressing room against me. He played well under Mark McGhee and I suppose he's disappointed Mark has not taken him to Wolves. After all, he took Steve Corica, who was a big favourite with the Filbert Street fans; because I allowed him go to Wolves, that's another nail in my almost completely nailed-down coffin. As I will later discover, Parker is the exact opposite. He wants to do well. He's not a troublemaker, not the manipulator I think he is. He's actually a very good midfielder. Although not the quickest, he can pass the ball all over the pitch. Perhaps I can't see this right now. Perhaps I don't want to see it.

Watts will start in the team as one of three centre backs. In terms of numbers the club may be short of genuine talent in midfield, wide, or up front, but we could fill a stadium with centre backs and I've just bought another one. Who needs another bloody centre half that few have even heard of? Or a reserve from Chelsea that no one knows either?

Izzet is on the bench, naturally excited about the possibility of making his Football League debut sometime during the game and totally oblivious to all that will happen within the next two hours.

Of course, Sheffield United score, and their manager, the brilliant Howard Kendall, gets out of his dugout to applaud their goal. We huff and puff but cannot make things happen in their penalty box. The frustration around Filbert Street is both audible and visible. Those supporters directly behind my dugout are letting me know that my presence is not welcome. The substitutes hear every word of their utterances. I don't even want to look at Muzzy. He must be wondering what the hell he's let himself in for. The manager who has brought him here might not even see the week out.

Then it happens. With less than twenty minutes to go, Sheffield United score again. It is 2–0. Cacophonous booing erupts all around Filbert Street: 16,000 people rhythmically roar in unison: 'Fuck off O'Neill, Fuck off O'Neill . . .'

I'm standing up. John Robertson, my assistant, stands with me giving me support, which I appreciate greatly. We don't look at each other, but stare directly ahead. I'm looking into blank space, beyond the stand opposite me. And maybe beyond even that, into the abyss. In future years John will often remind me, particularly after big successes together, about these sixty seconds of our lives.

'It's wild, isn't it,' I say to him.

'Yes, it is,' he replies.

There's nothing I can do to quell the volcanic anger at Filbert Street. But I do bring on Muzzy Izzet, and his first touch in the Football League is something special. He controls a tough pass, pirouettes between two Sheffield United players and takes the ball away with a grace and poise that is totally incongruous with his surroundings. Suddenly, if only for a few seconds, the crowd gasp at what they have just seen from this weedy kid whose shirt looks as if it's been borrowed from the wrestler Giant Haystacks. But the awe is ephemeral. The barracking continues until the final whistle and I am booed off the park.

'Pack it in, O'Neill! Go back to Forest!' are the last words I hear going down the tunnel. I reach the relative sanctuary of the dressing room. The players have heard the reaction of the crowd, aware that I have borne the brunt of it. This, in turn, allows them some distraction from their own performance.

'You may have given up the ghost,' I say to them, 'but I swear to you this will not defeat me. We will still make it.'

The press conference and post-match interviews, and there are a few of those to deal with, carry the same defiant tone. How quickly events can unfold. Just months ago, I left Wycombe Wanderers. Life was good then. I was coming off four years of unparalleled success and I could do no wrong. I cannot believe it has come to this. But I take some consolation from the fact that my adversary today, Howard Kendall, felt the wrath of the Good-

18. With two men who had a big impact on my life: George Best (*left*) and Ivor Beeks (*right*), the Wycombe Wanderers chairman.

19. A double year in 1993: winning the Vauxhall Conference with Wycombe and promotion to the Football League for the first time (*left*); and (*bottom*) celebrating the FA Trophy with the Wycombe players and staff.

20. The Wycombe Wanderers team who played against Carlisle United in our first-ever appearance in the Football League.

21. (*left*) Winning the play-off for promotion to the Premier League with Leicester City in 1996. 22. (*right*) With Steve Claridge after winning the Coca-Cola Cup final replay against Middlesbrough.

23. Support from the fans in 1998, pleading with me not to leave.

24. With Matt Elliott after the second League Cup win in 2000.

25. Winning the Scottish Premier League with Celtic: lifting the trophy, and (*below*) getting out of the way of the players celebrating.

26. Dejection after the extra time loss to Porto in the UEFA Cup final in 2003.

27. Celebrating victory over Rangers at the Ibrox Stadium in 2004 with John Robertson and Steve Walford; both men were integral to the successes achieved.

28. Helping the officials with their timekeeping as Aston Villa manager against Man City in 2007.

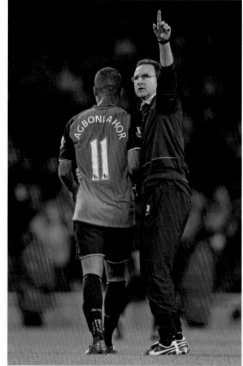

29. Embracing Gabby Agbonlahor, a brilliant player for me at Villa.

30. Facing Alex McLeish in the English Premier League, he for Aston Villa and me for my boyhood club Sunderland.

31. With FAI chief executive John Delaney ahead of being unveiled as the new Republic of Ireland manager.

32. (*left*) Leaping at Shane Long's winning goal against world champions Germany during the Euro 2016 qualifiers.

33. Saluting the fans after qualifying for the Euro 2016 competition for only the third time in Irish history.

34. (*right*) Celebrating with Roy Keane after beating Italy at the UEFA 2016 Euros.

ison Park faithful before he turned it around for Everton and brought them great success a decade ago. And he had even been a hero as a player there.

I don't get a chance to see Howard after the game to maybe seek his advice on how to handle my situation. Instead the club secretary, Ian Silvester, comes to tell me that my car should be brought round the back of the stadium and that it would be safer to leave by that exit. I have much regard for Ian, and I will hold him in even greater esteem when he puts his job on the line for me some months later; but I tell him, 'Sorry, Ian, I'm going out the front door and will deal with whatever and whoever confronts me.'

My voice sounds strong enough for him to say, 'OK – it's up to you.'

I'm not sure my courage is singing from the same hymn sheet as my voice, but I take the keys from Ian and head off. As I am leaving, I discover that a few of the directors are in a room with fifty or sixty supporters who have demanded to see the chairman and some of the board members. They want to voice their anger at today's performance and the general goings-on at the club. I've got to show my face. If I'm the one being vilified, I should have a right of reply, even if it's not accepted.

I knock on the door and enter the room. There is a stunned silence. I ask the crowd to hear what I have to say.

'First of all, I apologize for today. It's entirely my fault, but all I'm asking for is just a little patience. I'm in the job three months. If I'm serving this up in twelve months' time, you won't even have to demand that I leave. I'll walk away. There's not a blade of grass on the pitch and it's very hard to play proper football on it. But I promise you that I will turn this around. I just need a little more time, please.'

I'm not saying this solves my problems, but at least the supporters thank me for coming to face the music. I leave with my wife and my daughters through the front entrance. My car is not far away in the car park, but the crowd gathered there still have their say.

There is silence in the car until we pass the Fosse Park shopping centre and get onto the M69.

'That was really bad, Dad, that shouting from the crowd during the game,' says one of my daughters.

'Yes, it wasn't good, was it?' I reply.

There is a Radio Leicester phone-in the following Monday evening. I ask the presenter if I can be on the programme and of course he accepts. I defend myself reasonably well, but I'm not sure that speaking nicely to five or six callers in half an hour is enough to secure my future. I'm still shaken by my reception at Filbert Street a few days before. And tomorrow, a midweek game awaits.

We travel to London to face Charlton at the Valley. Muzzy Izzet starts his first game. We play strongly and win. Dare I hope that things are looking up? We come back to London the following Saturday and win again, this time 1–0. Steve Walsh, our centre half and captain, has the game of his life. He heads everything that Palace throw at him. A defeat, an unlucky defeat at that, at home to West Bromwich Albion a few days later, doesn't elicit the same reaction as against Sheffield United ten days earlier, but it's still a big setback for any promotion hopes we might have.

And then we start to get some momentum.

We win three home games in a space of ten days and we're in the hunt for the play-offs. We need to win the last game of the season at Watford – nothing less will do – and even then, we will be waiting on a couple of results elsewhere going for us too. At half-time at Vicarage Road, we are goalless. The players are desperate to hear what is happening elsewhere, but I press home that we must prevail ourselves.

Then the scraggly youngster Izzet, who only four weeks earlier no one at Filbert Street had heard of, comes up big and he scores. We anxiously wait another five minutes before it's finally confirmed: we are into the play-offs. Ipswich, our competitors for the final spot, have fallen short.

We will play Stoke in the semi-final over two legs and I make my peace with Garry Parker. The first leg, with Stoke at Filbert Street, yields a goalless draw. Kevin Poole, our goalkeeper, makes a breathtaking save to keep us in the tie and so ends the Filbert Street season. If we beat Stoke City at their Victoria Ground, Wembley beckons.

Parker, restored to the team, not only gives a brilliant performance but scores the only goal just after half-time. There are joyous scenes, perhaps too joyous, in our dressing room. For me it's a relief. We're down to one game left. Would I have taken that when I joined the club just before Christmas? Absolutely.

In the corridor I see Martin George, who has swept down quickly from the director's box. He wants to remind me that getting to Wembley is not enough. As if I don't know that. Just for good measure, he makes me aware of a report from KPMG, the accountancy firm, that is about to be officially put in front of the board. The report has been commissioned by some of the board members.

'What's it about?' I ask.

I can tell by his tone that it's not good news.

'The club is looking to float on the AIM market, and this is a feasibility study by KPMG. It's not very complimentary about either of us,' he says. 'They want rid of you, but Barrie comes out of it with flying colours. Hardly surprising that, given his long interview with the two men from KPMG,' he adds with a hint of sarcasm.

'You might think that KPMG would have interviewed me, the manager,' I say. 'After all, it is a football club.'

Martin interrupts to remind me that we have a game to win at Wembley.

'I'll do everything I can,' I say.

'Just win the game. That's what I brought you to the club for.' And with that, he turns away.

On the bus back, I don't know what to think. I've got the team to Wembley, but my suspicions about some of the board members' intentions seem to have been confirmed. I wonder if a KPMG report on a football club, without one word from the manager, will see the light of day. And what if we win at Wembley? Will the report be pulled?

Steve Walsh interrupts my rumination for a moment, blasting out 'Something Inside So Strong' by Labi Siffre, forcing us to all join in, but soon my thoughts return to my conversation with Martin. I don't need a report to motivate me for a Wembley play-off final – I won with Wycombe Wanderers against Preston just two years earlier. But Martin has made doubly sure that losing is not an option.

Wembley is upon us. Crystal Palace, led by the redoubtable Dave Bassett, are our opponents. Although we beat them at Selhurst Park earlier in the season, they were by far the better team that day. We have momentum behind us but they are the favourites.

We're soon behind. Palace score early but then, slowly but surely, we start to come into the game. At half-time we're still behind; I'm concerned, but not panicking. There will be plenty of time for that later.

Although we are playing well, that means very little if we don't get the equalizer. I don't think the 35,000 Leicester City fans who have travelled down the M1 will forgive me if we play well and lose. They've seen too many play-off finals at Wembley, and too many defeats in the last ten years, to accept another Wembley loss.

With about fifteen minutes left and defeat looking likely, Izzet breaks into the penalty area. He's brought down for a penalty. Garry Parker will take the spot kick. I've had my spats with him but now that he's back, he's responded brilliantly. There is no one else in the team today who I would rather have take this penalty

– a possible career-defining moment for me – than the lad who's confidently picked up the ball and is striding over to place it on the spot. He takes a few steps back, comes forward and drives the ball past the Palace goalkeeper.

We go into extra time. I know from my experience that teams get tired at Wembley, more quickly than at other stadia. All week I've prepared for penalties in my mind. Kevin Poole, who has performed brilliantly for the team in recent weeks, is agile but small for a keeper. My reserve goalkeeper, Zeljko Kalac, a £750,000 signing by Mark McGhee, is six foot seven inches tall. But he's had a poor time since he joined the club, and was left out by Mark just before I came to Leicester.

Kalac has been less than impressive in training. However, that doesn't seem to bother him greatly. Letting in soft goals each morning doesn't affect his self-confidence one jot. Quite the opposite. He came into my office less than an hour after the most inglorious morning in training and insisted he was ready to come back into the team. And actually, I quite like him.

I have decided to put Kalac into goal for the penalty shoot-out, should the game head in that direction. At the very least, his size will be intimidating. But Kalac has got to be on the field when the referee blows the final whistle, and I will wait until the last possible moment to do this. There is just over a minute to go and the ball goes out of play. The move is on. Kalac, already aware of what I'm planning, puts on his gloves and I wish him good luck.

'Don't worry, boss, I'll win it for you,' he says, with such confidence that he genuinely makes me believe he will. On he goes to take his place in goal.

But he never touches the ball. We attack for the very last time of the whole season. Steve Claridge gets an opportunity and although he doesn't get proper connection he still directs it goalwards. Incredibly, almost in slow motion, it deceives the Palace goalkeeper and ends up in the net.

The referee blows almost immediately – and we have won. We will play Premiership football next season.

We spend the late afternoon and early evening on the famous hallowed turf of Wembley. This is no hardship; it's what I craved back in December, and the day can go on forever as far as I'm concerned. Even after the team has collected medals we seem to start all over again. There must be a finite number of times I can hug Lennon, Izzet, Walsh, Claridge, Heskey and of course Parker.

I seek out Martin George. Martin isn't into giving or receiving too many hugs, but this time it's different. I am relieved for myself, but I couldn't be more pleased for him. Martin can be haughty and somewhat brusque to those he doesn't really have time for – but he knows his football, just like he knows his wines. He has a feel for the game that some other board members may never have.

'I'll meet up with you towards the end of the week. That KPMG report should be interesting reading for you,' he laughs. And he leaves me to continue my celebrations.

The bus trip back to Leicester is one I cannot forget. The music is still blaring loudly; the players have been fantastic today. They have played with a spirit and determination that will be the hallmark of Leicester City for the next few seasons. Every success that will follow stems from this performance. They have courage in adversity and the will to keep going to the very end. Today I feel there could be something special happening.

Now the end of the season has arrived, Martin George will vacate his role as chairman and I will have to fight my own battles. The KPMG report looks hollow now, but it's nevertheless been published and is there for all to see. It's a damning report for me and the fact that it emerged even after promotion beggars belief. But it's also an embarrassing document for some of the board – and possibly for those who wrote a report on a football club without ever interviewing the incumbent manager.

I know I will miss Martin. Yes, he is opinionated, particularly concerning football matters; but he hired me against a backdrop of rancour and disharmony and, as the KPMG report will testify, my appointment was heavily influenced by Martin. He could just as easily have decided to line up with the board for an easier life. To his eternal credit, he is just not that type of man. Before he steps down, I thank him for choosing me as Leicester City manager and say that my office is still in exactly the same place and that his steadfast opinions on players will always be welcome.

Tom Smeaton is the new chairman. He is a genuinely warm-hearted individual who has been pushed out in front by some of the other board members, who tell us both that there is a substantial transfer kitty for the manager to spend. Despite the promotion, I'm still not sure I have won over all the Leicester City fans; there is some anxiety in their midst over the lack of transfer activity in the summer. However, I have proven myself, and my self-confidence is completely restored.

A scheme by the board to raise £5 million falls by the wayside. Instead, with less than forty-eight hours before the start of the season, I recruit Spencer Prior, a centre back with whom I worked at Norwich, and Kasey Keller, an American international goalkeeper. They arrive at Filbert Street for a combined total of less than £2 million. It is not overwhelming news according to the fans, but it's a start: we need both players to bolster a squad that doesn't look strong enough or large enough to survive a season in the Premier League. Both go into the team for an opening fixture at Roker Park, home to Sunderland, the team I supported as a kid. We draw 0–0 and the two new lads do remarkably well. A big home win against Southampton on the following Wednesday, with Emile Heskey now playing centre forward and scoring two storming goals, gives us four points from two games.

Heskey is a phenomenal talent. He has everything in his game to become one of the Premier League's greatest players. He has worked tirelessly and unselfishly for the team these last few months at outside left, but now his time has come. Centre forward will be his position for the rest of his career, and what a wonderful career it will prove to be.

I sign Ian Marshall from Ipswich soon afterwards. A big, curly-haired Scouser, Ian is a top-notch centre forward who can play centre half in an emergency. He looks every bit as scruffy as Steve Claridge both on and off the field. And when he settles at the club, which in fairness takes about eight minutes, he has a lot to say for himself.

A hammering by Liverpool at Filbert Street serves as an indicator of how far we have to go and perhaps, in a strange way, of how far we've come in the last few months. We get on a bit of a roll in the Coca-Cola League Cup. An early round victory sees us paired at home against Manchester United. They leave a large number of their first team out but still bring Roy Keane, Paul Scholes, Karel Poborský, Jordi Cruyff and Brian McClair. We win 4–2 to take us into the quarter-finals away to Ipswich. Before we get there I know we need to bolster our squad, and I take the opportunity.

I know all about Matt Elliott the Oxford United footballer, but I have no idea about Matt Elliott the man. I just know I want him to sign for Leicester City. When I was at Wycombe Wanderers, I watched Matt many times. He even played against Wanderers in one season. We are now in a bidding war with Southampton, who have tabled a £1.6 million deal for his signature. I say to Denis Smith, Oxford's manager, that we will match Southampton's bid, if only to get the opportunity to speak to the player.

Tom Smeaton, John Robertson and I travel immediately after our evening FA Cup tie win over Southend United to meet Matt and his wife at a hotel on the outskirts of High Wycombe. It's very late at night but the lad doesn't seem to mind. He insists that whatever transpires tonight, he wants to speak to Southampton tomorrow morning.

John and Matt's wife, Cathy, share a packet of cigarettes between them. Tom and I almost bore the player to death talking about all the great plans we have for the football club. In fact, Tom actually divulges more to Matt tonight then he has done to me these last few months, but if it works to get his signature, who cares?

By the end of a long evening, we've done our best and can only wait until tomorrow. The following day, Matt gives us his answer. He will sign for Leicester City. His arrival at Filbert Street gives the club an almighty boost, and Elliott will bring his personality and sheer footballing talent to become one of Leicester City's best-ever players. Like that of Lennon, Izzet and Claridge, his arrival lifts the club to another level.

I also sign up Steve Guppy from Port Vale. After we worked together at Wycombe Wanderers, Steve's move to Newcastle United under Kevin Keegan didn't go according to plan and he was sold to Port Vale. But I know he is capable of playing at the highest level. He just needs a little extra encouragement and his self-confidence will return. And it does, with great distinction. Not only does he become a major part of Leicester City's success story, but he wins a prized international cap for his beloved country too. The manager who picks him for England? Kevin Keegan. Just now, like Matty Elliott, Steve is cup-tied, but they are both here for the long haul and I couldn't be more pleased.

On a late January evening at Portman Road, we play Ipswich in the Coca-Cola Cup. Mark Robins produces the goods for us, and his goal takes us into the semi-final. We are also in the fifth round of the FA Cup, facing the might of Chelsea with a severely depleted squad.

The FA Cup game is on a Sunday for TV, yet the Coca-Cola Cup semi-final against Wimbledon is scheduled for Tuesday evening. Despite our protests, it is not moved to the following Wednesday night. We will play our two most important games of the season in the space of just three days. We fight back gallantly from a 2–0 deficit to earn a terrific draw against Chelsea, managed by Ruud Gullit. He makes a couple of post-match comments that we were 'lucky' and that 'set pieces kept us in the game'. Comments like these, from managers who expect to beat us but don't, become increasingly irritating over the season.

Ten days later, in the replay, Chelsea beat us by a goal so controversial it will be debated in the House of Commons by the prime minister, John Major. The game is in extra time and heading for a penalty shoot-out. A Chelsea player, Erland Johnsen, hurls himself into the penalty box and Mike Reid, the referee, points to the penalty spot. TV pictures clearly show that Johnsen has dived and no Leicester City player even got close to fouling him. But Chelsea score from the resulting penalty, which ironically can also be described as a 'set piece'.

It is deeply upsetting to go out of the FA Cup in such circumstances. A penalty shoot-out, of course, does not equate to victory, but at least we would have had a chance. The prime minister, a Chelsea supporter himself, admits that the penalty should never have been awarded. On seeing the incident back, the referee agrees. But Chelsea accept their gift and go on to win the FA Cup against Middlesbrough in May.

We've got to pick ourselves up and prepare for our second-leg semi-final tie at Selhurst Park against Wimbledon. The first game ended in a 0–0 draw at Filbert Street. A night of drama unfolds, with thousands of City fans making the awkward journey to South London. It's a long evening, with little separating the teams until Marcus Gayle's first-half strike gives Wimbledon the lead.

We now need a goal; otherwise Wembley will be beyond our grasp. Then, just after half-time, Simon Grayson heads in a Parker free kick and we are level. Extra time. If we can hold onto this draw, the away goal rule will see us into the final. Resilience in the team is our mantra. And we see it through.

Wembley will welcome us once again.

This time, I go to Wembley knowing that I have the support of the Leicester City fans. Winning the Coca-Cola Cup will be an enormous achievement if we can do it. That is a big 'if' just now, though, because Middlesbrough, our opponents, have three out-standing international footballers in their team.

They have Emerson, a midfielder from Brazil with all the talent in the world; Fabrizio Ravanelli, an Italian centre forward; and Juninho Paulista, also Brazilian, and possibly the best attacking midfielder in the Premier League. He showed us just about everything when he single-handedly demolished us at Filbert Street a few weeks ago. If we allow him to roam free at Wembley, it will be a long old day for us.

I decide that he must be man-marked in the Coca-Cola Cup final and I designate Pontus Kåmark to do the job. He's a Swedish international footballer with great intelligence, good discipline and a strong mind. He has been beset with injuries since his arrival at Filbert Street but it is good to see him back and fit again. I know that he will not manhandle Juninho, but will keep him in his sights. He will have to be the first one to close the Brazilian down when he gets possession of the ball.

Pontus takes the instruction in his stride. 'I will do my best, gaffer,' he says just before the match.

'That's all I can ask, Pontus,' I reply. 'It's just that I know your best will be good enough to win the cup for us.'

He just smiles back.

Leicester City fans have big, big numbers at Wembley on 6 April 1997. It's a glorious sunny day and we're ready to win against Bryan Robson's team. The FA Cup match at Stamford Bridge now pushed to the back of my mind, I remind the players how brilliantly they have played this whole campaign – and that it will count for absolutely nothing if we do not win this trophy.

The club have contested FA Cup finals many years back, but we have not won a competition in thirty-three years. This is our chance to make our own history. And of course, the winners of the competition will be in Europe next season.

It is a poor first half from both teams, with nerves accounting for a lot of misplaced passes, but thankfully Kåmark is subduing Juninho so far. There is more purpose to our game in the second half, but our attempts at goal do not cause Middlesbrough any real problems and at the other end of the pitch we repel their attempts on goal. Juninho races into the penalty box to meet a cross coming in and is set to head the ball into the net, when Kåmark comes from nowhere to get in front of him and save the day.

A war of attrition ensues, and it continues into extra time. Then Ravanelli scores for Middlesbrough. From what has preceded his strike, this should be enough to win the cup. But we somehow find the strength and willpower to stage a last-gasp recovery. Heskey heads up onto the bar, Claridge has his shot saved, and Heskey bundles the ball over the line. We live to fight again.

The replay at Hillsborough is just as tense. Kåmark once more keeps Juninho at bay and both managers know that a single goal either way is likely to decide the fate of the 1997 Coca-Cola Cup. We reach extra time again and it's draining – both physically and mentally – for all concerned. But we have come so far, so rapidly, that we must find that resolve to win this cup. We get a free kick and Parker floats it towards Walsh, who heads into Claridge's path. The centre forward bought from Birmingham to attain promotion does it again, sending the ball into the back of the Middlesbrough net.

The travelling Leicester City fans are in dreamland, but the realization that there are still twenty anxious minutes left does not afford me the same luxury. The fans too are jolted back to reality when they witness a magnificent save by Kasey Keller from Emerson to maintain our fragile lead.

'Come on, referee! Time's up two minutes ago!' I shout into the night air. On cue, he blows the whistle.

We have won the cup and qualified for Europe! All of our team are heroes. Kåmark, in quelling the threat from Juninho, is a key element to the victory, but the player I am most pleased for is Parker. Our arguments in the dressing room are now long forgotten. He's won trophies before in his excellent career, but given how things went last season, this one must be pretty special. And I thank him for his major contribution.

John Robertson, my assistant manager, Steve Walford, the first-team coach, and myself exchange congratulations and we all share the same thoughts: last season's victory at Wembley has made all this possible. Without it, we would most likely have been shown the door. There are emotional scenes on the pitch and on the terraces. No one wants to go home, just to stay here and drink in the atmosphere. The cup is now in the hands of our captain, Steve Walsh, who has also won the man of the match trophy. He has seen some dramatic days since signing as a young man for this club – now he has something tangible to show for all his efforts. The trip back to Filbert Street takes an age, but no one seems to care. The Coca-Cola Cup is on the bus and that is all that matters.

This victory has cemented my relationship with the fans. 383 days ago, I was in serious trouble and they were demanding my dismissal. There didn't seem to be any way back. But over the course of this season I have silenced the remaining doubters, particularly with the two cup runs and some remarkable league victories along the way. The most difficult thing for a manager to do is to change supporters' minds once they have been made up. Typically, respite might come for a while, but the next slip-up is usually fatal. This feels more permanent.

That awful journey to Filbert Street, which I used to dread on match days, now has celebratory blue-and-white bunting hanging from lampposts. The old factory that used to sport my painted name, daubed across the brickwork in hatred, has been cleaned up. All this can change in a heartbeat, but the transformation is incredible. My focus now is to keep the club in top-flight football for the next season, and then celebrations can truly begin in earnest. Five games remain and we are thirteenth.

We are at Stamford Bridge on the Saturday. Before the start of the game, the Chelsea players shower the team with bouquets of flowers to recognize our achievement. It's a nice gesture, but I wonder whether some guilt remains after the penalty debacle in the FA Cup replay a few weeks ago. Understandably, we don't have the same energy levels since Hillsborough, and we lose at Chelsea and at home to West Ham. When we draw against Manchester United at Filbert Street, we still need a victory over Sheffield Wednesday to secure our status. We do this, and a win at Ewood Park on the last day of the season sees us finishing in ninth position in the Premier League. A top ten finish, the Coca-Cola Cup in the boardroom cabinet, and European football next season. It has been a sensational turnaround in my eighteen months at Filbert Street.

I have a year left on my contract. The supporters are concerned that I might be lured away by so-called bigger clubs, but I want to stay at Filbert Street. I want to sample European football with a club I have a strong affinity with. Even the boardroom squabbles have taken a back seat, although they will later re-emerge with more vigour and rancour than ever.

I sign a two-year extension and get ready for the 1997/98 season ahead. Some players leave the club and I bring a few others into Filbert Street. Twenty-two-year-old Robbie Savage is signed for £400,000 from Crewe. He was a teammate of Neil Lennon there and perhaps he has seen how well the Ulsterman has done at Filbert Street and wants to sample some of the same success for himself.

Robbie makes himself at home quite quickly, buying a flashy car that indicates some newfound wealth. I politely ask him to change the vehicle, saying that he can do anything he wants when he's established in the first team. It's difficult not to like this shy extrovert, if you get what I mean. He settles down, forces his way into the team with his energy, running power and absolute commitment. His positivity matches his popularity in the dressing room, he becomes a mainstay in the team over the next few seasons and, despite our occasional disagreements, his performances in a Leicester City shirt make him one of my favourite players at the club.

I'm sad to see Jamie Lawrence leave Filbert Street. Although not a regular starter, he has produced some big moments for me in his time at the club; and he has a big heart, which counts for a lot in football. Bradford City get a bargain at £50,000. Lastly, Tony Cottee, that brilliant little striker of West Ham and Everton, signs for us.

When the fixture list comes out, our start to the season looks incredibly daunting. Our first four fixtures read: home to Aston Villa, away to Liverpool, home to Manchester United and then home to Arsenal.

But we are ready. We beat Aston Villa, win at Anfield, draw with Manchester United and then, in an epic night at Filbert Street, we draw 3–3 with Arsenal. This game will forever be known as the Dennis Bergkamp show, since he scores a wonderful hat-trick. What is later forgotten is that we fight back in a pulsating last few minutes to snatch the draw. Everything that I've tried to put into this football club is encapsulated in the final minutes of this classic match. We are 2–0 down with only a few minutes to go. Heskey scores what might seem to be a consolation goal for us; but that's not how we see it, and his goal galvanizes the team for an all-out assault on the Arsenal goal.

When the clock at Filbert Street shows the ninety minutes are up, we have everyone forward. Matt Elliott, our brilliant centre half, collects the ball outside the Arsenal penalty area, makes room for himself, and fires a low shot into the corner. The fans go wild. It may only be an equalizer but it seems like the night at Hillsborough all over again. Surely the whistle will now sound. But play continues. Arsenal break forward; Bergkamp controls a through pass and, with wonderful skill, guides the ball into our net for 3–2. The Arsenal players surround this magician, and so they should. The referee must now finish the game and leave us distraught. But Arsenal's celebrations for Bergkamp's goal allow us time to just force a corner. Walsh heads across the goal, Prior heads it back towards the back post, and Walsh comes in to power a final trademark header into the roof of the Arsenal net.

Three goals are scored in added time. Arsenal will go on to win the Premier League and we again finish in the top ten, but tonight's performance epitomizes the grit I had hoped I might foster at Leicester City: a never-say-die spirit, a ferocious determination to compete against any team and a system that will suit the players at the club at any given time.

It would have been hard to believe, eighteen months ago, that we would ever be lining up for European football. We face a star-studded Atlético Madrid team in the first round. Atlético's owner, Jesús Gil, has invested very heavily in the squad, recruiting big-name players from all over Europe including Juninho, newly signed from Middlesbrough. They are one of the strong favourites to win the UEFA Cup and, as much as I like Madrid as a city, I would have liked an easier fixture.

Still, what can beat Vicente Calderón Stadium on a balmy September evening? This iconic venue is still etched in my memory from when Northern Ireland played both quarter-finals of the 1982 World Cup here, against Austria and France.

Ian Marshall gives us a shock lead early in the game and we play well until two late goals, including a very debatable penalty, push the tie in Atlético's favour. It is 2–1 to them and all to play for at Filbert Street in two weeks' time.

30 September 1997 comes around quickly, and I've never seen Filbert Street so animated and colourful. The fans have been looking forward to this home game since the draw was made and they are even more enthused now that the second leg is in the balance. Unfortunately, what should be a magnificent occasion is marred by the most bizarre refereeing display, from Frenchman Rémi Harrel, that I have witnessed in a long, long time.

Our three clear penalty appeals are furiously waved away, and Garry Parker is sent off in the second half for a dubious second bookable offence: taking a free kick too quickly. Two late Atlético

goals do not paint an accurate picture of the game and at its conclusion, we are cheered up and down the field by our supporters
as if we had won. My post-match comments about the referee's
performance are scrutinized by UEFA but no action is taken,
particularly when the UEFA panel are shown a video of the game.
The referee himself is suspended by UEFA.

On 24 October, history is again made for the club, this time
from the commercial side. Leicester City Football Club is floated
on the stock market at a value of £36 million. This is a momentous decision by the board members, but unfortunately the share
prices soon fall dramatically and continue to drop over the next
few weeks. By early 1998, our stock sells for less than half its
original price. Now it is the board's turn for some criticism.

Tom Smeaton, the chairman, breaks cover in February 1998
by telling the local media that my net spending since my arrival
is over £5.5 million. I'll publicly dispute the figures and argue my
own case for the last two seasons. However, my struggles with
the board, which have been dormant for quite some time, now
resurface with a vengeance and come to a head on the final day
of the season. We are at Upton Park on a Sunday afternoon, a
game we need to win to have a chance of qualifying for the UEFA
Cup again through our league position. That's an indication of
how well we have played.

All Premier League games on the last day of the season kick off
at 4 p.m. We travelled down to London the night before, as we
normally do for any games that are a reasonable distance away from
Filbert Street. Pre-match meals are served a little later than normal
due to the timing of kick-off, but everything else remains the same.
In a brilliant match, we are defeated 4–3 at Upton Park, narrowly
missing out on Europe. In fact, the way other matches go means
that even if we had won, we wouldn't have qualified. The dressing
room is quiet post-match; there is the sense that a good season
could have been even better. Nevertheless, it is a solid performance.

There is a knock on the dressing-room door and in comes Ian
Silvester, club secretary. I know that Ian has had a difficult time

with some of our board members over the past eighteen months, often fighting battles on my behalf. But I often don't hear about these skirmishes for some considerable time afterwards, by which time things have generally moved on.

Today he comes over to tell me that the board members who have travelled today to Upton Park are furious about our overnight stay in London the previous evening.

'Why?' I ask.

'Their complaint is that we shouldn't have been wasting money on an overnight stay because today's kick-off time is four p.m., not three p.m.' Ian looks embarrassed.

'Are you serious?'

'I wouldn't be telling you if it wasn't true.'

He knows what my reaction is going to be, and he also knows that when he's alone with them, he's going to cop it for this.

'I'm going up to see them right now,' I say, and I don't even change my clothes before I race up to see the directors.

'You are complaining that we've stayed overnight in London because kick-off was four o'clock and not three o'clock? You haven't got a clue, have you?'

I look straight at Terry Shipman. Terry's family is entrenched in Football League history, his father Len being League President some years ago. 'I'm amazed at you, Terry,' I say. 'These other members of the board have no understanding about what it takes to win football matches. I know one thing – your father, if he was here, wouldn't be taking your side today.'

I look at Barrie. 'Don't forget, football clubs live or die by what happens out there on the pitch. Not by the number of lunch covers sold on match days.'

I turn and make my way back to the dressing room, where I tell the players that we are not going home this evening. If there are rooms available at the hotel we've just been in, we will stay there another night. We spend the night back at the hotel in Cockfosters and arrive back at Filbert Street the following afternoon.

Ian Silvester leaves the club shortly afterwards to take up a similar role at Leeds United under chairman Peter Ridsdale. There's more boardroom upheaval: Tom Smeaton is deposed as chairman and instead they opt for one of their colleagues, Phil Smith, a decision which has the approval of Sir Rodney Walker, the chairman of the PLC. But John Elsom, who is deputy chairman, is being ostracized completely.

I phone Rodney Walker to tell him that it's Mr Elsom I wish to work with, not Smith. Rodney is in a bit of a quandary: he's reluctant to upset Barrie Pierpoint or Roy Parker, but doesn't want to go against me either. In the end, John Elsom is installed as the new club chairman. He proves to be brilliant in the role, and a great friend. His influence has a great stabilizing effect and he oversees a terrific couple of years at the club.

To replace Ian, I mention that Andrew Neville, with whom I worked for a short while at Norwich City, would be the ideal replacement. He is a bright, intelligent, inquisitive young man who loves football and knows the job inside out. He is interviewed and he becomes Leicester City's new secretary.

In the summer of 1998 I'm invited by the BBC to come to France and cover the World Cup as a pundit. We will be stationed in Paris, which is no hardship. Learning on the job becomes a priority but there is no shortage of excellent teachers: Mark Lawrenson and Ally McCoist are both excellent pundits, each particularly witty in his own inimitable way. And Alan Hansen and Des Lynam have by now formed an incomparable partnership that reaches its apogee in this tournament. Both men are peerless in their craft. One particular Saturday afternoon, I am working with both of these gentlemen. Robbie Williams strolls into the studio, wanting to meet Des. He had a big hit last year with 'Angels' and he's performing this weekend in Paris. Des invites him onto the live show. I interrupt proceedings by saying to Robbie that he has done magnificently well since leaving Take That, considering he doesn't write his own songs and isn't much of a singer. Robbie takes it in the spirit it was meant, but afterwards I think that, with millions of records sold, Robbie might be a better singer and songwriter than I had first imagined.

Despite the constant boardroom wrangling, these are heady days at Leicester and I'm thoroughly enjoying my time there. But the most emotional moment comes when Leeds United ask permission to speak to me after George Graham leaves to take over at White Hart Lane in October 1998. We have a midweek home game against Tottenham Hotspur and everyone inside Filbert Street seems to be holding banners printed with the words 'Please stay, Martin!'. It is a tumultuous reception for me that sways any decision I may have to make, and I will stay at the club for two more brilliant years. I love Leicester City Football Club, and on days like these, who wants to be anywhere other than the Filbert Street touchline?

We go on to have two more top ten finishes and our love for the League Cup continues with another two visits to Wembley: a loss to Spurs in 1999 and a victory over Tranmere Rovers in 2000. Leicester are guaranteed European football again. Our ongoing success leads to boardroom talk of a new, bigger stadium – I do not yet know that this will not happen under my tenure.

I have done a lot for this group of players but in truth, they have done so much for me that it is impossible to quantify. Tony Cottee wins a medal that he has craved throughout his terrific career. Heskey heads to Liverpool just after the League Cup final, and Tim Flowers demonstrates at Filbert Street why he has been one of the best goalkeepers in the Premier League. Although by now Steve Claridge has left the club, his goals will be forever talked about when the story of Filbert Street is retold.

John Elsom tells me that a substantial portion of the £11 million we get for Heskey will be used to rebuild the team in the summer of 2000. Meanwhile, one of my daughters has just got a place at Cambridge University and the other is enjoying her life at school; Geraldine and I are very content. But what happens next comes out of the blue.

11

THIS IS PARADISE

'If you ever get a chance to play for Celtic, son, take it immediately and don't even stop to think,' were my father's words when it was reported that Jock Stein was sending a scout over to watch me play for Distillery. Well, the scout did come, and he saw, but I certainly didn't conquer on that particular day against Crusaders. So the chance to play for Glasgow Celtic, as they are referred to by most older Irish supporters of the club (as distinct from Belfast Celtic, defunct since 1949), was lost.

But the chance to manage Celtic is an equally treasured opportunity. And so I am sitting in the boardroom at Parkhead in June 2000, having signed a rolling (one-year) contract, already agreed with Dermot Desmond – Celtic's largest shareholder – and the chairman, Brian Quinn. Dermot Desmond is strikingly impressive. I have been interviewed by him and the board members some days earlier in a London hotel and have been given the job. I don't suppose he has got to where he is by being indolent but his energy is limitless, as is his desire to put Celtic back on the football map. There were many excellent options available to him when the Celtic manager's job became available, but he has chosen me. That is both a boost and a worry, the worry being that I fail in Glasgow. My final season at Filbert Street with Leicester City was one of immense joy and satisfaction both on and off the field; I'm genuinely sad to be leaving a place I have grown to love. But I feel that if I turn this opportunity down, it won't come round again.

A crowd of Celtic fans are gathered outside the main entrance. Apparently they have come to welcome me to the club and wish me well, and although they are in very good spirits, they are not leaving until they hear from their new manager. Encouraged by the directors, I open the main door, stand on the steps and address the group, which has formed a horseshoe shape round the barriers.

'Thank you very much for coming this evening,' I start. 'I greatly appreciate it. I will do everything in my power to bring success to the football club.'

Some clap affectionately, others are a little more boisterous with their cheers. I'm starting to realize for the first time just what this institution called Celtic means to these people. Lots of fans go to a football game to forget about their trials and tribulations for a few hours and immerse themselves in the atmosphere of their club. Here, though, it seems that Celtic is at the heart of many supporters' very existence. They need their new manager to show them, perhaps not necessarily this evening, but in the days, weeks and months ahead, that he shares their passion for the club.

As I go back indoors the crowd disperses, all but one or two who would wait until midnight if they thought the new manager might bring some respite and cheer remain. The light is beginning to fade as the sun starts to disappear over the stadium. I climb to the very top of the Jock Stein Stand, sit in the back row and survey the empty arena. It is an inspiring monument even in its untenanted state.

If Jock Stein could see it now, he might have some difficulty recognizing the place where he once reigned supreme. Old film footage of a big lorry being driven into Parkhead with the club's manager, players and the European Cup all on board comes into my mind. I think back to that famous night in Lisbon, in 1967: I was still a boarder at St Columb's College in Derry and because Celtic were in the final of the European Cup, the Dean allowed us to watch the game in the big hall. We were all Celtic supporters in the college, even if in rare cases it happened to be someone's second team after Manchester United, Spurs or Liverpool.

As kick-off approached, we had a bit of a problem. Our black-and-white TV wasn't functioning properly and the picture was intermittently disappearing. Wires were checked at the back, but it made no difference. Eventually one of the priests, growing tired of our ineffectual efforts, walked up to the TV and thumped the top of it hard with his fist. Miraculously, the jumpy picture steadied itself and remained perfect for the rest of the evening. We thought that Celtic would surely win now that a hand closer to God than ourselves had intervened.

Back in the present, the players at the club are obviously my first concern. Mark Viduka, a centre forward of immense talent, has decided that he no longer wants to play for Celtic. He has fallen out with our CEO, Alan MacDonald – over what, I'm not sure, and for what it's worth neither is Alan. But Mark is a player I would dearly like to keep at the club if at all possible. We are about to start preseason training. I phone him and leave a message. He returns the call.

'Mark, it's Martin O'Neill here. I'm the new manager of Celtic. I'm not sure what the reasons are for you wanting to leave, but maybe we can talk about them. I would really want you to stay if the problem can be resolved.'

'It won't be resolved, and Alan MacDonald knows why,' he says abruptly.

'Actually, he doesn't, Mark. Maybe just tell me now.'

'Nothing to tell you. I just want to leave the club.'

'Where are you calling from?' I ask.

'Melbourne,' comes the reply.

'I guess you won't make it in time for training tomorrow morning, then?'

Mark goes to Elland Road soon afterwards for £6 million. I don't actually meet him until a number of years later, by which time he has made his name as a brilliant player for Leeds United. As a replacement I bring in Chris Sutton and his arrival is a landscape changer. What he does for the club over the next few seasons is unquantifiable.

It is a bright evening in the city of Dundee and tomorrow is our first game of the season. The talking – and there has been much of that in the last few weeks – is done and now we're ready to go. I've been able to strengthen our defence with the signing of Joos Valgaeren, who has just played an excellent tournament for Belgium in the Euros. Normally I wouldn't even consider signing a player strictly on the basis of his performance in international games, preferring to see what he's capable of at club level. But Joos has so impressed me with his speed and bravery, as well as his genuine desire to come to Celtic, that I've set aside my usual reservations.

Chris Sutton will partner Henrik Larsson up front. Larsson, the darling of the Celtic fans, has recovered from a bad leg break some months ago and fought his way back to fitness just in time for Sweden's European Championship campaign over the summer. While he is still not completely match fit, it's a boost for all concerned that he is in the line-up today. Eyal Berkovic will play midfield. I'm not convinced, based on what I've been able to see of him during my few weeks here, that his heart is really in the club, but he assures me that I've got that wrong and that his commitment is real. There is no question that the lad is a good player but I feel that when he is in possession of the ball, he is looking for that pass that no one else in the stadium can see. Sometimes it actually reaches its intended target, and then of course the crowd gasp in awe and Eyal looks like a Superman. The only problem is, the ball doesn't *always* reach the intended target and then people like me, the manager, can become more than a little frustrated. When the percentages drop, my blood pressure rises. However, Eyal can deal with the ball, which is why he's in the team. Young Stiliyan Petrov is playing alongside Paul Lambert in midfield, giving us energy and guile.

The game is live on Sky Sports on a Sunday, with a 6 p.m. kick-off. The endless press conferences I did pre-match on Friday actually persist right up to kick-off. I say to the press guys that we obviously face a difficult task, not just today but over the whole of the season, to get some sort of parity with Rangers.

One journalist asks a question I am not ready for: 'With

Rangers winning at Ibrox yesterday, do you think that if you don't win here today at Tannadice, the league is over?'

This is not said in jest, but as a serious question. League over? In July? Evidently Rangers are not expected to drop too many points this season. In fact the question may have more merit than I initially think. Rangers lost only two games last season, winning the league at a canter by twenty-one points. Since then, they have strengthened their squad considerably in the close season for their two-pronged attack on domestic affairs and their Champions League ambitions. Still, I'm somewhat taken aback, and I say that we hope we can compete better than last year. Are Rangers that good, and might we still be that bad?

It is both a comfort and a spur to walk to the dugout and look ahead at the thousands of Celtic fans in a blaze of green and white, filling the stand behind the goal at Tannadice. The pitch itself seems to slope a little but, as the old saying goes, 'same for both teams'. The referee looks for the last time at his two companions on either line, gives a thumbs up and blows his whistle.

Dundee United are not just stubborn. They're causing us problems and the pace of the game is surprisingly quick. Our own play is hardly vintage but once or twice we look as if we can break through, which is encouraging. Then, about eight or nine minutes from half-time, Larsson scores to give us the lead. I wish the referee would blow for the end of the match right this minute to get our first win on the board. But Dundee United equalize in the second half.

I take Berkovic off and replace him with Tommy Johnson, a young Englishman who has a decent pedigree. Berkovic is annoying me anyway. When we lose the ball he's not just slow to track back and defend, he's refusing to do it at all. I feel better about the substitution and exhort our players to find the winning goal. With only a few minutes left, Chris Sutton strikes. It's too late for an unlucky Dundee United team to respond. We have won the game. I know we can get better but today, victory is all that matters. Players respond to your words, your encouragement and your exhortations so much more.

Winning is just a wonderful feeling and the players are mostly exuberant, although Eyal Berkovic is in a corner, looking none too pleased at his substitution. He reminds me of myself in my grumpy Forest days. But victory always vindicates the manager's decision and I say well done to him anyway. Judging by his facial expression, I'm not sure he accepts my praise. For at least a week, we are level on points with Rangers and my words to the players that we can take the title off them this season don't yet sound hollow, although only one game is gone.

The week's press coverage is a mixed bag, I'm told by our press officer, Iain Jamieson. I will learn over the years that Jamieson is just brilliant at his job, knowing exactly when to intervene if I'm floundering in a press conference, usually with a tap on the knee under the desk. In good news, Steve Walford, my coach, is making a favourable impression on the players judging by the feedback on the training ground. I am still trying to get John Robertson out of Leicester City and make us a trio again.

And so to Saturday's game, at home to Motherwell. The crowd fills up quickly after the players finish their warm-up and in the dressing room I ask for some quiet. I have worked with managers who have allowed conversations between players to take place as they themselves are trying to speak. It doesn't work, and the manager loses out completely.

Again, we are far from a coherent football team, and Motherwell are doing unexpectedly well considering this is Celtic Park. There is a little uneasiness beginning to thread its way round the stadium. It's a long way off from agitation since it's my first home league game, but I don't want it to unnerve the players. Memories of last season's collapse are still too recent and too raw. Patience is preached by me at half-time, encouraging the players to believe that the goal will come – and so it does. Petrov is the goal-scorer. We don't concede and see the game through to the end. It is far from convincing, but it's another win. We will improve the performances without a doubt when I get to know the players working under real pressure.

We now have six points on the board and a little momentum. It's nothing that will make those at Ibrox sit up and take notice, but it's a start. Next up is a workmanlike victory over Kilmarnock at home before a stiff test against Hearts at Tynecastle in Edinburgh. If we have any aspirations of staying the course with Rangers, then here is where we need to win. Suddenly the shackles are thrown aside and we blitz Hearts in a thrilling first half, scoring three goals. Although they make a spirited match of it in the second half, we win 4–2 and go level again with Rangers.

One of our scorers today is Lubo Moravčík, a thirty-three-year-old Slovakian signed by Dr Jozef Vengloš a few seasons ago and second only to Larsson in popularity with Celtic fans. It isn't too difficult to see why. A wonderfully gifted two-footed player who has played for a number of European clubs during his twenties, Lubo has been terrific this afternoon. I take him off with about twenty-five minutes left, thinking he is getting tired. That's not unexpected, given his age and lack of proper game time since the start of the season. Lubo doesn't look entirely pleased, but he will have a big part to play next Sunday in my first Old Firm game at Celtic Park.

The week is short, the build-up long. Every day, columns and columns of newspaper print are devoted to this match. It seems that just about everyone in Scotland has something to say. And sometimes the opinions expressed become absolute facts even though the game has yet to be played. Most of me wants Sunday to come round fast; yet there is a nagging percentage of me that wishes the game could be pushed further down the calendar until we have properly hit our stride.

During a training session I ask Tommy Boyd and Alan Stubbs, two of the senior players, how they feel. 'We're ready to go,' they answer, and Tommy adds with a smile, 'That's if I get picked.'

I like these two players and they are brilliant professionals. This little midweek conversation actually gives me a boost, although I'm well aware come match day that actions, not words, are what's needed.

I book my wife and our daughter Alana into the Crutherland Hotel, not too far from East Kilbride on the outskirts of Glasgow. It is situated in an extremely pleasant location and ideally quiet. I will stay there myself all week up until Saturday morning and then, after training, I will join the players and coaching staff for our own overnight stay in another hotel in Glasgow, leaving us a shortened journey into Celtic Park. Geraldine and Alana will make their own way from the Crutherland on Sunday morning to the ground by taxi and I'll see them after the game, regardless of the result.

The staff at the Crutherland have been especially cordial and welcoming and evenings have been as unobtrusively peaceful as I could wish for – but then something peculiar happens. I get back to Celtic Park from the Barrowfield training ground on Saturday and Debbie, my secretary, has had a call from the hotel. They want Geraldine and Alana out of there immediately. I can't imagine what has happened.

It transpires that the Rangers manager has been told that my wife and daughter are in the hotel. Rangers use the Crutherland as a base for many of their games and have a contract with them. If Geraldine and Alana don't leave immediately, Rangers will cancel their contract with the hotel.

I'm shocked, especially as I have been staying there all week; perhaps the hotel manager might have let me know at some point that there could be a problem with Saturday evening's accommodation for my family? No. Not a thing. I phone Geraldine. She doesn't know a jot about the situation and she's still in the hotel bedroom. Just as I am speaking to her, however, there is a knock at her door: it's the manager. She is about to give Geraldine the same news I've just given her.

'A porter will come up and help you with your bags,' she says, 'and also for your daughter's room.'

Geraldine refuses to leave until a proper explanation is given

to her. None is forthcoming but she is told that on their departure, she and Alana will have to leave by the back-door fire escape
because the Rangers team will soon be at the hotel and her presence is not welcome. Their paths just cannot cross. My wife tells
them that it's the front entrance or nothing. Anyway, I'm not so
sure that Stefan Klos and Claudio Reyna are carrying pictures of
my family around in their breast pockets and, although some of
these Rangers players are extremely well known in the footballing
world, my wife, with only a few weeks of Glasgow experience
behind her just now, is unlikely to recognize Dick Advocaat if he
walked past her. Anyway, a new hotel is found by Debbie and a
potential altercation between Geraldine and the Rangers manager is averted.

The dressing room is tense. Bobby Petta has forced his way
into the team and he's almost a reborn footballer. He has had a
rough time at the club, but he is regaining confidence on an
hourly basis. I give him plenty of encouragement and insist that
he takes full-backs on, telling him not to be concerned if he loses
the ball a few times trying to do so. When he does go past them,
he will be able to deliver the ball into the right areas for Sutton
and Larsson to attack.

I look over at Stubbs and Boyd. They give me a nod of
approval. I'm hoping that Jonathan Gould, our goalkeeper, is prepared. A glance over at Moravčík. He is putting on his football
socks so nonchalantly, so utterly casually; there is not a trace of
anxiety in his face. It must be an extremely beautiful feeling for
him to know that his instant control of the ball with either foot
will never desert him, even in front of 60,000 people. Petrov
looks so young, like a lad plucked from some youth club and
dropped into the dressing room by mistake. But he has a massive
heart, and that counts for almost everything today. You never
know for sure whether the players are ready, and this match is
not for the faint-hearted. We know we cannot allow Rangers to
dictate the game. They have written their own terms for ten years
and if they dominate us today, it could be another ten years

before anything is done about it. We need to start fast and set down a marker.

I have been in the game a long time and experienced some incredibly high moments both as a player and a manager, as well as a host of disappointments. But I'm not sure I'm prepared for the noise that booms from every part of the stadium as the two teams take the field. It is Celtic Park, in early afternoon sunshine, in its gladiatorial magnificence.

Two minutes in, and we get a corner. Moravčík fires an in-swinger. The ball is not cleared, bounces a little and finds its way to Sutton, who side-foots it into the net. A few minutes later another corner goes to us. Moravčík varies the pace and length of his kick. Young Petrov comes fearlessly into the penalty box, out-jumps the Rangers defence and heads the ball into the net. 2–0. A few minutes later, Moravčík, inside the penalty area, swivels as only he can, leaves his opponent sprawling and passes into the pathway of the oncoming Lambert, who fires into the bottom right-hand corner of the net. It is simply unbelievable. We are 3–0 up.

The stadium is absolutely rocking. Our fans are in a state of delirium, urging more and more of the same. I ask John Clark how long to go. He tells me thirty-four minutes. He thinks I mean half-time. No, how long till it's over? Seventy-nine minutes, he calculates quickly. I want it to end right now. Clark, a great player for a great Celtic team who has been through experiences like this many times in his career, knows exactly how I'm feeling at this moment. He too may want it to end; but Rangers are far from finished today. Sure enough, they get a goal back, Reyna forcing the ball past Gould. Just before half-time they seem to have scored again, but to my relief, Wallace is judged to have been offside.

'The next twenty minutes are absolutely vital,' I tell the players at half-time. Lambert has had to leave the pitch and Johan Mjällby joins the fray in midfield. This man will soon find his proper position in the heart of our defence and become one of my favourite players, but today I'm telling him not to stray from the middle of the park. I have enough players going forward as it is. He should certainly go up for corner kicks and free kicks, but otherwise stay there in front of the back three and protect, protect and protect. Within minutes of the second half he's at outside right, helping Jackie McNamara, and I am roaring to him to get back into position. It's his only aberration and he soon rejoins Petrov and Moravčík, who are starting to tire. But not before the magnificent Larsson scores a goal that very few other players in the world could do. Picking up a chested-down ball from Sutton, he drives forward, deftly beats two defenders and chips one of the best goalkeepers in Europe to give us a 4–1 lead. As it hits the net, the two young ball boys behind the goal jump into the air with unbelievable glee and utter admiration for a genius at work.

The game ends at breakneck speed. Rangers win a penalty and score: 4–2. Larsson scores a header for 5–2. And Sutton scores his second goal when Stéphane Mahé drives forward on the left and whips in a glorious cross which he converts: 6–2. The referee, Stuart Dougal, blows a few minutes later and we have won.

Today a sea change has taken place at Celtic Park. Years of Rangers domination may not come to an end after one victory, but the result has given both players and supporters genuine hope that good times might be returning. The victory gives me incredible confidence and belief that we can compete with Advocaat's men.

Today's result is not a flash in the pan. We press on, adding a couple of players: Alan Thompson from Aston Villa and Didier Agathe from Hibernian. Both will prove critical for this season and the seasons to come. Our form through August, September and October is excellent, dropping a few points only at Aberdeen and Motherwell.

Significantly, my assistant manager John Robertson joins me, and for the first time since he was fifteen years old comes back to Glasgow to live with his family. We are now three, with Steve Walford and his wife also in the city. Together we make a tight-knit unit; I have complete trust in both of them. We naturally discuss players, tactics, opposition and everything else related to the game, with strong opinions voiced on occasion, but in public we are in total agreement – and even more importantly, in the dressing room, where it really matters.

I am enjoying life in Scotland and we find rented accommodation for the family in Edinburgh, a strong Gavin Hastings kick from Murrayfield Stadium. We have enrolled Alana in a school not far from our rented house. Both Geraldine and I feel that if by chance things don't go well for me at Celtic, then Edinburgh might be a safer haven for our daughter. The taunting may be less severe, if it's even an issue at this school.

Rangers are having some autumn problems. After two big wins in the Champions League they have lost European momentum, which has burrowed its way into their league form. By the time we play them at Ibrox in November, we are still unbeaten and hold a number of points in hand. But we know we need to show proper character at Ibrox. The owner of Rangers has responded to the club's dip in form by spending £12 million on Tore André Flo, who has left Stamford Bridge to come north of the border.

Ibrox is a magnificently intimidating stadium. Our team bus pulls up under police protection as close to the main entrance as possible. The ten yards I have to cover from the bus to the entrance is a memorable experience in itself. I bear the brunt of the expletives hurled by the Rangers fans gathered round the bus, but honestly, I am expecting this reception, just like Dick Advocaat would get at Celtic Park. If this 'welcome' is anything to go by, the fans certainly haven't given up the fight, and soon the battle will commence. I take my place in the dugout, not wanting to look behind me. The hostile roar from kick-off reminds me of Celtic Park in August.

Rangers attack immediately and should score in the first

minute. That they don't is down to sheer providence and nothing else. Their blinding start only serves to switch the volume button to another level. The atmosphere within the stadium goads the Rangers players to drive forward in numbers, and we cannot quell the rampage. Unable to help myself, I glance over my shoulder: it seems that thousands of Rangers fans have actually been waiting for this very moment, because they're staring straight at me with contumely pouring from their mouths. I've learned my lesson: if you want to look around at Ibrox, make sure that you're winning the game and there are only ten seconds left.

We are actually level at half-time, with Larsson equalizing for us, but the second half is one-way traffic and Rangers are too strong. Alan Thompson, playing in his first Old Firm game, is sent off the field for two reckless challenges and we are bullied for the rest of the match, with Rangers scoring at will from corner kicks and Tore André Flo getting on the score sheet on his debut. Our unbeaten run has ended. But it seems more than that. We couldn't compete – or didn't compete. I know that Rangers will get, as we did last August, an enormous injection of confidence and self-belief from this result. They have shown themselves to be what I have known all along – a top-class soccer team.

Maybe I got my tactics wrong, although I think Advocaat actually changed his own system and played Reyna at right wing back to match us up and take Petta out of the game. In the dressing room, I have my say. I tell Thompson that I thought he wanted out of the game, so poor were his challenges; but really I'm just getting a few things off my chest. The players are down, and I want them to be down. I want them to feel what it's like to be hammered by our fiercest rivals. All this talk about being too hard on players, and that at that their lowest point they need lifting – well, to hell with that theory. Today is for feeling real pain. Today is for being absolutely at rock bottom. Today just cannot pass without bucketloads of soul-searching.

Dermot Desmond suddenly appears in the dressing room. He has never been down before since he made me manager. He starts to speak to the players and there's complete silence for him. He has a quick look round the dressing room before he starts and I think he's pleased that there is sheer and utter devastation all around, and that defeat is hurting.

'I just came down to see how you all were,' he says, 'and while defeat is obviously hard to take today, and I see now that it hurts you, you have to go through this to be successful and some days you just have to suffer. I now know we have a team capable of winning the championship and I know we have a manager who will take us there.'

With that, he turns and walks out the door. It is the biggest boost of restorative confidence that one could possibly get – and in front of the players, too. I'm called to the press conference with Dermot's words still uppermost in my mind. While I'm still devastated inside, I say that Rangers are strong, which I've always believed. It is a salutary lesson for me and the players, but our unbeaten run had to come to an end sometime. We will try to pick ourselves up and start all over again on Wednesday night at Easter Road.

It is absolutely freezing when Wednesday comes; the wind is blowing hard and the pitch is rutted. We draw 0–0 against Hibs, and in truth I'm relieved at the result. We don't play well, and five points are dropped in two games. Naturally, the press are wondering whether the wheels are coming off.

Rangers have been given hope tonight but we are still in front, and that counts for a lot. Having said that, Saturday's game against Dunfermline Athletic at Celtic Park takes on monumental proportions. We should win, and ten days ago we would have looked forward to the game, but just now I've become rather anxious about the match.

We need to start fast – but it doesn't go to plan, and Dunfermline score in the first minute. The stadium is stunned into momentary silence. But what happens next I will remember for a long time. Like a smoking volcano about to erupt, 60,000 people decide to change the course of this match, and perhaps

Celtic's history with it. This is not the roar of disapproval heard so many times last season, when a goal for the opposition signalled discontent and opprobrium. No, this thunderous cacophony is one of complete and utter encouragement to the players. This is a sure sign that Celtic belongs to the fans; it belongs to all of us. If the players need a lift like never before, they seem to be saying, then we are not going to stand idly by. We are going to do something about it.

Moravčík the wonder man responds almost immediately with the equalizer. Larsson, treated by fans with the nearest thing to hero-worship since the phenomenal Jimmy Johnstone, gives us the lead in twenty minutes – and there's no going back now. We win in style, and this match will feel more and more like a tipping point as the season goes on.

Neil Lennon has finally arrived at Celtic Park, his spiritual home. I have attempted a number of times since the summer to sign him for the second time in his career. The new Leicester City manager, Peter Taylor (no relation to Peter Taylor of Nottingham Forest), refused to sell him some months ago, so I had more or less given up hope of bringing the midfielder north of the border, at least for the season. But then, out of the blue, Taylor called me to see if I was still interested in a deal. I don't know what made the manager change his mind but a £5.5 million deal is arranged and the ginger-haired lad from Lurgan, County Armagh signs in time for a debut at Dens Park in December. This is a pivotal signing for the club. Lennon has been extremely influential in Leicester City's successes. His personality alone is enough to drive on relentlessly but add that to his ability on the pitch and you have a winner. Now he will bring all of this and more to Parkhead, both as a brilliant footballer and then as a terrific manager. He will go on to have a career of which most people can only dream.

Coping with football injuries is just part of the game, but when illness hits a player, that is something else. Morten Wieghorst, a splendid Danish international, was rushed to hospital in

October, where he will spend a long time trying to recover from Guillain–Barré syndrome, a rare brain condition. Only sheer willpower from the lad himself and excellent medical care pulls him through. Morten will recover eventually and head back to his native Denmark to play for Brøndby, resurrecting a very good career.

In November, Alan Stubbs also got bad news back from our doctor. Medical tests confirmed that his testicular cancer had returned and that his life, not just his career, was in jeopardy. Stubbs will fight this in the same way that he has fought throughout his career and will come through his battle with cancer. But we will not see him on the field until May. The lack of his presence in the dressing room is a big loss. The senior professionals at Celtic have a strong positive effect on the younger players, which makes for a better dressing-room environment. To offset the loss of Stubbs, Ramon Vega joins on loan from Tottenham Hotspur and December sees us win six consecutive games, totting up twenty-three goals in the process. A 6–0 victory over Kilmarnock at Celtic Park preludes a three-week winter break in Scotland.

Even though we are on a tremendous run, I am thankful for some respite. My plan is to give the squad a week's family holiday and then fly to Florida for some training in the sun. This suggestion proves a winner with the players. Dermot Desmond invites me and my family out to Sandy Lane Hotel in Barbados for five or six days. Such an alluring invitation cannot be turned down, and I fly from Bridgetown to Florida to meet up with the squad. One could get used to this kind of life.

The winter break, both physically and mentally, works wonders for the team. Despite big dips in temperature – from balmy Florida to Scotland in January – we are ready for the second half of the season.

A testimonial match for Tim Sheppard, my physiotherapist when I was at Norwich, on our immediate return from Florida sees thousands of Celtic fans flock to Carrow Road on a cold late

January evening. But after that, the show is back on the road again and we continue from where we left off. In February we are drawn against Rangers in the semi-final of the League Cup at Hampden Park, and while we have immense respect for them, confidence could not be higher in our camp.

Sutton and Larsson score early goals. Rangers pull one back, but we run out 3–1 winners, and reach the final. We cement our superiority over the Ibrox club a few days later at Celtic Park, where a hard-fought 1–0 victory courtesy of a goal by Alan Thompson effectively ends their challenge for the league title.

On 18 March 2001 we play in the final of the League Cup against Kilmarnock, managed by Bobby Williamson, an excellent motivator and tactically very bright. Nevertheless, we are expected to win. We haven't lost a game in any competition for almost four months. Despite that, it is my first cup final for Celtic and I'm anxious about today. All those things I said last June, about doing everything in my power to make this club successful again? Well, here's my first chance to do something about it.

Rab Douglas and Agathe are cup-tied, so unavailable. Jackie McNamara and Alan Thompson are suspended, so they too miss the game, and young Petrov is still recovering from an injury sustained at St Johnstone. A young lad from Cork, Colin Healy, will start the game on the right-hand side but with Petrov sidelined, we could be lacking just a little depth. Both teams have a change of kit, Celtic being in yellow shirts and green shorts. In my dreams, Celtic will win a cup final at Hampden Park and the famous green-and-white-hooped shirts will be on parade. John Clark and I agree that whenever possible Celtic should always wear the hoop shirts, home or away, when they don't clash with the opposition. But for whatever reason, no hoops today.

Within ten minutes Petta is off the field, having been clattered a few too many occasions even in that short space of time. Stephen Crainey, a young Scottish lad with much promise, takes his place on the left side. Petta's injury disrupts any flow we might have, and in truth I'm glad to get into the dressing room at half-time with the game scoreless.

Kilmarnock have played very strongly, don't seem intimidated at all, and in fact are relishing the challenge as supposed underdogs. Maybe it's the cup final; maybe it's my desperation to win something for Celtic; or maybe it's my own anxiety, but it feels that whoever scores first may well win the game. That's how close it seems to be.

But I'm not anxious in the dressing room. In fact, I am remarkably calm. There is room to play when we have the ball, I say. Take real care with our passing, openings will appear, and don't forget who we are. Within two minutes of the second half, Colin Healy fires a shot that their goalkeeper, Marshall, saves. From the resulting corner, the ball drops inside the six-yard box and Larsson – who else? – hooks it into the net. We have the all-important first goal.

Just when I think we can press for another and put the game beyond Kilmarnock, Chris Sutton is sent off on the hour mark for a poor challenge on one of their players. If Kilmarnock score next, the game could be extremely difficult to win with just ten men. Sutton's sending-off puts us under needless pressure.

But then Lubo Moravčík plays a wonderful through pass to Larsson, who controls and attempts to chip the ball over the goalkeeper's head. The ball takes a deflection, loops up over Marshall and into the Kilmarnock net: 2–0. Excitement and relief in equal measure. We can see this through to the end. But Larsson is not finished yet. He outstrips the Kilmarnock defenders, drives into the penalty area and has the composure to drag the ball with his right foot past a sprawling Marshall and tap it into the net with his left foot for his hat-trick.

What a performance from the mercurial Swede, who guides us to our first trophy. In the Scottish footballing lexicon, the League Cup is behind the Scottish Cup in importance. But we can only win what is in front of us, and this is the first trophy on offer this season. We are also in an unbelievably strong position in the Scottish Premier League, and just last week we beat Hearts at Celtic Park to take our place in the semi-final of the Scottish Cup. So we will be back here at Hampden Park next month.

Later tonight I will allow myself, for the first time, to think that the improbable Treble is within our grasp. The immortal Jock Stein did it way back in 1969 but, incredibly, it hasn't been done since. I remember Brian Clough once saying in a reflective interview after retirement that he felt that winning the Anglo-Scottish Cup, when Nottingham Forest were in the Second Division, was a breakthrough moment for the club. It was his first trophy on the mantelpiece and its importance should be stated. Not for one second have I underestimated our achievement in winning the Scottish League Cup. I feel that we are on the cusp of something very special. And the celebrations continue into the small hours of the morning.

There are thirty-eight games in the Scottish Premier League calendar. After thirty-three matches, the twelve-team table falls into two sections. Those who finished in the top six will play against each other one more time, and those who finished in the bottom half will do the same in their section, making a total of thirty-eight games altogether.

On 7 April 2001, we are at home to St Mirren. If we win, we win the league. We are a good distance in front of Rangers and even if we get beaten today the title will be ours next week, or the week after that. The Celtic fans turn up in carnival mood. I know it's going to happen sometime, but I just want it to be today, in front of our own fans. They deserve it: our average home attendance of close to 60,000 people proves the point. And the morale-sapping pain of the previous season has eased. It's our day today.

We play patchily but we get a goal before half-time from Tommy Johnson, and that will prove enough to win the title. There are glorious scenes at the end of the match with much jubilation in the stands. Celtic Park truly is paradise this afternoon. For whatever reason, the legendary Jock Stein fills my thoughts;

how did he feel when he clinched his first championship? Was he even conscious of the impact he had already made at the club? Just this minute, the championship trophy bears testimony to my own impact, and a natural feeling of both pride and privilege runs through my veins. This is what I have come here for.

But we have unfinished business. The Scottish Treble, to which I turn my attention, is now the focus. Proper celebrations will have to be put on hold. In eight days' time we play Dundee United in the semi-final of the Scottish Cup at Hampden Park. Larsson breaks the deadlock with a bullet header from a brilliant cross by Sutton. We score two more goals in the second half and duly reach the final. Incredibly, the Treble is now a distinct possibility. There is only one more hurdle: Alex McLeish's Hibernian, back at Hampden Park.

Before that, a visit to Ibrox in the league looms large. I get the same reception as I received last November. This time I stop, look at my aggressors and, in a rather arrogant tone, say, 'Champions.' It provokes more invective in reply, but I may never get the chance to say that at Ibrox again. Once the game gets under way, we turn it on in style. We sweep Rangers away 3–0, banishing last November's mauling to the underworld. Moravčík is simply sensational, scoring two magnificent goals. The season's domination of Rangers is complete. Next year will come round soon enough, but in the meantime, our 6,000 travelling fans bask in unadulterated glory at the home of our fiercest rivals.

The league has been won. We have lost only one game, and that was at Ibrox back in November. That game against Dunfermline started a run of fifty-two points out of fifty-four. With two league games to play before the final at Hampden, I do not want injuries to affect us if we can avoid it, and so I make a lot of changes to the team. Naturally, I still hope to win, but I'm aware that the games have no significance. However, regardless of team selection, two successive defeats is not the way to go into a cup final and that's exactly what occurs. We lose 2–0 at home to Dundee and then 1–0 away at Kilmarnock.

In retrospect, I wonder what was I thinking. I've prevented the team from accumulating a hundred points for the season, which would have been a remarkable achievement, and I might have put a little question mark against the extraordinary confidence prevailing in the squad. I have only myself to blame if things go wrong.

It's a bright morning over Glasgow, and I haven't been able to sleep at all. A few miles from our hotel lies Hampden Park, scene of our League Cup victory over Kilmarnock in March, and where this afternoon we will try to win the Scottish Cup against Hibernian. We already have two trophies back at Parkhead, but a third today will give us the elusive Treble, the clean sweep. The thought of it all last night prevented my sleep and has me walking around the hotel perimeter as the clock strikes 7 a.m.

Back in the bedroom, I start to imagine different scenarios for the game. An early goal for us, an early goal against, an early injury setback, set pieces for and against; but I try to stop myself thinking about the final whistle, whether we're beaten or victorious. The Scottish Cup has always fascinated me. Usually held the same day as the FA Cup final in England, one might get glimpses of what has happened at Hampden Park when it's half-time in the English final. There always seems to be an incredible atmosphere in the stadium, and although Hampden Park has been modernized over the years, the arena still evokes memories of past glories.

The journey into the stadium starts to excite the closer to Hampden Park we get. We pass little pockets of Celtic fans who either wave encouragingly at the team bus or salute us with raised clenched fists, like I'm sure William Wallace must have done to exhort his clan to victory on the battlefield.

Then Hampden comes into view. The supporters are here in greater numbers, and they too raise fists in defiant gestures. Adrenaline runs through my veins. Although we have won two trophies, defeat today would be a massive disappointment; I even start to think it might spoil the season. But the players, I sense, are ready.

An early setback: Moravčík is injured and cannot continue. Jackie McNamara, who could easily have started in the match, comes on to take his place. As against Kilmarnock in the League Cup final, the game is evenly poised. Alex McLeish has his team well organized, as one would expect from an acolyte of Alex Ferguson and an important cog in that splendid Aberdeen team of nearly twenty years ago.

Then it happens. Didier Agathe, driving forward, evades a couple of challenges and pushes the ball into McNamara's path on the left-hand side of the penalty area, but onto Jackie's weaker foot. However, the baby-faced Scotsman, sometimes underestimated by me earlier in the season, gets his left foot round the ball and squeezes it into the net past both defender and goalkeeper. There is an explosion of emotion from the Celtic fans as McNamara is hugged by his teammates. Teams can be at their most vulnerable just after they have scored a goal, but there are only a few minutes to half-time and we reach it without incident.

'The next goal belongs to us,' I tell the team, and it resonates with the players. Just after half-time, it comes, from the boot of that superman Henrik Larsson. An excellent move brings McNamara into play, again on the left-hand side of the penalty area. He pulls the ball across the face of the eighteen-yard line and Larsson sweeps it into the roof of the net with his left foot.

The cheering celebrations of Larsson's goal finally recede, but only for the crowd to recover its breath. A thrumming sound, like band members tuning their instruments before going on stage, signals some sort of imminent happening, and then all the Celtic fans in unison begin to chorus 'The Fields of Athenry'. It's a familiar ode, but now taking on a meaning all of its own. This is the last time this season that it will be sung, and the sound almost lifts the Hampden roof from its rafters.

Larsson is brought down. A penalty is awarded, and he scores himself to make it 3–0. There are ten minutes left for me to relax, take it all in, soak up the atmosphere and enjoy those precious moments that are seldom afforded to you. I stand with John Robertson and Steve Walford. Together we have been a strong unit, recognized and appreciated by the players all season long. Steve and John's interaction with the squad, both on the training ground and in a social context, has been profoundly important to our success. I want to take it all in, but instinct kicks in quickly.

'How long to go?' I ask John, with a trace of anxiety still in my voice.

'Three minutes,' he answers. 'Just enjoy it!' he adds.

The scenes at the end of the game are unforgettable. Hampden Park, half in sun and half in shade, bears testimony to another Scottish Cup final, and tonight will close its doors on another season. The trip back to Celtic Park with the Scottish Cup at the top of the bus is pure exhilaration. There is a gathering of fans as we reach those very steps that I stood on almost a year ago, when I promised to bring some success to the club. The assembled crowd is much larger than it was last June, but that's only natural considering there is something tangible to celebrate, with all three trophies now at Celtic Park. I have kept my promise.

After the obligatory photographs on the pitch and in the boardroom with the silverware, I have a few moments with the family to take it all in. Then I corner Dermot Desmond, who is talking to some of his fellow directors. I interrupt their conversation to thank him for taking a chance on me, when other options were available to him last summer. The trophies are carefully put into the cabinet and closed behind the glass case. John, Steve and I round up our families and walk out the Parkhead doors.

The evening light is beginning to fade, but the sun seems reluctant to drop behind the high-rise flats in the distance. What has been achieved today will stay with me for the rest of my life. We decide to grab something to eat together.

'Have you booked anywhere?' I ask John.

'I think we'll get in somewhere tonight, don't you?' he replies.

'It's a beautiful evening, isn't it?' I say earnestly.

John answers with a smile. 'It's always a beautiful evening in Glasgow. This is Paradise, you know.'

Because of the three-week winter break last January, the off season in Scotland is very short. Our defeat of Hibernian in the Scottish Cup final was on 26 May, which means the players will only get a month off to recuperate from the exhausting work they put into winning the Treble. While the first game of the season against St Johnstone is not until the end of July, preseason must start at least a month before. There's no proper rest time. But it is what it is. And at least I'm not going into my training sessions with little knowledge of the strengths and weaknesses of the squad, as was the case last year. If I don't know every nuance of the players' characters and abilities by now, I shouldn't be managing any club, let alone Celtic.

Within a blink of an eye the opening league fixture is upon us. In time-honoured fashion the Scottish Champions' flag is unfurled at Celtic Park before kick-off, a final reminder of last season's triumphs. As it is stored away somewhere in the bowels of the stadium, we start again, with no advantage other than greater self-belief than the team have had for a long, long time.

A goal from Mjällby and two from Lambert set us on our way, and when Larsson scores the only goal at Rugby Park the following week to beat Kilmarnock, my thoughts shift quickly to our midweek Champions League qualifier against the formidable Ajax of Amsterdam, which will be played over two legs. My first European game last season as Celtic manager was just a qualifying game for the UEFA Cup against Jeunesse Esch of Luxembourg. This is an entirely different proposition. Ajax are very strong favourites to overcome us and take their place in the Champions League group stage next month. But our concerns about the quality of the opposition are balanced by our belief in our chances at the hallowed Amsterdam Arena.

The coach journey from the hotel to the stadium has that indescribable Champions League feeling. Hordes of Ajax supporters, dressed in red and white from top to toe, are thumping the bus as it inches its way through the stadium gates. This can either inspire you or scare you to death. They have a terrific young team with pedigree including Rafael van der Vaart, Shota Arveladze, Mido and Zlatan Ibrahimović.

But we have a secret weapon. I know that their young Romanian defender Cristian Chivu will not be able to cope with Didier Agathe's pace if we can isolate one versus one on the right-hand side of our attack. Very few left-sided defenders can. And Bobby Petta will want to perform well back on home soil. One thing for certain is that we are coming to attack. How can it be otherwise, with players like Alan Thompson and Paul Lambert, Lennon in midfield, and Sutton and Larsson in attack? We will not lose wondering what might have been in this atmospheric arena. And the Celtic fans are out in force, and their support can do nothing but act as a stimulus.

We are blindingly brilliant from the whistle. Petta opens the scoring with a left-foot shot into the roof of the net. Agathe blitzes past Chivu to score the second goal and although Ajax get one back just before half-time, Sutton makes it three when he powers home a header from Agathe's cross. We miss two great chances to increase our tally, but we have performed with distinction and given ourselves a proper chance of making it through to the group stages with three away goals. Our fans give the team a standing ovation and I travel back to Glasgow positively glowing. I wish the return leg was tomorrow.

Two weeks to ponder the next game is too long, but sure as night follows day, we are back at Celtic Park for the second leg. A couple of enforced changes to our line-up doesn't help and the element of surprise, so crucial in the first leg for us, is no longer a weapon. Ajax score halfway through the first half and we become very tentative, totally understandable considering the club's lack of Champions League experience. They sense our nervousness but still need two more goals.

We have character in abundance and refuse to allow that imperious performance a fortnight ago to count for nothing. Slowly but surely, we edge towards the finishing line with our lead still intact . . . and we see it through. We have reached the group stages of the Champions League for the first time, a huge financial boost to the club and the opportunity to experience Celtic Park on Champions League nights. Tonight's showing may not be enough for every journalist tomorrow morning, but the result is the only thing that matters. There will be better productions in the future.

Porto, Juventus and Rosenborg are our group opponents. The former two are seeded and obvious candidates to qualify for the knockout stages. Our first game is a home tie against Porto, and with our massive support at Celtic Park I feel we can spring a surprise. The game is scheduled for Wednesday evening, 12 September. Tuesday's training is over for the morning and the players can have lunch at Celtic Park if they wish. But as is routine, we will meet up later to spend the evening in a hotel a little distance from Celtic Park in an attempt to have a quiet night away.

I leave my office and head up to the restaurant area. There I see Jim Crockwell, who organizes the lunches. He has the television on and beckons me across to have a look at what's on the screen. The Twin Towers in New York are ablaze with black smoke and Jim has just witnessed an aeroplane crash into the second tower. This is not a tragic accident, as it first appeared.

As we leave Celtic Park in early evening, the whole world is aware of what happened in New York a few hours ago. It is no surprise that UEFA call off Wednesday's games as a mark of respect for those people killed earlier today. To be playing so soon after such horrendous and shockingly sad circumstances would not have been the right thing to do.

The following week, we start our campaign in the storied Stadio delle Alpi in Turin against Juventus, one of Italy's finest. Almost thirty-four years since winning the European Cup, Celtic will finally make their Champions League debut tonight, but a daunting task lies ahead. Gianluigi Buffon, Paolo Montero, Lilian Thuram, Edgar Davids, David Trezeguet and Alessandro Del Piero all feature in the starting line-up and to cap it all, they are managed by Marcello Lippi, lauded as one of Europe's greatest coaches.

It is difficult for me to gauge just how we might perform this evening. Will Juventus's reputation be so intimidating that we just freeze on this big occasion? Will we cope at all in the big club competition in Europe? Well, a 2–2 scoreline with only minutes to play gives an indication of how excellently we have played. We are fully deserving of this vital point we are sharing with Lippi's team. Then the referee intervenes. He awards Juventus a penalty when one of their players falls over in the penalty box. It is a terrible decision, and one that will be of significant consequence further down the line.

That we manage to fight our way back into contention in the group speaks volumes for the players and the Celtic supporters. On a glorious December night we take revenge on Juventus at Parkhead with a simply awesome performance, winning 4–3. Chris Sutton has the game of a lifetime and he's not alone in that regard. Our first crack at the Champions League has yielded nine points, but it is not enough to go into the knockout stages. This still remains one of the very few occasions in Champions League history when nine points are not sufficient to go deeper into the competition. The atmosphere in the stadium is charged. It only makes me want this sort of experience every year from now onwards. It's what the crowd want. I now hope it's what we demand of each other.

There is no winter break, for the first time since the Scottish Premier League began in 1998/99. We drive on regardless and although we lose an epic Scottish Cup final to a last-minute Rangers goal we are runaway winners of the SPL, amassing 103 points with only one league defeat throughout the season. Our Champions League experience has no doubt fuelled our appetite for more success, hence the triumphal march to the championship, and by the season's end we are already setting our sights on Europe again.

That's what Celtic fans are now demanding. There has been a real sea change from two years ago. But these are exactly the challenges I want to face as manager of this club.

It is difficult to imagine a season in which Celtic do not win a single trophy but which is considered by many fans to be right up there in the history books. But that is what is about to unfold. We have won the league for the second consecutive season and with an inordinate number of points, but ever since last Christmas, when Alex McLeish replaced Dick Advocaat at Rangers, the Ibrox club has gritted its teeth again and found a new resolve. They beat us in the last minute of last season's Scottish Cup final and they will be breathing down our necks this season. That's a certainty.

With the season barely started, we face a qualifying tie against Basel of Switzerland to reach the group stages of the Champions League. The Scottish coefficient has improved with our efforts last season in this very competition but because of the way UEFA works, the benefit is not immediately granted. So qualify we must, in a tough two-legged tie against the best Switzerland have to offer. It does not help that their own season is well under way and they have a big head start on us in terms of match fitness and competitive games.

At Celtic Park the fans are in holiday mood, not surprising given that many people are doing exactly that. This time last year was different. We were not expected to beat Ajax, and so we were lifted high by fans both in Amsterdam and back here at Celtic Park. In the lead-up to this game, there is a presumption gathering modest momentum that we should easily knock Basel out and take our place once again in the group stages. But our hopes are soon shattered.

Disaster strikes within ninety seconds. Some fans haven't even taken their seats in the stadium, and we are a goal down. The dreaded away goal. We fight back, and Larsson scores a penalty almost immediately to level affairs, but it's plain to everyone now that this will be a difficult match for us. We score in the second half and add a third goal, which we hope will be decisive when the tie has finished.

One of my daughters is acting in a Dylan Thomas play, *Under Milk Wood*, at the Edinburgh Fringe with some of her fellow Cambridge students this month. Geraldine and I promise that we will take in at least one visit to see it. But even with a fortnight between the two Basel games, taking time out to watch a play seems a dereliction of duty with so much at stake; so I meet my daughter in Edinburgh for a cup of tea, but don't go to see her play.

Iain Jamieson, our PR man, subsequently gets in touch to tell me that I've been spotted in the city with a young blonde woman and that the newspapers are likely to print some photographs the next day. I tell Iain it's my daughter I've been with and if they want to print the photographs, let them do so. He replies that he thought there was probably nothing in the story because no young women would want to be seen with me anyway.

Basel is a beautiful city on the Rhine in north-western Switzerland. But as lovely as it is, today we can only focus on the St Jakob-Park Stadium, where over 30,000 fans have congregated. They get the goal they were searching for. Then they score again before half-time. I tell the players not to panic and that chances will come our way. But we do know we have to score. We are pressing strongly, incredibly so, towards the end of the game. Every player on the field save Rab Douglas seems to be in the Swiss team's penalty area. The momentum is in our favour.

The ball is passed through. Larsson, with his back to goal, lays a little pass off to Sutton, who caresses the ball towards the far post. Time stands still. There is hardly a sound in the stadium. The ball passes a stranded goalkeeper. It's in! It's in the net! It must be. But it isn't.

The ball shaves the post and goes agonizingly wide. A roar goes up. People outside the ground must think a goal has been scored, so loud is the noise. But it is the celebration of us not scoring that has inspired such tumult in the stadium. The referee blows almost immediately and we are out of the competition. We have come so close to a second successive Champions League foray, but have fallen short.

Basel are a good team – in fact, a very good team. I have known that from the outset. It will come as no surprise to me when they qualify for the second group stage by beating Spartak Moscow both home and away, knocking Liverpool out of the Champions League. But for the moment, none of that matters. Our dressing room is deadly silent. That ineluctable fact of defeat is written on every face, mine more so than any.

Heads are bowed, except for one. One of the youngest players on the field lifts his face from his towel and says, 'We will just have to win the UEFA Cup now to make up for this.' Stiliyan Petrov is only twenty-three years old. But like the fallen angels hearing Lucifer's defiant voice in Milton's *Paradise Lost*, the players hear his words, remove the towels from their buried faces and take the first steps on the road to recovery.

We grasp Petrov's challenge with immediate enthusiasm, opening our UEFA campaign by thrashing FK Sūduva from Lithuania over the two games, winning 8–1 at Celtic Park and 2–0 in Marijampolė. We are then drawn against Blackburn Rovers, who are going strongly in the Premier League. They are managed by Graeme Souness, who was a brilliant midfielder for Liverpool in their glory days. As manager of Rangers in the mid-1980s, he not only changed the fortunes of the struggling Ibrox club but helped to reverse the haemorrhaging of quality players from Scotland, bringing international footballers to Ibrox.

Now he's here in Glasgow, in charge of an excellent Premier League team, and the press lads renew their love-in with him. One of the redtops draws contrasts between Graeme's swagger and my unwillingness to divulge much information to them about, well, anything. The tie is incredibly important to Scottish football. A loss against Blackburn Rovers, not considered a Liverpool or a Manchester United, could invite prophecies of doom, or at the very least encourage detractors of the game up North.

Blackburn play exceptionally well for almost all of the game – better than I expect them to on our home pitch, even though I saw them at Highbury a few days previously, where they defeated Arsenal convincingly. But we score late in the game through Larsson and although we do not deserve it, we take the spoils 1–0. Within minutes we get to hear one of Blackburn's players telling the press that tonight's game was 'men against boys'.

The return leg assumes a new importance as the media hyperbolically dub it 'the battle of Britain'. Ewood Park holds a special place in English football history and Blackburn Rovers were founder members of the Football League. More recently, under Jack Walker's guidance, the stadium has been renovated, and Chris Sutton won the Premier League with them just over eight years ago.

About a mile or so from Ewood Park there is a rather steep hill which our bus descends. It's dark outside. There is a tightness in my stomach, but there is always a tightness in my stomach around this time before a game, as silly thoughts flit around in my brain. A few moments later the road levels off, and soon we will be there.

The road is brighter now and the bus slowly passes a pub on the left-hand side, essentially the first sign of life in the outside world for the last ten minutes. The pub is crammed with Celtic supporters who, on seeing our bus, rise to their feet. They either deposit their pints and clap the bus or raise their glasses in the air, not seeming to care whether beer spills or not. They want to tell us that they are with us every step of the way, and I take comfort from their gestures.

Before long, we are in the dressing room. John Robertson sneaks out to the tunnel to have a cigarette. As he opens the dressing-room door, I can hear the noise of the crowd outside. The players haven't been out for their warm-up, yet it's a deafening din. I walk out down the tunnel and look to my right: the stand behind the goal is filled to capacity with thousands of Celtic fans. We are still about an hour away from kick-off and Celtic are already holding sway. It's a sight that gladdens my heart. I give them a wave and the response is so powerful that I know, I just know, we will win tonight. The Celtic fans have decreed it.

We play brilliantly. Larsson latches onto a through ball and chips Brad Friedel, the Blackburn goalkeeper. I will sign Brad in a few years' time, but not for Celtic. Our football is slick, purposeful and threatening and continual encouragement from me is all that's needed at half-time. Sutton scores with a header from a corner and while that wraps up the scoring, the Celtic celebrations continue long after the final whistle. Scottish football is still alive, and pretty vibrant if this game is anything to go by.

In the next round we are paired with Celta Vigo of La Liga, the Spanish league. We play in two tough games: a 1–0 victory at Celtic Park followed by a 2–1 defeat in Vigo. But John Hartson's vital away goal carries us through, and Celtic will play European football after Christmas for the first time in twenty-three years.

This season, the winter break is reinstated in Scotland and we will have three welcome weeks in January to recuperate. A dogfight for the league title between ourselves and Rangers is hotting up. We drew 3–3 with our rivals at Celtic Park in October, then they beat us 3–2 in early December a few days before our second leg game in Vigo. It will be a fight to the finish. Rangers have no European football to concern them, having lost early in the UEFA Cup. That will eventually prove to be decisive.

In February 2003, we play Stuttgart in the next round of the UEFA Cup. Hartson is suspended and Larsson has a broken jaw so cannot play, a major loss to the team. Shaun Maloney, a very gifted but very young player, will partner Sutton up front for the first leg. On the plus side, the opposition will know very little about this lad. His ability to beat markers with his quick feet will definitely surprise Stuttgart. I find myself in the stands once again, serving another UEFA ban for unbecoming conduct during the Celta Vigo away game.

A reshuffle of the defence is also needed with Mjällby injured. Stuttgart are managed by Felix Magath, an old adversary of mine from the 1980 European Cup final when Forest beat Hamburg. And just to add more flair to a stadium already filled with vigour and brio, Pierluigi Collina, considered the best referee in the world at the time, takes charge of affairs. The crowd, mindful of the long stretch since Parkhead last hosted European football at such an advanced stage of the season, is in full voice. Tonight Celtic Park is the only place to be in the world.

Disadvantaged by injuries and suspensions, we need to attack early to keep the crowd at fever pitch. Petrov is brought down while latching onto a through ball, and the Stuttgart defender is sent off. This certainly helps, but even with ten men Stuttgart, who have been in great recent form, take the lead when the much-vaunted Kevin Kurányi sends a flying header into our net. Maybe this is as far as we are meant to go. The thought fills my mind for two whole seconds, but I dismiss it. There is still a long way to go; they have ten men; we have 60,000 people urging us forward. I have instilled character and a strong mentality into this team – and will we need it.

Paul Lambert rifles in an equalizer. He has been a splendid professional footballer all his life; he is now in the autumn of his career but still possesses the fitness of a twenty-two-year-old. He is also the proud owner of a European Cup medal, won when playing with Borussia Dortmund when they beat Juventus in the final in 1997. How good must that have been for him? To leave Scotland, to go on trial in Germany. To be taken on by Dortmund, to get into the team, to stay in the team and to learn the German language. And now, at Celtic, he has been a big influence in a dressing room filled with big characters.

Maloney, reading Sutton's knockdown, scores to give us a half-time lead. That didn't seem possible fifteen minutes ago. Only one message for the players: keep going forward in the second half. And we do. Petrov scores the third goal, squeezing a shot past their goalkeeper. The crowd is ecstatic. Roars for a fourth goal do not go unheeded but try as we might, we cannot get it.

In the circumstances it is a brilliant win. And while there is a general acceptance in football that the best referees are the ones you don't notice, Collina's presence on the field and his supervision of the match lend the evening an extra layer of significance.

We must then play Stuttgart away for the return leg. We score twice in the first fifteen minutes but Stuttgart fight back, and with time still on the clock they are leading 3–2 on the night. In fact, Douglas blocks what looks like a fourth goal for them. If it had gone in, Stuttgart would only need one more goal and they would be through. The very thought of this possibility disturbs my concentration.

Minutes earlier, I heard a laugh coming from behind me; two of my medical backroom staff are sharing a joke, seemingly oblivious to what is unfolding before them. They simply aren't getting the danger that we are in. They don't think Stuttgart can score twice in a couple of minutes even though they are shredding us just now. I turn round and throw a few expletives of warning to them: this is no laughing matter, save the jokes for after the bloody game.

From being in total charge of the game we are hanging on for dear life, completely out on our feet. At last, to my great relief, the whistle blows and we are through. I shout behind me, 'You can finish your bloody joke now.' It has been a tense and uncomfortable evening in this south-eastern German city.

I seldom need reminding about how difficult it is to win football matches domestically or in European football, but tonight has been a lesson for me. We were 2–0 ahead after fifteen minutes. Stuttgart then needed at least five goals to qualify. Did I take the eye off the ball myself? Did I think the game was over then? I'm not sure myself, but I'm just mightily relieved we are in the quarter-finals.

I remind myself about Stuttgart when our quarter-final opponents are up next – Liverpool. I honestly believe that Celtic Park has never been louder. 'You'll Never Walk Alone' is sung by both

Celtic and Liverpool fans together just before kick-off, and it moves you like nothing else. John Robertson looks over to me. We know each other's thoughts. This is what football is all about. This is what Celtic Football Club is all about. Celtic Park on this very night cannot be matched for atmosphere anywhere in the universe.

Within ten minutes, Larsson forces the ball over the line to give us the lead. A Liverpool equalizer through Emile Heskey follows almost immediately. The game threatens to explode with goals, but they do not materialize. Unsurprisingly, the match drops in intensity before half-time, and then the second half is full of skirmishes but no real patterns of play. A draw looks the most likely outcome long before the referee blows his whistle, Liverpool more pleased with the result than ourselves. It means that whatever happens at Anfield, we have to score a goal at least. If we don't, Liverpool's away goal will prove decisive. But we are far from out of this tie. Anfield will be rocking, but so will we. Of course, this is Scotland versus England once again: Scottish football is on trial, just as it was when we played Blackburn Rovers a few months ago.

In our Anfield dressing room before the game, I sense tension among the players. This is the most atmospheric stadium in England; I know as much from my playing days with Nottingham Forest. We came here once as European champions, full of terrific players – and spent the first fifteen minutes never getting out of our own half, so on top were Liverpool that day.

I actually mention this to the players in the dressing room, but tonight will not be like that at all. Yes, we will have to face an expected early onslaught, but we will not only survive it but we will find the strength of character we know we possess to overcome the opposition on this evening of all evenings. Years later, I learn that my words before they take the field tonight are regarded by some of the players as one of the most inspiring team talks of their footballing careers. Well, if that's the case, I draw the very same inspiration from the players sitting in that room, ready to fight Celtic's cause.

Liverpool do come on strongly, forcing us back towards our own goal. But soon we get a foothold in the game. A free kick is awarded to us; Larsson pretends to shoot, but runs over the ball. Alan Thompson fires a low drive into Jerzy Dudek's net and wheels away in utter joy. We are in front.

And now we take command of the game. Into the second half, and a second goal for us will surely be enough. John Hartson has scored a lot of goals in his football career, many of them for this club. But I doubt he will score a more beautiful goal than the one he rockets into Liverpool's net this evening. The ball is hit with such force and precision that Dudek cannot do anything about it. For a split second the stadium is silent, so stunned are the fans by what has just happened.

But that silence is just the cue for the loudest roar ever heard by away fans at Anfield. Within minutes, 'The Fields of Athenry' resounds throughout the Celtic end of the stadium. John's goal has sealed the most memorable of victories, and staunch supporters of the Scottish game will definitely take their hats off to this Celtic team.

Seville is on the horizon. Surely we won't trip up against Boavista over two legs. We don't, but it takes a late Larsson strike in Portugal to save the day and guide us through. Semi-finals are supposed to be tough, though, aren't they? Larsson's goal triggers the rush for tickets, and the Road to Seville is set.

Congratulatory messages pour into Celtic Park. The prime minister, Tony Blair, sends a good luck letter to me, and suddenly Celtic is the talk of British football. We are still contesting the Scottish Premier League with Rangers. The title race will go to the very last kick of the very last game of the season.

I want to win the SPL for a third consecutive year, but if given a choice, the UEFA Cup takes preference every time. The prestige of winning a prized European trophy has to be the desire of all Celtic fans – it is certainly mine.

We are going to Seville. It's unbelievable.

Porto will be our opponents there, having thrashed Lazio in the semi-final. But there is little time to think about all that now. We have Rangers at Ibrox in a couple of days and we have to win there first. The UEFA Cup has brought immense happiness and joy to our Celtic supporters all over the world, but it has also brought us a heavy schedule of matches to play in a very short space of time. An extension to the season is discussed as a possible way of helping Scottish teams in cups, but this doesn't materialize, so midweek fixtures with no respite are the order of Celtic's day from the beginning of May.

It is a Sunday at Ibrox. Celtic fans most certainly have a sense of humour: many have turned up wearing shorts, flip-flops and sombreros, with a taunting catchphrase gathering momentum: 'We're in Seville, while you're watching *The Bill*.' We beat Rangers, and the possibility of three consecutive titles is still holding firm. And to cement that desire to stay in the race for the championship, we win three league games in the space of a week.

Seville is now only eleven days away and it is almost impossible not to give it some thought in quieter moments. Jim Duffy, the Dundee manager, does us a big favour by bringing forward our match at Celtic Park with his team by a few days to allow us a week's preparation for Seville. It will be our penultimate game of the league, with the last match against Kilmarnock at Rugby Park on the Sunday after our UEFA final.

John Robertson says that this hectic schedule of one big game after another, with precious few moments to draw breath, reminds him of our playing days at Nottingham Forest – and of course he's right. But we were players then, carefree, no responsibilities other than to ourselves. We both agree that we would never have considered what Clough and Taylor might have had in their minds with regard to team selection and planning in such a condensed period of time.

Goal difference is becoming a more and more significant factor in the championship race with Rangers and although Jim Duffy has helped us with the scheduling, we still need to win this game – and, if possible, score some goals. As it turns out, a 6–2 scoreline to Celtic looks impressive, but I'm absolutely livid about the needless concession of a late Dundee goal, which I feel in my bones may play a significant part come Sunday week. Still, it's hard to be angry with a team that has put aside thoughts of Seville and scored six goals in its quest to remain champions of Scotland. My ire cannot and does not last long in the dressing room, but I brood over it for the next few days.

A week to prepare for the UEFA Cup. Seville is on every Celtic supporter's mind and lips. Rafael Carmona, the security chief for this UEFA final, dismisses the highfalutin notion that Celtic will not only take up their allocation of tickets but will want more. Carmona thinks 50,000 extra tickets is a total exaggeration and that 5,000 is a more realistic number. My, is he in for a surprise.

Arrangements are made for the team to stay in Jerez, not Seville, and so, with the obligatory new suits on view, we leave Glasgow Airport behind and travel south to Andalusia.

Billy Connolly is staying with us in Jerez. And so are the Lisbon Lions. A glittering combination. Billy, when opportunity allows him to return to Glasgow, often pops into our dressing room at Celtic Park before matches to have a word with the players. It is a genuine pleasure to be in his company. I have seen him at the Hammersmith Odeon, when I paid for him to make me laugh, but he's doing it today for free. Now that's generosity. Some months ago, he invited my family to his house in Aberdeenshire to be part of a big celebration for his sixtieth birthday. It was a two-day event but we could only get there on the second day and as we made our way up the driveway, the actor and comedian Robin Williams whizzed past us wearing full Lycra for an afternoon bicycle ride in the Scottish countryside. We were told the previous night at dinner that Robin had made one of the great impromptu rhyming odes to a haggis, performed as Robbie Burns with the accompanying Scottish accent.

While we are preparing for Porto, Rangers are at Tynecastle on the Sunday. I am hoping against hope that Hearts can get a draw. If so, then the league is totally in our own hands with just the one game left. It is scoreless at half-time. Can Hearts hold out for another forty-five minutes? They can't. Rangers score with about twenty minutes to go, and add a second a few minutes later. We cannot do anything about it. That's gone now. Leave it until we get back home. Porto on Wednesday night, nothing else. Still, dinner is pretty unappetizing this evening, all because of the result in Edinburgh over 1,000 miles away.

The day of the final. The team boards the coach but the bus driver must think the match will only start when he arrives, so unconcerned is he that there is anxiety building amongst his passengers. The police escort in front of the bus may well not be there at all, so little are they doing to help us get there in time.

Despite the efforts of our driver, we finally reach the stadium. Our inspection of the pitch yesterday morning revealed a rotted, discoloured surface, which is helping no one's mood. For a UEFA Cup final, I'm afraid to say it's a disgrace. I honestly think most amateur clubs would turn their noses up if asked to play a final here.

Even for an 8.45 p.m. kick-off, the temperature is still red hot. The game may take a little time to get going while the players get used to the boiling conditions. Save for an area on the far side belonging to the blue and white of Porto, the stadium is awash with green-and-white shirts.

Celtic supporters in full voice is something magnificent to both see and hear. Last night's sing-songs in the tavernas of Seville were just a warm-up for tonight. 'The Fields of Athenry' is sung with such fervour and emotion that the noise reverberates around the stadium like a hymn to the gods. The game itself is evenly contested, but even at this early stage it is clear that the young, inexperienced referee is having a tough time.

The Porto players fall to the ground at the merest hint of contact and this trend, once allowed to go on unchecked, continues unabated. There is no need for such gamesmanship considering the abundance of talent in their team. Porto's president has been quoted as saying that this is the team's best squad of the last fifty years, better than the team that won the European Cup in 1987. We are mentally strong, wise and battle-hardened after the last eighteen months, but it is difficult for our players not to be irritated with the way the game is being handled, with some Porto players turning theatrical tumbles into an art form.

Then, just before half-time, Porto score. A bad time to concede, but we just have to get over it. We have been behind at half-time quite a number of times over the last couple of seasons. We have got to keep playing, forget about the heat and put heart and soul into the second half. These opportunities to win big, big medals in this old game come round so seldom, they might never occur again.

Within minutes of the second half Larsson equalizes, climbing high to head back across goal and into the net. A magnificent goal from a magnificent player. The Celtic crowd are in a state of delirium. The dream is still alive. But Porto score again. Then we equalize: Larsson again, with another splendid goal that maybe only he could have conjured. The teams are level once more. Extra time looms. The noise in the stadium is at fever pitch; we look physically stronger just now, but the heat is still in the stadium.

The referee blows, and the UEFA Cup of 2003 comes down to at least another half an hour and possibly penalties to decide the winner. Bobo Baldé is sent off for a second bookable offence – a rash challenge to make when you know you're already on a yellow card – and Porto breathe a sigh of relief. Eleven versus ten, with twenty-five minutes left in 32°C heat and having already played ninety minutes, gives you a big boost.

They score a goal. A soft goal. In fact, I don't see it. The situation appears to be under control and I look upfield for a split second to see what might be on when we move the ball. At that moment, the ball slips from Rab Douglas's grasp and Porto take advantage: 3–2. It is a devastating blow and one from which we cannot recover. And then – to add insult to feigned injury – Porto's goalkeeper, Vítor Baía, catches the ball and then falls in a heap. He rolls over a few times, signalling for the physiotherapist and two or three doctors to boot, who all arrive on the scene to examine this man who may never play again, so bad is the injury the physiotherapist cannot find.

The referee blows his whistle for the very last time, and we have lost the UEFA Cup final.

Celtic fans cover themselves in glory in Seville. The largest green-and-white army ever assembled in the city, and not one arrest. Stories abound about the journeys taken and the sacrifices made to undertake such a pilgrimage. The pain I feel about the match has been partly lessened in recent years, purely because everyone I have spoken to since says that Seville was one of the most wonderful experiences of their lives.

However, the season is not over for us. We must fly back to Glasgow, discard our disappointment and prepare for Sunday's game at Rugby Park against Kilmarnock. We are level on points with Rangers, but they have a one-goal advantage. They play Dunfermline at Ibrox. We must score one more than they do. First of all we have to win – then, if we can secure that, goals will be at a premium.

The effort put in by the team this afternoon in Scotland borders on the superhuman. With very little rest, the same group of players who gave everything in Seville are solely focused on trying to win the league title at Rugby Park. Everything is done in an attempt to stay at pace with the goals we hear of being scored at Ibrox. We even miss a penalty in all of this drama. Eventually, our 4–0 victory is not enough: we fall short by a goal.

Afterwards, the dressing room at Rugby Park is silent for a long time, the players too exhausted even to take off their boots. They have used every last ounce of their energy to win. They deserved more. This season has yielded not a single trophy. And yet, even today, many Celtic fans regard the 2002/03 season as one of the most memorable in all their years of supporting the club.

I break the silence, telling them that their efforts will not go unrewarded. We will come back even stronger next season. I tell them to remember what I'm going to say next: 'We will win the league next season by a distance.'

And we do.

For the 2003/04 season we have some Champions League qualifying games to negotiate before securing our entry into the group stages, in which we are drawn against Bayern Munich, Lyon, and Anderlecht of Belgium. I have extended some contracts for the players who have performed so brilliantly over the last few seasons, but there have been no major additions to the squad. Stanislav Varga, on a free transfer from Sunderland, proves exceptionally good value with Mjällby fighting against constant fitness battles throughout the season. We are prepared to put all the disappointments of last season behind us.

We open the league campaign with a 0–0 draw at Dunfermline, which proves unreflective of the season we will have. We win the next twenty-five league games in a row on our way to winning the SPL by eighteen points from Rangers, scoring a record 105 goals in the process. We go on to complete the Double when we claim the Scottish Cup with a 3–1 win against Dunfermline at Hampden in May. A stellar season.

The Champions League group stage will tell a more frustrating story. In our opening fixture at the Olympic Stadium in Munich we swamp all over Bayern Munich, taking the lead early in the second half. Bayern's equalizer I can accept, but their winning goal in the dying moments of the game is very hard to take: a cross evades everyone in the penalty box and ends up in the back of our net. I am mightily disappointed on the trip back to Glasgow, having been dominant against the German champions for so long.

By the time we face Lyon in December, we need a draw to see us through to the knockout stages of the competition after Christmas. We fall behind early, but a John Hartson equalizer puts us back in position. We then concede a soft goal, shot from almost forty yards out; it's almost a spirit-breaker, but again we rally to force another equalizer, and this will be sufficient to see us through. Then, with less than three minutes remaining, Bobo Baldé needlessly handles the ball in the penalty area and Lyon take the lead. There's no time left to rectify the situation. Our place in the knockout stages is thwarted.

At the end of the season comes news I have been expecting, but am still disappointed to hear. Henrik Larsson is leaving Celtic.

He will sign for Barcelona. I will miss him and so will the fans –
he's been a fantastic player for this football club. He will be
extremely difficult to replace. The draw for the Champions League
is glamorous but not very kind: Henrik's new club, Barcelona, will
be in our group, and so too will AC Milan and Shakhtar Donetsk.

As replacements I take Henri Camara, on loan from Wolves,
and Juninho on a free transfer from Middlesbrough. Juninho has
been a brilliant footballer in his prime, but recently he has been
unable to recapture the form that made him such an attacking
threat some seasons earlier. I hope that I can help him get back
some of his former glory, but a free transfer granted by Middlesbrough, where he is revered, doesn't sound promising. And so it
proves. He makes his debut in a victory over Rangers, playing well,
but is unable to consistently play to the level he was once capable
of doing. Camara, on the other hand, is a live wire on the pitch,
scoring quite often in the early part of the season. Younger players
are coming into the team and making their mark, and our league
form continues to be strong. Rangers, having been obliterated by us
during the 2003/04 season, have regrouped as expected and are
strong again. The race for the title will be head to head.

At home, we receive bad news. Geraldine had been having
chemotherapy treatment for cancer that looked to have been
successful, but test results now say otherwise. Geraldine's doctor,
Professor Linch, tells us that there is an experimental stem-cell
treatment. It is fraught with difficulty but it is Geraldine's best
chance – actually, her only chance. She needs a blood match but
one of her sisters, Kathleen Ann, has that match, and she will do
anything she can to help. All of this takes time to organize, and
the treatment is scheduled for late 2005.

In September 2004, Brian Clough dies. While I'm aware that
he has had a few health problems in recent times, the news still
comes as a shock, probably because I thought Brian Clough was
immortal. It is sad to realize that this extraordinary football manager will no longer be in our midst, popping up now and again,
even in retirement, with some classic vignettes of footballing life.

The following month I hear from Barbara Clough, Brian's wife. She and her family would like me to give one of the three speeches paying tribute to her husband at his memorial service. This remains one of the biggest honours of my life. As I prepare, I think about his first-ever day at Forest; his lambasting of me one Friday evening in a game at York City; the praise he gave me in the European Cup final in Madrid; and the incredible journey he took Nottingham Forest on, and which it was a privilege to be a part of.

The end of Celtic's 2004/05 season is climactic. We need to win the last game of the league season at Motherwell – if we can do that, the Scottish Premier League title will be ours. With just a few moments to go, we are leading 1–0. We should be out of sight in this game. But a combination of great goalkeeping by them and bad finishing by us still allows Motherwell a chance to get something from the game. They take it and score. Rangers win against Hibernian, pipping us for the championship. Defeat today is raw and painful and we are left to rue the afternoon.

A few days later, I announce that I will be leaving Celtic Park after the weekend's cup final against Dundee United at Hampden Park. If not for my wife's health problems, I would not be leaving the club – well, at least not of my own volition. I have had the most enthralling time managing this institution called Celtic Football Club; and I believe I have restored the pride and passion that had disappeared, or rather remained dormant, for much of its previous decade. At least, that's what the Celtic fans tell me.

But Celtic, in return, has given me so much. Had Dermot Desmond passed me over for one of the other candidates, I would never have had such an opportunity, and I am so grateful to him for that chance. Geraldine tells me that her time in Glasgow was simply magnificent and that this fabled city is rooted in her bones.

We beat Dundee United to lift the Scottish Cup. My last-ever game as manager of Celtic. It's a poignant end to a resplendent time in our lives.

12

A RETURN TO THE MIDLANDS

The June afternoon sunshine pours through the patio doors, lending a languorous warmth to the refined lounge in which I am sitting. The house in Four Oaks, Sutton Coldfield belongs to Doug Ellis, owner of Aston Villa Football Club. I am in the company of Steve Kind, Doug's operating officer. I know Steve from my time at Leicester City. He had a somewhat similar role at Filbert Street some years ago. We are sipping tea, waiting for Doug's appearance. A second cup has been poured.

Within ten minutes the octogenarian enters the room and I am somewhat taken aback. He is dressed in a pressed white tennis outfit, with shorts displaying a pair of legs that a stork might be embarrassed to own. A tennis racket is in a firm grip as he practises imaginary backhands. A visitor might form the impression that he has been playing a big game, but more likely, judging by the lack of sweat on his face, he is just about to play. I do not know Mr Ellis at all but his legend, much of it self-proclaimed, is widely familiar in the footballing world.

I also do not want to lose the opportunity to manage Aston Villa so early in the conversation, but I cannot resist a little jibe. 'Is Roger Federer in the bathroom?' I ask.

He gives me a reproachful look but passes no comment. In football parlance, it's a bad back pass by me. I'm hoping it's not an own goal. A number of days have elapsed since he removed David O'Leary from office. He is looking for a new manager and he's conducting this interview in his splendid abode, fifteen minutes' drive from Villa's training ground.

My wife, Geraldine, is feeling better by the day since her stem-cell treatment the previous November and I want to get back to work at club level. Doug starts to talk. And talk. He is aware of my interview for the England manager's job a few weeks earlier and asks how it went. I don't get three sentences in before Doug interjects and continues his monologue. Within fifteen minutes I determine that the man is rather full of his own ideas.

He tells me that, among a number of exceptional firsts during his life, he invented the bicycle kick in soccer. I'm thinking that I might have seen an archive photograph of David Jack performing such a feat at Wembley's first FA Cup final in 1923, a year before the eighty-two-year-old Doug was born, but I keep that fact to myself. In fact, maybe because I am, if not totally transfixed by, at least very attentive to these immodest ramblings, I am offered the job of managing the monumentally historic Aston Villa. I think back to the legendary European Cup final victory in 1982 and the immortal words from Brian Moore for his ITV commentary: 'There's a good ball played in for Tony Morley. Oh, it must be and it is! Peter Withe!' That's where I would want to be with this iconic club.

Doug says that there is a bid of £4 million from Portsmouth for Gareth Barry.

'Does Gareth know about this offer?' I ask, rather naïvely.

'Yes, and he wants to go,' says Doug. Seemingly last season was the final straw for the player.

'Whatever Aston Villa do, you must keep Gareth Barry,' I say, taken aback. 'You haven't accepted Portsmouth's offer yet, have you?'

'We're quite close,' says Doug. I pause.

'Selling Gareth Barry would be a bitter blow for the fans and for the club's chances in general. Selling him for £4 million would be absurd,' I pipe up, having composed myself.

Despite his apparel, Mr Ellis – or Deadly Doug, the sobriquet that the great Jimmy Greaves once gave him – is nobody's fool. He has ruled over Villa Park for more than twenty years, many fans would say with a rod of iron, and he is now in his second spell at the club. He has a reputation of being unwilling to let managers manage, which may explain the number of comings and goings within the last two decades. Last season, in particular, has been disappointing, with Villa avoiding relegation from the Premier League by the skin of their teeth.

The fans are in uproar, inveighing against the beleaguered chairman with a staunch refusal to renew season tickets, which at this time of year are at an all-time low. There is talk of him selling the club to interested parties, hardly a new topic at Villa Park these last few years. But it does seem that the chairman is now willing to sell, as long as (in his words) the new owner promises to take great care to enhance what he has built. There are a number of consortia with serious interest, according to reports, but in truth only one contender is in a position to buy the club.

Doug tells me that Randy Lerner, an American who currently owns NFL stalwarts the Cleveland Browns, has been the most impressive of the bidding parties. Lerner is who Doug would like to succeed him as the new owner of Aston Villa.

A football club manager is never more vulnerable than when a club has been taken over. Understandably, new owners have their own ideas, their own visions and their own people in mind. Before I accept the job at Villa, I need to speak to Mr Lerner. I want to know if, should he succeed in buying the club, he will still want me to be its manager. Thankfully, I get the chance and we meet in London.

'You do what you think is best for you,' Randy says, 'but rest assured, if I do get to buy the club and you are the manager, whether that is in two weeks, two months or at Christmas, I will not be wanting to make a change. I think I'm the only one who doesn't need a consortium and if Doug and I can agree – and we still have some way to go – I want to own Aston Villa Football

Club. The history of the club, where it's positioned and what it stands for remind me so much of the Cleveland Browns.'

I sign for Aston Villa fifteen days before the start of the season and later that afternoon I hold a press conference as the new manager. I am well received by the fans, who are naturally looking for an improvement on last season's near-fatal plunge down the Premier League. The following morning, I travel over to join the squad at their preseason training camp in Germany, in enough time to introduce myself and catch the afternoon's match.

Although it's only a preseason game – and these games can be misleading – it's not too difficult to see why the team struggled last season. Gareth Barry is here in body, if not in spirit. He has been at the club for a long time now, a firm favourite with the supporters. An FA Cup final visit to Wembley six years ago, losing to Chelsea, was as good as it got for this talented player and he has dropped out of the international reckoning, making him rather unsettled just now.

Portsmouth and Tottenham Hotspur have shown interest in Gareth, the former club tabling their £4 million bid. I think he has his mind set on a move to the South Coast club. Trying to convince Barry to stay is my main objective over the next few days. The afternoon's performance convinces me that we need to keep him, otherwise we will be in trouble again in the coming months. Players like Lee Hendrie and Kevin Phillips are towards the end of their careers, despite being terrific players.

I have a chat with Gareth just after lunch on my second day in camp. He's prepared to listen to what I have to say, my plans for the club, the real possibility of a new owner who wants to make Villa big again.

'How long is it since you were last in an England squad?' I ask him.

'About three years,' he answers.

'I promise you, regardless of the team's progress in the upcoming months, you will not only be our main man but you will also be back in that England squad before the end of this coming season.'

At least I've given him something to think about. I also mention that if things don't work out the way I hope they will, the club won't stand in his way at the end of the season. Thankfully, a few days later he confirms that he will stay at Villa Park and see how it goes. It's a terrific boost with the season about to start.

The opening day of the 2006/07 season comes up on me much too quickly to bring any new players to the club, and I have had less than a fortnight to prepare my team. Of all places I would rather not be, it is the Emirates Stadium. We will, in some little way, make history, being the first visiting team to play Arsenal in a Premier League match at their brand new home. Personally I wish the Gunners had been able to redesign Highbury but there's no stopping progress, I suppose.

Arsenal's new home houses 60,000 people who are anticipating an easy victory against a team that just managed to stay up last season. The Gunners' last competitive match in May was the Champions League final in Paris against Barcelona. They may have lost, but even so it's not a bad starting point for their next hundred years in a brand spanking new state-of-the-art stadium.

We repel customary early Arsenal pressure and even have the temerity to take the lead. Olof Mellberg becomes the first-ever scorer of a Premier League goal at the Emirates. It's a long afternoon after that, with Arsenal swarming all over us. But we resist, showing a strong mindset and a willingness to help a teammate when he's in trouble – traits that I want my team to have in abundance if we're to have any hopes of being successful. I hope to improve the squad as time goes on but . . . It's a healthy start.

As we start to tire in the second half, we get ragged. When we do get the ball we cannot keep it long enough to build attacks. Despite this, Arsenal have not been able to penetrate us and we are still holding onto that precious lead as time ticks away. Then it happens. With six or seven minutes left in the game, the Brazilian Gilberto Silva scores for Arsenal. The noise in the stadium is absolutely deafening, the crowd well aware that there is still time for a winning goal. I signal to the bench for Martin Laursen to get ready quickly. Martin is a centre half from Denmark who played exceptionally well for AC Milan a few seasons ago, but who has been plagued with injuries since his transfer to Aston Villa. Indeed, if truth be known, injury and Martin Laursen have been joined together his whole career.

A fortnight ago I met Martin for the first time in the training camp. He was actually running with a profound limp. He told me that he would be OK this season. He needed a little more time and would not be able to play two games a week for a little while, but he would be able to manage one game a week while his knee got stronger with rehabilitation.

'Are you sure, Martin?' I queried. 'If you don't mind me saying, your limp suggests you might not manage one game a year.'

'Don't worry, my limp will go away soon and I'll be fine,' he replied.

'I'll take your word for it,' I said, but I was not totally convinced.

I have little choice today, anyway. Arsenal, in their quest for the winning goal, are forsaking their passing game and going more directly into our penalty area. Martin, who will prove to be a colossus for us in the next few seasons, throws off his tracksuit and enters the fray.

I still believe he's running with that limp, but he's bursting with desire and enthusiasm as he takes his place at the heart of our defence. During the next few minutes he heads two dangerous crosses away from our goal in quick succession, disregarding his own safety in doing so. He gives us a lift and we see the game through to the end. We have a draw against the mighty Arsenal, on their own pitch, with a team that has been hastily put together in the last seven days. I receive a cursory handshake from Arsène Wenger at the end – a common occurrence over the next few seasons – but it bothers me not one jot.

We have a point on the board, a precious away point, and at the Emirates of all places. There are naturally jubilant scenes in our dressing room. In the immediate aftermath, I have just about completed the post-match talk to the players when Doug Ellis walks into the room. I haven't invited him. This is my territory, not his. But I stop myself from saying anything to him. We don't know each other very well; this may be something he routinely does, and has done for years with other managers. We've just earned a brilliant point today and he may not be the owner of the club in a few weeks' time.

He comes over and congratulates me. As he turns away, he asks to see me on Monday after training.

'No problem, Mr Chairman. I'll be there.'

It's Monday afternoon in Doug's office. We discuss the merits of the game and I say I think Gareth Barry is going to stay, at least for the season. I offer him my first impressions of the team, which may well change when I get to know the players a little better. But he stops me in my tracks.

'Why did you put Martin Laursen on with only a few minutes to go on Saturday?'

I am more than a little flustered. Doug's manner suggests that I shouldn't have made such a substitution.

'What did you say, Mr Chairman?' I ask as if I hadn't heard him correctly. He repeats himself.

More than a little perturbed, I say, 'I put Martin Laursen on because we were under severe pressure, which you yourself could see from the director's box, and because Arsenal were going long in the last few minutes of the game. Martin actually got two important headers to clear danger.'

His reply is unexpected.

'It's just that Laursen is on £3,000 an appearance, and he gets that even for those couple of minutes.'

I am totally flabbergasted. So that's what was bugging Doug in the dressing room after the game, and all weekend. He will have to pay Martin the appearance money for just five or six minutes' work.

'Well, Mr Ellis. I don't think about appearance fees when I'm managing a team on match days. I try to utilize what I have at my disposal, that's all. I've been here for less than a fortnight. I have no idea yet about wages, appearance fees and bonuses for play-ers. Anyway, it's your fault! You gave Martin the contract,' I say facetiously, with a wry smile. I think I detect the tiniest grin on Doug's face.

I finish the tea given to me and remind him that we have a big game on Wednesday night against Reading. 'I might need Martin again, if that's OK with you, Mr Chairman?'

I walk out the door and don't hear the reply, even if there is one.

We are the last Premier League team to be beaten this season, taking fifteen points from the first nine games before losing at Anfield. I am back together with John Robertson and Steve Wal-ford. Jim Henry, my fitness coach at Celtic, also travels south to join me and in a few weeks Seamus McDonagh will become my goalkeeping coach. We create a support network for each other. All managers know the importance of strong backroom staff and in these lads around me I feel as if I have an unbreakable bond.

By now Randy Lerner has bought the club, and I am pleased that he has done so. Villa's training facilities need a complete overhaul. Doug Ellis had started to do some work on them, but left it for the incoming owner to do as he saw fit; Randy has ambitions there and also plans to refurbish parts of the famous Holte End at Villa Park, so that the fans can have a little more comfort there on match days. He is also aware that the first-team squad needs addressing and is instrumental in the purchase of Stiliyan Petrov from Celtic for £6 million. A poor run in December gives us a reality check, and by the time the transfer market deadline is reached in late January we have also added Ashley Young.

At £8 million, with add-ons going up to £9.2 million, it seems a lot of money for a lad just out of his teens. Bringing such a young boy into a team that hasn't quite found its feet is a slight concern. He will have to play with a weighty price tag round his shoulders. But I've seen enough of Ashley at Watford to know that even with a modest start, he will have the character to see over the horizon and light up the park in seasons to come. Randy Lerner backs my judgement and I am grateful to him.

John Carew, Shaun Maloney and Phil Bardsley are also added to our squad. Carew is playing at Lyon under Gérard Houllier. Gérard wants to sign Milan Baroš from us, and we decide a swap deal is the easiest outcome. Shaun is out of contract at Celtic come the end of the season but for £1 million to Celtic, I think we should do the deal now. Randy gives me the go-ahead. I also know a lot about Carew. He played exceptionally well for Valencia against Celtic a few seasons ago in the UEFA Cup, and since Baroš hasn't really hit it off at Villa Park, this will be a good swap for us.

John Carew will become a very popular figure with the fans and in the dressing room over the course of the next few seasons and mostly for good reason. When on song he is majestic. So powerful is he that most defenders cannot dislodge him. Keeping John motivated for a full season becomes a pleasant chore, and his more than occasional love of the bright lights in London is fine so long as his performances for the club remain at their peak.

As a loving son he keeps in constant touch with his beloved mother back home in Norway, who sometimes makes health decisions on behalf of John from afar. The lady herself might detect a sore throat in his voice during a phone call and, as any good mother would, advise John that he shouldn't play at the weekend. Sometimes John may need a little convincing from our doctor that he is actually perfectly all right and that his services are needed for our trip to the City of Manchester Stadium. John not only takes a couple of paracetamol, but single-handedly takes Manchester City apart a few days later.

With the January transfer window closed, I am refreshed by these four additions. We let other players out of the building and a nine-match unbeaten run to end the season gives me zest for next year's assault on trying to bring European football back to Villa Park. It has been a good year for young Gabby Agbonlahor. During the previous season Villa sent him out on loan to a number of clubs and it must have been a disappointment to him that his loans were not extended. But since being in my starting line-up for our first game at the Emirates, playing wide in a three-man forward attack, he has improved beyond recognition. He is exceptionally quick and will need to improve his first touch, but as he gets physically stronger he develops as a footballer. He moves to centre forward and it becomes a role he will fill with success.

Randy is making a home for himself, too – literally. A few miles from our training camp he is busy building and refurbishing a house that he intends to make his English home, with thoughts of school for his children. As for me, I am reasonably pleased with the season, although eleventh is the lowest I've finished in my time in the Premier League, having had four consecutive top ten finishes with Leicester City. The Aston Villa fans have turned out in mightily big numbers and I believe they see progress in the offing. Randy tells me that we will push strongly next season to take the next step.

The summer of 2007 is busy for me at Villa Park. A number of players leave the club: Gavin McCann goes to Bolton, Aaron Hughes and Steven Davis to Fulham, and Liam Ridgewell to Birmingham City, for a combined total of £8 million – promptly reinvested in the acquisition of Nigel Reo-Coker from West Ham United. My belief is that Nigel will add that strength and dynamism in midfield that I think we are lacking just now.

Stiliyan Petrov, after an exceptionally bright start, has faded somewhat and is struggling for his proper form. I see him in the canteen one day, fetching himself a coffee after doing some extra fitness work in the gym supervised by Jim Henry. I approach him, give him a big hug and say, 'You handsome bastard' – and he is. Stiliyan would probably have been on the cover of *GQ* if he hadn't chosen this other profession.

I join him with a coffee and we have an honest conversation. I tell him that I think he may not recover his form at Villa Park and that a move away might refresh him. Of course, this would be a blow to both of us, since he was my first signing last season and one that I placed so much faith in. After all, we have had so many shared successes at Celtic. He agrees that it's been tough for him but says that given another chance he will not only fight his way back into the team but will be a big success. I acquiesce and say, 'OK, let's see how it goes.'

He walks towards the door, opens it and looks back. In his soft Bulgarian accent he says, 'You wait and see, gaffer. You wait and see.' He is as good as his word and he will become an integral member of the Villa team and figure in the success that follows.

A couple of friendly games abroad – one in Toronto, the other in Columbus, Ohio – gives the owner an opportunity to bring me and the team to watch the Cleveland Browns prepare for the new season in the NFL. I really enjoy this experience, being a massive NFL fan, and as a coach I am intrigued by the strategy of the game. I get an opportunity to converse with my opposite number at the Browns. Randy looks at home in this environment, and the Browns players either embrace him or shake him warmly by the hand when he approaches the group just before they start to exercise. I get to see the 'war room' where the general manager works. A list of potential recruits lines the walls of this workhouse. Randy thinks we should have a similar room at Bodymoor Heath, Aston Villa's training ground, and there is certainly no disagreement from me. In fact, Ian Storey-Moore, our chief scout, could do with a larger office at the Heath.

This will also be good news for our bright young data analyst, Patrick Riley, who I inherited when I first came to Villa Park. Alert and clever Paddy, as I know him, will go on to push boundaries in later days. Just now he will be delighted to get a bigger room in which to work.

Back on the other side of the Atlantic, Gary Cahill, a young centre half, wants to play regular first-team football. Gary has already written his name in Villa folklore by scoring a wonderful goal against Birmingham City the season before last, effectively keeping Villa in the top flight and at the same time condemning the enemy to relegation. I do not think that at this stage of his fledgling career he can deal with ten or fifteen consecutive Premier League games. So he joins Sheffield United on loan, and in January 2008 Bolton Wanderers make an offer of £4 million and add-ons, which we will accept. Gary will spend four years at Bolton, later moving to Chelsea and winning the Champions League with the club in 2012.

A new crest on our shirts featuring a star to represent the European Cup win in 1982 is revealed for the 2007/08 season, but it does not bring us any immediate fortune. In the opening game of the season at Villa Park, we lose to a last-minute Liverpool free kick in front of almost 43,000 fans. I sign Zat Knight from Fulham for £3 million and on his debut we beat Chelsea 2–0 at Villa Park. Zat scores the important first goal with a powerful header just after half-time and Agbonlahor completes the scoring some minutes later. This will be the last Premier League match that José Mourinho presides over in his first spell as manager of Chelsea.

November 2007 is a splendid month for the team. A brilliant win over Birmingham City at St Andrew's Stadium falls in the middle of four successive Premier League victories, but just when we look to have matters well in hand, December sees us lose the momentum with two points from four games. A brilliant 4–4 draw with Chelsea at Stamford Bridge on Boxing Day gets us back on track.

Randy is in fine spirits. I am in contact with him by phone when he is in America, and when he travels over to England the staff at Villa Park are always glad to see him. The refurbishment work at both Bodymoor Heath and Villa Park have been well received by players and fans alike.

Two losses in seventeen games refreshes our hopes of European football next season at Villa Park, only for us to slip up again with a trio of defeats. But we stand our ground and surge back for more with a 4–0 win over Bolton Wanderers, a 6–0 hammering of Derby County and a fantastic 5–1 demolition of Birmingham City at Villa Park.

Led splendidly by Gareth Barry, Aston Villa are back among the footballing elite. We finish sixth in the 2007/08 season with an exhilarating brand of counter-attacking football, scoring seventy-one goals from the thirty-eight matches. Only Manchester United with eighty and Arsenal with seventy-four have scored more goals than we have, and they finish first and second respectively in the Premier League.

We've qualified for the Intertoto Cup, a gateway to the UEFA Cup. This of course means a short summer break and a very early start to the season. I have been at the club for almost two years and I am enjoying every minute of it. Our sixth-place finish has given rise to optimism that we can gatecrash the top four and grab a Champions League spot. That is my ambition for this club. The little star on the crest is a constant reminder of that glorious evening in Rotterdam in 1982.

The European Championship is being held in Austria and Switzerland and I have been asked to do some punditry on television, something that has become a regular feature when the major competitions come round biannually. Around this time, I am alerted to a tabloid article which has appeared that morning back in England. Gareth Barry has done a piece with a journalist essentially stating that I should be not in Austria but back at home, conducting a move he wants to make to Liverpool.

Some weeks earlier, on my way to a reserve game at Villa Park, I answered a call. It was Rafa Benítez, the Liverpool manager. He wanted to take Gareth to Anfield. Within seconds he started to mention a few players that we could have in exchange.

'Hold on, Rafa,' I said. 'Just a minute, you're going too fast. Firstly, I don't want to sell Gareth Barry. Secondly, I will inform Mr Lerner about this conversation. I think he will have something to say about it all. And I actually may not want any of the players you have just mentioned.'

That's how things started, but Gareth's criticism in this article has stung like hell. I phone him immediately. He hasn't got the club's permission to do the article and it isn't the way he's going to force a move to Liverpool. I speak to Randy, who is more than upset with how this is all panning out. We agree that if Barry wants to leave, Liverpool will have to meet our asking fee. Randy is very strong on this issue. It's £10 million, take it or leave it. Liverpool's offer is nowhere near acceptable. Randy is not budging. Liverpool's next offer is still not acceptable. Randy is still not budging: £10 million. Take it or leave it.

Liverpool make a final offer of £8 million and say they cannot go any higher. Randy is immovable and Liverpool end their interest in a now very disgruntled player. However, a few days later Robbie Keane leaves White Hart Lane bound for Anfield. The fee is a reported £20 million. Now, at least, Gareth's ire is aimed at Liverpool. He is disappointed with them for not coming up with the extra £2 million, but then spending £20 million on another player only days later. Benítez throws a few barbs in my direction in the media and gets his strike in first.

I am disappointed with the whole saga. Gareth doesn't need to go to a newspaper to sort his future out. He's been superb in his last two seasons under me for Villa, and he's back in the England squad, which is what I promised when I first met him. Maybe Randy would have taken a softer attitude to the transfer if a different approach had been adopted. But he has been steadfast both in his dealings with Liverpool and in his support of me. He knows what type of effect this solidarity has on a dressing room. Players will see that they cannot easily bypass the manager and converse with the chairman without being sent back down the line again.

I've taken the whole affair much too personally. You think you have built a special rapport with some special players, only to find out it's not really that special at all. I'm afraid that's the way I've managed. The lesson is here to be learned. Unfortunately, I never do. A similar scenario will arise with another player whom I put into that special category. This particular saga will have more serious consequences, and James Milner's proposed transfer to Manchester City in two years' time will hasten my departure from one of the all-time great clubs in English football.

By being joint winners of the Intertoto Cup, we qualify for the group stages of the UEFA Cup. These Thursday evening games in Europe will tax our resources to the limit and mean that we will play Premier League games the following Sunday. Psychologically, Thursday/Sunday games feel totally different to Wednesday/Saturday matches, even though it's the same recovery time. Your preparation time seems different, and sometimes by playing Sunday football you feel you're playing catch-up football from the previous day.

I have had these 'catch-up' experiences with Celtic for some years so I know there's a different mindset required for the continual Thursday/Sunday programme. We will be playing European football up until Christmas at least, so it's just something to which we will have to adapt. However, last season's aim to be back in European football has been achieved and these forthcoming games should be enjoyable experiences.

My aim this season is to try to break into the top four and secure a Champions League position. This will take an almighty effort from everyone involved with the club but I emphasize to the players right from the start that this target is worth going for. There is universal approval of this aspiration in the dressing room and our ambition pays off with an explosive start to the season. We score four goals to beat Manchester City at Villa Park, Gabby Agbonlahor running riot with a hat-trick. Barry settles down to play some of the best football he has ever produced in an Aston Villa shirt.

A few weeks before Christmas we play Manchester United. Alex Ferguson visits our coaches' room after the game to have a chat, as has always been his custom. He will win the Premier League by May next year and contest the Champions League final, only to lose to Barcelona. He asks when our Intertoto games began.

'About the third week in July,' I say, 'if memory serves me.'

'It's a long time to be playing competitive football. You don't change the team too often,' he adds.

'Well, as you know yourself, you go to the wall with the players you trust.'

'I know,' he answers, 'but burn-out is something you'll have to look out for.'

Our brilliant run of sixteen domestic matches without defeat stretches from mid-November to the beginning of February 2009. We are also making significant progress in the FA Cup, a competition I hold in the highest regard, especially as the trophy has so far eluded me both in my playing and managerial career. We are drawn against Everton at Goodison Park for a fifth-round tie. I have, not unexpectedly, a few injury concerns and Gareth Barry is suspended. But I go with as strong a side as I can muster, even though the bench contains a number of very young players. Watching this cut-throat cup tie from the dugout, with the possibility of getting on the pitch, is an experience that will stand them in great stead as their careers progress.

We lose a pulsating cup match 3–1; Everton will go to the final at Wembley only to lose to Chelsea. But today, on the bus back to the Midlands from Liverpool, I am reflective. Disappointment and losing in this iconic competition has to be tempered by our position in the Premier League. We sit in third, a few points ahead of Arsenal.

In three days we will play a home tie against CSKA Moscow

in the last thirty-two of the UEFA Cup. I speak to Randy. My priority is the top four. We will go as strong as we can at Villa Park and then take stock after that. We can only manage a draw in the tie. The second leg in Moscow will be played on an icy artificial pitch. Some of the players have been carrying knocks, bruises and tightness in the last few weeks. Some of them are getting tired, having hardly missed any games since July. I am reminded of Sir Alex's words a couple of months ago.

Before we go there, Chelsea await. Gus Hiddink is the Stamford Bridge replacement for the recently sacked Luiz Felipe Scolari. The team respond to the new voice in the dressing room and play more strongly today than they have done in weeks. I had been hoping that the expected change of manager would not take place until after this game, but it isn't to be. After they take the lead Ashley Young powers a terrific free kick against their bar, nearly bringing about an equalizer, but the fates are against us and we concede ground in the race for the top four. With Manchester United, Liverpool and now Chelsea in the top three positions, it is probably that enticing fourth spot that Arsenal and ourselves are contesting.

We travel to Moscow, late February. The weather is predictably freezing. Randy has travelled over to the game as well but is staying in a different hotel from the main party. I go over to see him and inform him of my intention to rest some of the players tonight. He's already guessing what's on my mind, since he is aware that a few have not made the trip. If Milner, Young or Petrov break down on this icy surface with the strains they have told the physiotherapist about, then our chances of taking that fourth position in the Premier League will recede. There will still be many senior players in the team.

I leave Randy's hotel not sure what he really feels about my decision. But it is certainly not without precedent. Tottenham Hotspur are also in the UEFA Cup with a two-legged tie against Shakhtar Donetsk. Their manager, Harry Redknapp, states publicly that his priority is keeping Spurs in the Premier League and that he has no problem playing an under-strength team against the Ukrainian side. This seems to attract universal approval. Tottenham lose the tie.

I make the call entirely believing in what I'm doing. With Brad Guzan in goal, Luke Young, Curtis Davies, Zat Knight and once-capped England international Nicky Shorey at left back, it looks a decent starting point. Three of those five played against Everton in the FA Cup match, as did midfielders Steve Sidwell and Craig Gardner. I'm not sure they would like to be called 'second string', as the media will refer to them in the next few days. Marc Albrighton and Barry Bannan will make their debuts, and Nathan Delfouneso, a young player with immense talent, will start up front. Albrighton will become a very good player, and a major force in Leicester City's Premier League title-winning season in 2015/16.

We lose the game to two second-half goals and so go out of the competition. But I do not expect the reaction to our defeat that follows. Given our league position this season, I think that the majority of Aston Villa fans would gladly place the UEFA Cup to one side and attempt over the last dozen games to break into the top four, thus acquiring a Champions League position for next year. But seemingly not, if the press reports are anything to go by. Vitriol oozes from every newssheet and given the reaction, it is as if I played an under-12 side at the Luzhniki Stadium.

We must win at home to Stoke City at the weekend in vindication for the team selection in Moscow. The players left at home feel fresher and we blitz Stoke early on in the game, but we cannot get that breakthrough goal. Eventually the Stoke dam breaks and Petrov scores. Carew adds a second and we are in cruise control. This is our forty-fourth game of the season – three more than we played last year, and still with a quarter of the season's games left to play. Maybe we think that Stoke, having a tough time at the other end of the table, have nothing more to offer.

But they do, and they score two in the last three minutes. We've dropped two valuable points at the end of the game. The stadium is stunned, as I am myself. It's a devastating blow and the dressing room is like a mortuary.

We end up finishing sixth, with two more points than the previous season, and European football awaits again for next year, if not in the competition we would desire. It's another incredible year and we have kept pace with the elite. Of course, in an ideal world we would have finished fourth, but Alex Ferguson was right. The fifty-five-game season did catch up with us. Maybe we might learn from it going forward. Next season we will compete again in Europe, although the UEFA Cup takes on a new format and is renamed the UEFA Europa League.

It is finally Gareth Barry's time to leave Aston Villa, and he goes to Manchester City for £12 million in June 2009. He's been able to put aside the whole Liverpool transfer saga, concentrating on matters on the field, and has played brilliantly over the season. He has been a great servant to the club over the years and my own belief is that his best form has been during these past few seasons. Unlike last time, he leaves with everyone's blessing. He will be sorely missed and we need a replacement for him.

Randy has made Paul Faulkner CEO of the club. He and I will work closely together. Randy and Paul go back some considerable time and Paul was previously Chief Operating Officer; but now he is in a completely different role, one where every aspect of football stares at you every single day and every minute of that day.

We have a preseason competition in Malaga, the Peace Cup, which we win. The prize money, quite sizeable, will be used for player acquisitions, but Randy is also funding other transfer targets. Last season's frustration at not quite making Champions League football is still bothering both of us, but there's spirit enough to think that the top four is achievable despite the loss of Barry. I tell Randy that players like Sidwell and Reo-Coker will have to come to the fore this season if we are to thrive without Barry.

Randy asks me my thoughts on the youth team coming through. I say that I wouldn't have contemplated fielding Bannan, Albrighton and Delfouneso in Moscow if I didn't think they had potential to be first-team players. And the young centre half Ciaran Clark has a chance – but all of these players are at least a season away from first-team football and would be little help this year if we are thinking about top six again, and top four if possible.

Paul Faulkner tells Randy that in his opinion, the young lads are ready now. I had hoped that Randy would prioritize my views on footballing matters, but they may think that I want to delve further into the transfer market rather than giving these young players their chance. Paul is possibly basing his judgement on the Peace Cup back in July, essentially a glorified set of friendly games. Some of the young players did exceptionally well but friendlies are indeed just that: friendlies.

We start the season poorly. Wigan come to Villa Park and win 2–0. Then we travel to Rapid Vienna and lose the first leg of our Europa League tie. We will go out of the competition on away goals just a fortnight later, so the pressure is on almost immediately. A massive victory at Anfield on Monday evening addresses the loss against Wigan, but with Curtis Davies needing an operation, I need replacements before the August transfer window closes.

I tell Randy that James Collins and Richard Dunne will cost £5 million each. He tells me that I can have one but not the two. I tell him this is incredibly important and we need both of them now. If we can do this, I will recoup £10 million in the January transfer window by selling, but right now we have no time to lose. Although Ciaran Clark played at centre back against Fulham and did well enough last week, he's not ready yet. Players like Milner and Young are valuable assets and if they eventually leave the club they will be worth at least double the price we paid for them.

It is with much reluctance that Randy agrees to do both transfers. We manage to complete Richard Dunne's prolonged discussions with his former club, Manchester City, and he becomes an Aston Villa player, transfer deadline having almost elapsed. We travel to St Andrew's immediately after the international break and both players are in the team that triumphs over Birmingham City, Gabby Agbonlahor sending the travelling Villa fans into ecstasy with a late winning goal.

With just two league defeats in seventeen games, we are right back on course. And our League Cup run is beginning to blossom. A quarter-final victory away to Portsmouth in December takes us into a two-leg semi-final against Blackburn Rovers, to be played in January 2010. This is something that the club has not budgeted for, and the TV revenues are quite significant. If we can make it to Wembley, not only will this be a day for the supporters to savour but it will help swell the coffers. I share my thoughts with Randy but he isn't having it. I just want him to be a bit more enthusiastic about our league position and a possible Wembley appearance, if we can overcome Blackburn Rovers. But he is still thinking about our early-season transfers and my agreement to recoup the money.

We play very well to win the first leg of the League Cup tie at Ewood Park, with James Milner scoring the only goal. We are obviously in a strong position with the return leg being at home. However, within minutes of the start of the match, Blackburn Rovers have scored twice and are winning on the away goals rule. An evening I was hoping would be one of great celebration is now provoking nervous tension throughout Villa Park.

Sam Allardyce, Blackburn's manager at the time, will later write in his autobiography that I paid too much for his left back, Stephen Warnock. Well, if ever a lad repaid a large chunk of his fee, Stephen Warnock does just that when we need it the most. He comes from nowhere to smash home the equalizing goal in the tie and re-energize the famous Holte End into a war cry, carrying us into a frenzy that I know will take us through. We end up winning a thrilling game 6–4 on an unforgettable night at Villa Park. This is exactly what the stadium can do when we are at one with each other.

We will go to Wembley – and Warnock, who will travel with the England squad for the World Cup finals in June, takes deserved plaudits for his game-changing goal. I am desperately hoping that all this will reinvigorate the owner of the football club. The following night after our dramatic semi-final, Randy Lerner invites all heads of department to a dinner in a Birmingham city centre restaurant to celebrate reaching the final. And indeed the evening starts off in ebullient mood, despite rumbling tension between Randy and myself over the £10 million recoupment situation.

During the latter part of the evening, he thanks everyone for their commitment and enthusiasm and sits down. He leans over to me and says that the catering lady has done a wonderful job at Villa Park. And indeed she has – last night there was not an empty table in any of the lounges, although of course it was semi-final night with a full house to boot. But Randy says it in a manner that suggests it was she, not James Milner nor Stephen Warnock, who scored the vital goals. I should let this comment pass, but I cannot let it lie. I say to Randy that there is no question she is doing a wonderful job and the hospitality at Villa Park is riding high just now, but it's the football results that drive the business. When there is a downturn in results it will be reflected in the number of unsold covers in hospitality, regardless of all the wonderful catering on offer.

Randy is not amused with my comment. Still, despite this little tête-à-tête and the mental reminder that I am seen as a head of department, I enjoy the night. We are in the final of the League Cup and we can win at Wembley, even though our opponents are Manchester United.

I have a big decision to make. Brad Guzan, a young American goalkeeper, has been at the football club for a while now. Seamus McDonagh and I persevered in getting him over to Aston Villa when he was first refused a work permit, and he has repaid us all in full with some fantastic performances during this League Cup run. In fact, we wouldn't be here today if not for his magnificent goalkeeping at Sunderland in an earlier round. But in the two semi-final games against Blackburn he was far from at his best.

Today, less than two hours before we take on Manchester United at Wembley, I have to tell him that I'm going to play our experienced goalkeeper Brad Friedel instead of him. Had this game taken place immediately after Guzan's heroics at the Stadium of Light, then he would have been an automatic choice. But I believe that today, Brad Friedel's expertise and experience will be invaluable to us; and so I tell young Guzan that he won't be starting in the game he's probably dreamed of since arriving at Villa Park.

Within minutes of the game starting, a controversial incident happens. Gabby Agbonlahor breaks free inside the penalty box and is through on goal. Nemanja Vidić, the Manchester United centre back, hauls Gabby to the ground. It's a penalty for us and an automatic red card for Vidić. That's the rule. The referee, Phil Dowd, awards a penalty but keeps the red card in his pocket. It's absolutely astonishing – Phil has made up an entirely different set of rules to those he should be adhering to. A neutral viewer watching on a TV screen may not want to watch a Wembley cup final with one team bereft of a player for the next eighty-eight minutes, but the rules are there to be obeyed.

James Milner scores from the spot but Vidić, a top-quality centre back, one of the best in Manchester United's great history, stays on the field unpunished. No one can tell for sure whether Aston Villa would have beaten ten-man Manchester United with Alex Ferguson in charge but we have a lot of pace in our team, with Young, Agbonlahor and Stewart Downing. Downing is an excellent footballer I've signed from Middlesbrough. He is now fully recovered from injury and is showing the class and verve that made me take him to Villa Park. He will prove to be a quality player both for us and later for Liverpool over the next few seasons.

Fate plays a big hand today. United take time to recover, equalize, and then force a second-half winner. I haven't been as angry about a referee's decision in a long, long time. It will have heavy consequences. Victory would have meant a major trophy for Aston Villa. It would have been a big positive step forward and guaranteed us European football next season. Instead, we face massive disappointment.

The Wembley dressing room is deathly quiet. One would not expect anything else from a vanquished football team. My anger at the referee has not subsided and once again I try to confront him, but it's over now and, life-changing or not, I just have to live with it.

There is a reception for the team in a London hotel. Again, there is a downbeat gathering of sullen faces fuming about Dowd's decision now that the incident has been replayed a hundred times. I'm hoping to see Randy there, as I would like to speak to him and his presence would lift morale, but he doesn't come. There can only be one reason, I think to myself: me! I'm the reason he's angry about everything, and has been probably for the whole season. I continue to wonder whether a victory today would have changed his mood, but that is only supposition on my part. Either way, I don't mask my great disappointment that he is absent.

We have another opportunity to go back to Wembley: we are in the quarter-finals of the FA Cup with an away tie at Reading. So there is limited time to mope and moan about what might have been. We come from 2–0 down at half-time to beat Reading 4–2, casting off a dismal first-half performance to put in a devastating goal burst and bring the fans an FA Cup semi-final.

But our quest for silverware is not to be. Chelsea beat us on their way to winning the trophy and will also go on to win the Premier League title. As the season approaches its climax, Aston Villa beat Birmingham City to complete the Double over our city rivals. We have sixty-four points on the board with two games left. Manchester City and Tottenham stand ahead of us in the table for that Champions League spot, and Manchester City at the City of Manchester Stadium are next up. We have to win.

Carew gives us an early lead, but two goals in a minute just before half-time put City ahead. We do everything we can but succumb to a last-minute third goal for them, and the race is over. Had we won today and next week at home to Blackburn Rovers, we would have taken a prized fourth position. We have gone so very close again.

We end the season in sixth place, once again playing in Europe next season. We have had an FA Cup semi-final against the eventual winners and a League Cup final appearance at Wembley against Manchester United. Furthermore, we have an improved points total on last year. Once I step back from the disappointments, I will consider it an exceptional year.

After the end of the season, Randy and I meet at his home near the training ground. We both accept that there has been much friction between us and we resolve to put matters right. He still feels that last January's transfer window should have yielded another outgoing permanent transfer along with Craig Gardner. I counter with the League Cup revenue argument, but he tells me that these are totally separate issues. That said, I leave the house feeling a little better, hoping that it has cleared some air at least.

In June, Aston Villa sign a new sponsorship deal with FxPro, a Cyprus-based broker. It is reportedly the biggest in the club's history. At the very same time, news comes through that James Milner wants to go to Manchester City. They have put in a bid in the region of £18 million for him, and he and his agent wish to have a meeting with Randy and myself to talk everything through.

I am bitterly disappointed; Milner's departure will leave a void. He has been magnificent ever since he set foot in Villa Park for a second spell here. I changed his position from wide on the right to centre midfield and he has never looked back, breaking into the England squad for the World Cup in South Africa this very summer. It's going to be very tough to get his wages remotely close to what Manchester City can offer him. I feel exactly the same way as I did a year ago when Gareth Barry was leaving for City. I should take the personal sentiment out of all this, but I find that difficult to do.

Randy asks me if I have any possible replacements in mind. I tell him Scott Parker could be available with a fee of around £7 million. In the meantime, Manchester City up their offer for James to an eventual £24 million.

A couple of days later, Randy speaks to me by phone. He wants to keep James at Villa Park regardless of their offer and says that we'll go and get Scott Parker as well. James will just have to accept that he's not for sale and Scott Parker's coming too, if it can be achieved.

This will be something special. I tell John Robertson about what Randy has said. 'Whoa!' he exclaims. 'That's some news.'

But within a day, Randy has changed his mind. Not only is he accepting Man City's £24 million offer for James, but Scott Parker is also off the agenda. This time, he is adamant about what he's just said. I relay the news to my backroom staff. 'That's some U-turn in twenty-four hours,' remarks Robertson.

Other potential recruits are mentioned, including Stephen Ireland. Stephen proved himself to be a really good footballer a couple of seasons ago but has had a tough time in the last eighteen months, which means there's a good chance he won't get a shirt number at his club. Manchester City want to offload him and probably see an opportunity for Aston Villa to participate in an exchange with James Milner. I mention this to Randy and say that with all this mind, Ireland could be acquired for next to nothing the closer we get to the deadline.

At the beginning of August we are playing Valencia at Villa Park. It's a Friday evening and the season will start in eight days' time; Randy will be in attendance. He phones me to let me know that he has agreed everything with Manchester City. Milner will go there for £24 million and Stephen Ireland will come in exchange, his transfer price being £7 million. I cannot believe it, but Randy is adamant that this deal will go through. I ask to see him after the game and he agrees – but after the match, it turns out he has to leave early.

I tell Paul Faulkner that I'm disappointed not to have seen Randy and I need him to call me tomorrow morning. The phone duly rings. I tell Randy that if he is downsizing I do not have a problem with that, as long as he is the one who will tell the fans. He says he cannot do that just now, and I say that I'll think about everything.

Over the weekend my friend Mick McGuire, former Deputy Chief Executive of the Professional Footballers' Association, tells me about a barrister, Paul Gilroy QC, who also works for the League Managers' Association. I speak to him on the Sunday and we have a lengthy discussion. We agree to meet in the morning the next day in Birmingham. I want to resign.

'Are you sure about this?' Paul asks very early on Monday.

'I am this morning,' I answer. After four years of strong progress, it's become obvious that the owner wants a change of manager.

'Take a deep breath, have another few minutes of quiet reflection and then let me know what you want to do,' Paul responds.

Within half an hour I have left Paul, driven to Bodymoor Heath and handed in my resignation to Aston Villa Football Club.

As far as I am concerned, I have been constructively dismissed. The matter is referred to the Premier League Managers' Arbitration Tribunal. The case goes all the way to a hearing but is resolved as Randy Lerner is being cross-examined by Paul Gilroy QC. It would be breaching confidence to say much more about the legal case – and it would be raking over old coals. All I will say is that I am very pleased with the outcome.

In fairness, I should add that some years after the event I bump into Randy Lerner in a hotel while abroad on holiday. We have a good conversation, and there are no outstanding issues between us.

13

A BOYHOOD DREAM

It's now over a year since I left Villa Park. There is a function in Manchester to celebrate Sir Alex Ferguson's achievements in football and I accept an invitation to attend. The great and the good have gathered here this evening and the guest of honour is on very good form when delivering his thank-you address from the podium.

It has been a fine evening and I'm about to leave when I get a tap on the shoulder. It's Sir Alex. 'Martin, don't stay out of the game too long,' he advises me. 'You get forgotten very quickly.'

Less than a month later, his words ring in my ears as the opportunity arises to manage my boyhood team, Sunderland, when Steve Bruce leaves the club. It is late November 2011. Chairman Niall Quinn phones me to offer me the job, or at least to invite me to speak to the owner, Ellis Short, an American businessman. From an excellent mid-table finish last season, Sunderland's results have declined in recent months.

I agree to meet Ellis at his home in London, and on a cold, dark winter evening I find myself sitting down in his elegant lounge. He outlines the position of the club and where he thinks it should be. Relegation is concerning him greatly. How can you run a business if you're not sure which division you might find yourself in come the next season? I say to him that Randy Lerner also hated relegation for the same reasons, but that's just the nature of the game here.

I would be very interested in becoming the new manager of

Sunderland. However, I'm not totally convinced that he wants me to run his football club, because his financial offer to me is dependent on what he has to pay in compensation to the departing management team. I tell him that any agreement we might reach should not depend on third parties, and he acquiesces.

Because I want to manage the club I supported as a boy and to lead them out of the doldrums into a new dawn, I accept his proposal and we agree that we will sign the forms in due course. After I leave his house I phone Paul Gilroy, who represented me in my Aston Villa tribunal case, to tell him what I have just done. Paul's chuckle indicates that I could have negotiated better terms for myself.

Paul travels north with me to meet Niall Quinn and pore over the contract. We have dinner in a local restaurant. Although the contract is not yet signed, the locals who come over to talk to us at our table assume it's a done deal.

John Robertson will not be coming as my assistant. Our last few months at Villa Park have taken their toll on him and as a result, his love of the game has diminished. This is painful to hear from such a magnificent player for Forest and Scotland. John has always lived for football – in fact, that burning enthusiasm has been a key reason for his brilliance. He has been a superb assistant manager all these years, but I fully accept his reasons. I make my plans without him.

Steve Walford and Seamus McDonagh both want to come. John will be badly missed, but along with Jim Henry, the fitness coach, we are determined to turn the club's fortunes around. Sunday finds me watching from the stands at Molineux as Sunderland lose, now having taken just six points from a possible twenty-seven.

Regardless, I sign the contract and prepare for a home game against Blackburn Rovers on Sunday 11 December. By the time the game kicks off, other results have put Sunderland into the bottom three. But there are twenty-four games left and I believe that's enough time to get to know the players, influence them and hopefully get our heads above water.

We have injuries to deal with. Nicklas Bendtner, on loan from Arsenal, picked up a knock against Wolves last week and is doubtful for the game. He and the club captain, Lee Cattermole, have been accused of being involved in an alleged incident in Newcastle during the week and have been questioned by the police about damage to some parked cars. I am confronted with this in my first week at the club. Bendtner also declares himself unfit to play against Blackburn Rovers. I almost plead with him to play, but he's adamant that he's not ready.

I turn to a young lad who showed much promise a few seasons ago at Ipswich – hence his £9 million move, a costly signing for Sunderland – but who so far hasn't really had a chance to shine. Connor Wickham's career is yet to fully take off, but I have no alternative other than to start him against Blackburn.

Encouraged by a large crowd of supporters, we start strongly but fall to an old sucker punch after less than twenty minutes. We are a goal down, and you can tell from the players' faces that it's a 'here we go again' situation. My half-time message is simple: we must keep playing as positively as we have been doing. If we do not concede another goal, we will get something out of this game. Maybe they've heard these words before, just told to them in a different accent – but I stress that we just have to win this game.

Relentless pressure on the Blackburn goal yields little and Wickham, having done as well as could have been expected, is treading water. I bring on James McClean, a Derry City lad still to make his debut for Sunderland. His entry into the game changes everything. A left-winger with some pace, he gets himself immediately into the game, running at defenders so positively that he takes the crowd with him. The way he's playing, you would think it's his hundredth game rather than his debut. He is whipping over some penetrating crosses. Unfortunately, we do not have anyone to take advantage.

Time is running out, and I'm beginning to feel that the breakthrough just will not come. But as we get into the last six or seven minutes, our little midfielder, David Vaughan, rifles a glorious shot into the net. It's a wondrous strike, and the reaction in the stadium is everything I imagined it would be. Almost 40,000 people make the noise of an erupting volcano. And it's just an equalizer. I jump into the air and celebrate, now believing that if we stay strong at the back, we can conjure another goal. McClean has been magical in his cameo role and given us just the lift we needed.

Then in the last minute we are given a free kick just outside the penalty area. Seb Larsson, a Swedish international player, is a very good free-kick taker. He stands over the ball, surveying all before him. He places the ball on a spot he has earmarked, steps back, runs up, and whips it over the wall and in off the post into the net.

It's the winning goal. If I thought the noise in the stadium was loud five minutes ago, the reception for this goal takes my breath away. At the final whistle I celebrate a priceless league victory with joy and relief in equal measure. We have stopped the rot.

Tottenham in London await us the following week. Cattermole and Bendtner declare themselves fit and I put them on the bench. We acquit ourselves exceptionally well but lose by the only goal of the match. Our position is still precarious, but at least the two aforementioned players will be available for the rest of the campaign.

Back in London a few days later, at an evening game against QPR just before Christmas, we have a sensational away following filling the stand behind the goal. Loftus Road is much smaller than White Hart Lane and the noise generated by our fans is fearsome. The recalled Bendtner gives us an early lead and Stéphane Sessègnon, a little inside forward from Benin, makes it 2–0 early in the second half. Even though it's only my third game it's easy to spot this young man's talent. He might be called a number 10 in the contemporary game and he is the most naturally gifted player on Sunderland's roster. When on form, as he is tonight, he can be unplayable.

However, old habits die hard, and we allow QPR back into the game by gifting them two goals. With minutes to play, we are holding on instead of coasting to victory. Somehow we manage to force a corner from a breakaway move. Wes Brown, the ex-Manchester United defender now plying his trade at the Stadium of Light, heads into the net for the winning goal. Overall, it's a deserved win but we've had to battle the whole evening through. I couldn't be happier and there are more than a few sighs of relief in the dressing room. Christmas can be enjoyed. Six points from three games is a great return for a team in such a lowly league position. We are not out of the woods, but an away win for a team in our situation is invaluable.

Two home games follow: Boxing Day against Everton and then home on New Year's Day against Manchester City, vying with Manchester United for the title. We work hard for a draw against Everton, roared on by almost 44,000 in the stadium. The result takes us out of the relegation zone and we can finish the calendar year in good spirits.

Keiren Westwood, our goalkeeper, cries off with illness less than twenty-four hours before the New Year's Day game against Manchester City. Simon Mignolet, the first-choice goalkeeper, is recovering from a badly broken nose and is wearing a protective mask on his face. His parents are coming over from Belgium for the New Year to see their son and expect to be sitting in the stand alongside him. But I need him to play.

We are decimated with injuries and I will go into the game with two midfielders playing as full-backs. Manchester City are exceptionally strong. Even with our best eleven on the field we would be hard pressed to get anything from the game. I ask Simon if he's up for it. He is surprised, but thinks he'll be OK. I tell him that even if he lets in seven goals this afternoon, he will not be blamed for anything. He's doing us all a massive favour. He says he'll go for it although he will still wear the mask. I am delighted by his courage and that he is prepared for the ensuing battle.

Manchester City swarm all over us, hardly surprising with Vincent Kompany, Pablo Zabaleta, Aleksandar Kolarov, Yaya Touré, Gareth Barry, Samir Nasri and Edin Džeko in their starting eleven. Seven of my starting line-up have played fewer than twenty games for the club. That encapsulates the task that is facing us. Amazingly, we have the first scoring opportunity, but Bendtner takes too many touches to control a great through pass by Sessègnon. However, Manchester City are soon back into their stride and drive us back.

Craig Gardner and Jack Colback, playing as full-backs, are coping with City's wing play and the Sunderland crowd are right behind the team. Even misplaced passes are not sneered at, so much heart is on display today. A team that shouldn't really be on the same pitch as Manchester City are fighting a rear guard action so splendid that it's almost beautiful. I bring on Ji Dong-won, a South Korean forward who has ability on the ball but is just not strong enough for constant Premier League football. I instruct him to take the ball into the corners to give us a breather, since the team is tiring rapidly and more players are getting injured all over the park.

Of course, he might not do anything of the sort, since he's young and raw and new to professional football in England. He just might dribble past some players, play a quick one-two with one of his teammates and put the ball into the Manchester City net. He chooses the latter option and has his moment in the fading sun of the Stadium of Light. The scenes are just fanatical – the roof almost lifts, so deafening is the noise. As Ji goes to the corner flag in celebration, I'm convinced he's never going to emerge from the supporters' grasp.

A moment later the whistle blows, and we have won the match against a team that will go on to win the Premier League in five months' time. Mignolet emerges with enormous credit, as he should. He and Seamus McDonagh work closely together and as a consequence he never looks back in his Sunderland career. He continues in goal, playing brilliantly, for the rest of the season and his goalkeeping the following year is largely responsible for the club's survival in the Premier League. He will deserve his £10 million move to Liverpool when the time comes.

But for now, in the Sunderland dressing room, both he and Ji are being toasted by an animated manager and a buoyant group of players. David Platt, assistant manager at Manchester City, comes to apologize for the rudeness of his boss in not shaking hands at the end of the game.

In fact, Roberto Mancini had already headed up the tunnel in disgust when Ji scored.

I tell David there is no need to apologize for his manager. I've seen it too often in the past to be concerned. The significance of the victory cannot be underestimated. The confidence, the belief, the resilience and the willpower to stay in the Premier League all stem from this win.

I take enormous pride in it all. This is why I have come to Sunderland – just to hear the roar of the crowds celebrating victory against the odds. Once called the Bank of England Club, those heady days seem a long distance off now. Perhaps one day, hopefully soon, Champions League football might be played in the Stadium of Light, and I would like to be leading the team when it happens. That is my own ambition for this club. The owner has seen enough today to think that we are safe and that, other than maybe a loan player or two in the January transfer market, there's no immediate need to spend money on players; and that is what transpires.

Twenty-two points from my first ten games in charge takes us through January and into February. Not a day goes by without some mention by our supporters of our big rivals Newcastle United, either spoken about disparagingly or with a degree of envy at their lofty position just now. So the imminent derby game against them at St James' Park has me excited for days.

Newcastle are big favourites to beat us. When they strategically

decided to position travelling away fans so far up in the stands –
closer to the gods than the pitch – perhaps they had Sunderland
fans in their thoughts! Nevertheless, so loud are our supporters,
I think they could still be heard in Gateshead. It's a wonderfully
bellicose atmosphere and we can't wait to get started.

We take the lead through Bendtner. That looks to be enough
to win the game, but a rash challenge by our centre forward in
our own box leads to a last-gasp Newcastle penalty and an equalizing goal. A draw is the result. We should have won and I am
incredibly frustrated.

Next up is the quarter-final of the FA Cup at Goodison Park.
This is one of the most intimidating grounds in the country for a
visiting team, as well as a visiting referee and his assistants. You
sense that the crowd could spill onto the pitch at any moment.
The irony is that it can be a tough place to play for the Everton
players, too, if things aren't going well for them. With all this in
mind, I extol our own strengths to my team and try to keep them
focused on the task in hand.

A fiercely contested match ends in a draw, and so we will
return to the Stadium of Light for the replay. The queue of fans
all round the ground for tickets is a sight to behold. It reminds
me of old photographs I saw way back in 1964, when Sunderland
played Manchester United in a quarter-final replay at Roker Park.

Just now, I really feel at one with this club. This is a chance
for Sunderland to make a mark this season. Two months ago we
couldn't even have dreamed of a semi-final appearance, but that
has become the ambition now the threat of relegation has been
removed.

We have the chance to give the fans an afternoon at Wembley
– and perhaps, given our strong run, that hope has become
expectation. Now I must win this match for them.

But I don't. We play poorly against Everton; we are weak
both physically and mentally. They bully us all evening and
we gift them the opening goal. We never recover, and we get
knocked out.

I think of all those fans who have queued, spending money to watch a disappointing performance on a night when we needed strong hearts and minds. I brood over this defeat for a long time. Despite a bright performance away at Manchester City to draw 3–3 in the Premier League a few days later, my mind is still on the midweek defeat by Everton. It will trouble me for some time to come.

The season moves on. We are in no danger of relegation and in fact, an excellent victory over Liverpool at home guarantees us Premier League football for next season, which was the task set by Ellis Short in the first place. The final game of the season is against Manchester United.

We are staying overnight in a hotel in Durham, as we usually do. The evening before the game I have a meeting with Short and Margaret Byrne, the club's CEO. I outline my plans for next season, telling them that despite some great results since my arrival, the team needs strengthening in a big way. I have so far cost the club not one penny in transfer fees and now is the moment, I feel, to state my case. I tell them that if we do not add quality to the team then we will find ourselves in the same trouble as earlier this season – and that, I emphasize, is not being dramatic. It's a simple reality.

Ellis looks at Margaret Byrne. Margaret looks at Ellis. Both are flabbergasted at what I've just said to them. Ellis accepts the fact that the on-loan Bendtner will return to Arsenal but feels that his replacement, whoever that may be, is the only player we will need for a top ten finish next season. Now it's my turn to be shocked. We leave the meeting, all of us with plenty to ponder.

The following day we are bit parts in one of the most dramatic afternoons in the history of the Premier League, with both sides of Manchester glued to what is unfolding at the Stadium of Light. Manchester United beat us 1–0, but United players are standing on the sidelines anxious for news from the Etihad Stadium. City are drawing 2–2 with seconds remaining. Then news of Sergio Agüero's unforgettable goal hits our stadium like a lightning bolt, and United are stunned. Ironic cheers ring out at the Stadium of Light, infuriating Sir Alex Ferguson.

Afterwards, he comes into my office for a post-match drink. The atmosphere is respectfully sombre. If I feel bad about losing a game, how must he feel about losing a Premier League championship in the final two minutes after a ten-month-long season?

He must be sick inside, but he doesn't show it to me. Even now, I sense that he is planning an all-out assault on the league next season.

A couple of minutes of background conversation among others in the room allows Sir Alex a little time alone with his thoughts. Then he gets up to leave, telling me that I've done well with the team but reminding me that reinforcements will be needed for next season.

I tell him that's what I said to the owner yesterday evening. Just as he is leaving the room, he turns back to me and says, 'You've still got my shirt.'

I laugh, and when he leaves I tell my backroom staff the context of his remark. It was the night of Ryan Giggs's testimonial game at Old Trafford; I had brought Celtic down as the opposition and 70,000 fans attended. After the game Sir Alex invited me into his office, suggesting that I stay the night at his house and travel back to Glasgow the next morning. I told him I had no fresh clothes, but he insisted. The following morning he produced one of his own shirts, a little larger than mine but perfectly laundered, for me to wear on the way back home. 'Don't forget to send it back,' said the Scotsman half-jokingly. I forgot to do so, prompting him to say every time he saw me, 'You've still got my shirt.' I still have it today.

We have been invited to the Peace Cup competition in Suwon, South Korea, as part of our preseason preparations. I bring some of the up-and-coming youth players with the senior group to let them gain experience and see if any of them are close to playing in the Premier League. They aren't. Our results and performances in later preseason friendly matches also don't augur well for the coming months. Michael Turner leaves for Norwich City for £1,500,000 and I bring in Carlos Cuéllar as a free transfer. And I still need a centre forward now that Bendtner has gone back to North London.

I would like to sign Steven Fletcher from Wolves, who have just been relegated. He is a very good player who I believe could do well for us. But there is reluctance from the owner and the CEO to do the deal – Ellis thinks that Wolves are asking for too much money. Surely there's room for negotiation, I reply.

Louis Saha's agent also calls, aware of our need for a centre forward. Louis, who has contemplated retirement after his release from Spurs and may well be lying on a beach somewhere not super close to Wearside, feels he's still capable of playing in the Premier League. With the season opener at the Emirates soon upon us and an impasse on the Fletcher deal, I have no alternative. Louis, still a fine footballer but at the wrong end of his career, comes to Sunderland and is a substitute against Arsenal, making his debut after sixty-five minutes in a goalless draw. It's a great point for us in the circumstances. But can we follow it up in next week's home game against Reading?

The winger Adam Johnson from Manchester City joins Sunderland, but a centre forward is still the priority. I again put forward a strong case to Ellis for Steven Fletcher, and thankfully the owner relents and agrees terms with both Wolves and the player.

Incredibly, our opening home fixture is postponed because of a waterlogged pitch – in August. A torrential downpour lasting maybe ten or fifteen minutes is enough for the referee to call the game off. After two games in the Premier League, we are already one game behind. Work that should have been carried out in the summer didn't get done because Bruce Springsteen was playing at the Stadium of Light in late June. I think Springsteen is brilliant, and his shows are special. I actually went with the owner to this very concert. But I also mentioned to the Chief Operating

Officer at the Stadium of Light that there would be little time to prepare the pitch for the start of the new season because of the lateness of Bruce's concert. I was assured there would be no problem with the new surface being laid in time for the opening match. But there was.

By the time we play Swansea away in our second game, Fletcher is in the starting line-up. We draw 2–2 and he scores both goals for us. We finally have our first home Premier League game against Liverpool halfway through September. We draw 1–1. Fletcher scores our goal again. A creditable draw against West Ham is our next game. Fletcher scores yet again. And in fact, he follows it up with the winning goal at home to Wigan Athletic. By the end of September, all Premier League goals scored by Sunderland have been down to Fletcher. With the fans now singing his name, his critical contribution justifies the purchase. With Mignolet's superlative performances in goal at the other end, the two will go a long way to keeping Sunderland in the Premier League.

Just before the transfer window closes I take a young left back, Danny Rose, on loan from Tottenham Hotspur. Danny has all the natural talent you could possibly wish for. Quick and with excellent ball control, he soon becomes a big favourite with the Sunderland fans, who love his intricate wing play and marauding runs down the left. It's plain that Danny responds to encouragement and I pour plenty of that in his direction. Some of the other players find it a struggle all season long. James McClean goes from hero to villain with the fans for his refusal to wear a poppy in November's game at Goodison Park. The captain, Lee Cattermole, finds it difficult to shake off some niggling injuries; Titus Bramble has played better; and defensively we are finding it difficult to cope.

In the January transfer window I sign Alfred N'Diaye and Danny Graham, but results in February are poor. There is now growing concern for our Premier League status, and Ellis Short summons me to a meeting in London saying that he would like me to meet some gentlemen in his office. They might be able to help with player recruitment, he tells me. This seems to suggest he is not particularly happy with the scouting system in existence at the Sunderland training ground which I have inherited. When I arrive, Ellis introduces me to the three men and we all sit around a very large table.

One of the men produces a laptop, opens it and proceeds to show me a number of players he has recruited for the Italian club he is still working for. He then shows me a list of potential recruits for Sunderland, many in a price range well beyond the Steven Fletcher bracket. Reading the room, it's clear that these three have had the ear of the owner for some time. The two-hour meeting concludes and I get a grim sense of what potential change is coming.

They are invited by Ellis to have a look around our training facilities and take in our home game against Norwich City. I see them again but I don't speak to them, and they don't speak to me. We can only draw with Norwich City. The following week, on 30 March 2013, we are defeated against Manchester United – strangely, this is exactly seventeen years to the day since I was booed at Filbert Street. What is it about this date?

After the match, as I'm heading back to our house in Durham with Geraldine in the car, the phone rings. It's Ellis.

'Martin, I want to make a change. I'm sorry I haven't been able to keep those promises I made to you.'

I am totally devastated. This is a hammer blow and a feeling that I have never experienced before. We turn the car around and head straight to the training ground to clear my office. I'm still reeling from the news.

And so my time at the Stadium of Light comes to a brutal end. We are sixteenth in the league, with thirty-one points from thirty-one games. Another five points from the last seven games will be enough to stay in the top flight, which I believe is well within our grasp.

When Paolo Di Canio is announced as my replacement, the

presence of the three men in Ellis's office suddenly makes sense. The appointment prompts David Miliband, former foreign secretary and vice-chairman of Sunderland, to resign, citing Di Canio's 'past political statements' regarding fascism. No sooner is Di Canio in the door than he announces that the players are not fit enough. This is no surprise, as he adopts the usual new coach's spiel of disparaging comments aimed at the outgoing manager.

This comment is re-emphasized after his first loss at Stamford Bridge, but remarkably not mentioned after victory over Newcastle at St James' Park and a follow-up home win against Everton. He does, however, revert back to the line after a complete month in charge of the team when they are trounced 6–1 at Villa Park. Only two points taken from the last three games is still enough to keep Sunderland up. They finish seventeenth, one place below when I left. But that doesn't matter as far as my personal involvement is concerned. I've now gone.

I watch Sunderland's results with interest at the start of the 2013/14 season. Di Canio has made so many signings from all over Europe, I've lost track. After five Premier League games they only have one point on the board. Ironically, when he is questioned about the fitness of the team when they seem to be struggling with the pace of the games, he replies that his preseason fitness regime will come into effect in the winter months. That's a new one on me, but either way, Di Canio doesn't get to see its results. Five games into the new season, he is sacked.

Margaret Byrne resigns over the Adam Johnson grooming scandal. Ellis Short finally sells the club. Despite the influx of players, Sunderland are relegated two seasons later.

14

IRELAND

After a lot of quiet introspection during the fallout from Sunderland, I question many things. How will I do things differently when I manage again? Where can I add a new direction to my style? What am I learning, and how? Like any manager, I am in search of fresh perspectives. And since John Robertson left the team, something has been missing.

Six months after my departure from the Stadium of Light, my phone rings. It's Dermot Desmond. 'Stop your moping and come and manage the Republic of Ireland,' he says. That position is now vacant, the legendary Giovanni Trapattoni having left the post following some disappointing results in the qualifying stages for the 2014 World Cup. Dermot tells me that I should meet up with John Delaney, Republic of Ireland CEO. I heed his advice and head down to London.

I am slightly hesitant. Managing the Republic of Ireland would truly be a great honour, but I have always been a day-to-day manager working at a football club, and the international post is a completely different proposition. If you start counting the number of days that you would be working with players in any calendar year, you won't get too far. The difference between the two jobs is extreme. Even though international football matches are now played in clusters rather than the sporadic matches that were typical when I was a player, the long gaps of days or weeks between games would be totally alien to me. Unlike club football, where a manager can quickly cement a previous good result or rectify a bad one, in international football there is a yawning time chasm between each success or failure.

John Delaney tells me my next contract would only be guaranteed if the Republic of Ireland qualify for the 2016 European Championship in France. I am fine with this and I decide that the honour of managing the Republic of Ireland outweighs any potential disadvantages. I am privileged to be asked and proud to accept the role. There will be two friendly games in November 2013: one at home to Latvia, the other one a few days later in Poland. The Euros qualification matches do not start until the following autumn.

I tell John I want to take Roy Keane as my assistant manager. At this utterance I race over to stop him from falling off his chair. John and Roy have famously had a few differences in the past, and his immediate facial expression suggests he might fear a déjà vu situation. But in all fairness to him, he tells me that he has no problem with Roy coming on board. In fact, once he regains his composure he jests with a broad grin: 'We'd better batten down the hatches, then.'

Roy and I have recently worked together as pundits covering Champions League games. On these trips abroad, while waiting for the games to start, we usually have a bite to eat before a match along with the rest of the crew. Over sandwiches, we once talked about international management and wondered – if the opportunity ever arose – whether working together would be appealing. I'm not sure we came to any conclusion. But when the Republic of Ireland job became available and John Delaney asked to meet me in London, I phoned Roy to see if he might consider being assistant manager.

Roy is a very intelligent man, erudite and easy company. His passion and commitment I take for granted. But in our conversations, he also spoke very thoughtfully about the game with an acute tactical insight that captured my attention. He knows football inside out and while I disagree with him when he tells me that Cork is the best county in Ireland, this man is Irish to the core. Galvanizing both players and supporters can only be easier with Roy Keane by my side.

I also take Steve Walford and Steve Guppy as our two coaches. Steve Guppy will deal mostly with forward wing play and Seamus McDonagh will be goalkeeping coach. At the end of the meeting we travel over to see Denis O'Brien, who has financed Trapattoni's salary and will continue to oversee the new manager's wages.

Before the manager and assistant manager announcement is made, the friendly game in Dublin against Latvia has attracted fewer than 10,000 ticket-holders. However, by the time we kick off at the Aviva Stadium there are 35,000 people in attendance. John Delaney will say later that he thinks the extra 20,000 are down to the appointment of the new management team.

Despite recent mediocre results, the national team are expected to win this evening. Roy and I have had a few days of training with the players. The atmosphere within the squad is exactly what I experienced as a player with the Northern Ireland team: these are players who want to play for their country, and who take special pride in so doing. It feels entirely different to managing a club team. Managing a club's expectations is one thing. Managing a country's expectations is something else.

My focus is to be in France in 2016. I recollect scenes that Jack Charlton created in the 1990s, when the Republic of Ireland came out en masse to welcome his team home from World Cup glory in Italy and America. That first taste of success had whetted the country's appetite for more, and Trapattoni had led Ireland to Euro success by getting to Poland in 2012 – although according to the Irish media, the poor performances there seemed to negate the good work done beforehand.

Unlike Charlton's star-studded group, we do not have too many players plying their trade at the top echelons of the game. Séamus Coleman is an exception, playing strongly at right back for Everton. Robbie Keane has been a terrific footballer in his glory days but is in the autumn of his career and may only be able to play periods of matches rather than whole games. Still, he is a proven goal-scorer playing in the USA for LA Galaxy and when I look round the squad, I don't see anyone else guaranteed to take a chance like Robbie might do in a game. Of course, none of this is any great surprise to me, because I am aware of most of the abilities of the squad I have at my disposal. But the few days we've spent together have given me a chance to discover their individual characters.

Roy and I get an enthusiastic welcome from the crowd. My message to the players beforehand is not only to recognize what an honour it is to represent your country, but that qualification for the Euros in France is our ultimate aim. The players know that there will be casualties along the way but this match, tonight, is their chance to stake a claim.

Robbie Keane scores the first goal when James McClean gets in front of the Latvian defenders to flick on our corner kick. In time-honoured fashion he comes away from his marker, swivels and sweeps the ball into the net. We're off and running. In the second half, Aiden McGeady fires in a second goal for us, and when Shane Long finishes off an excellent move involving Jon Walters and Séamus Coleman, the game is won. It's only a friendly, but it's a nice way to win my opening game.

I make wholesale changes for a second game in Poland. We manage a creditable goalless draw that makes a pleasing start to my international career.

There isn't another game until March 2014 – four long months away. Until then, I use my time to attend club matches across the UK and Ireland. Watching Irish-born players, or players who can potentially play for Ireland, fills my weeks. There are times when I leave a stadium at the end of a game and can't remember the scoreline, so engrossed have I been in watching a particular defender or midfielder. But I have to admit I do still envy those managers on the touchline, only yards away from where I am sitting, cajoling their teams with pointed arms and fingers. I realize that the international games come far too infrequently for me.

In January I head off for a holiday abroad. There is a Premier League game on TV that I want to see, but the game is not showing on the television in the bedroom so I head down to the bar area to see if it's on there. Someone else has the same idea and I bump into Eamon Dunphy, the RTÉ pundit and soccer writer for one of Ireland's newspapers. I believe he has to file a match report, even though by now both of us have missed the first thirty minutes of the game. Eamon, a former lower-league professional player in England, has been a pundit for years and is known for his vociferous criticism of Jack Charlton's reign. I haven't spoken to him since I won a case against RTÉ many years ago when Eamon, in his punditry role, managed to libel me on live television. It's an awkward moment with just the two of us in an empty lounge, but initial forced conversation soon transforms into a more pleasant tête-à-tête. I jokingly thank him for RTÉ's compensation from the case, to which he replies that it wasn't his money anyway. At least it's an ice-breaker, or so I think. He wishes me good luck in my role as the Republic of Ireland manager.

Friendly games do serve a purpose, particularly if experimentation is still high on the agenda. In March I test another formation against Serbia in Dublin, and we follow up with two more end-of-season friendlies against Turkey and Italy. I want to know the squad and how they respond to each other and the teams they face during the short period where only ranking is on the table. Defeat by a goal against Turkey and a robust draw against Italy give me plenty of food for thought. A few days later we travel to America to play Costa Rica and Portugal, both countries also heading for the World Cup in Brazil. Portugal are a class apart and expose many weaknesses in our team. The qualifiers for the Euros are three months away, but that really means I have only four days to work with the team and get us into real shape for that first game in Tbilisi in September.

It has been a long wait, but after almost a year in the job we are on the plane to play Georgia in our first qualification match. Robbie Keane, the captain, will start at centre forward but more than likely will not finish the game. I'm hoping that he might conjure a little magic for us in Georgia's penalty area before he departs the international scene. We are not prolific goal-scorers – the Republic never have been, Roy tells me, even when certain Ireland teams in the past have been loaded with quality players in other positions.

I have brought Aiden McGeady back in from the international wilderness and I'm hoping he can create some chances for us. A precocious kid at Celtic, Aiden possesses great natural talent, but putting that to its best use can be a problem for him. I am not sure he has quite grasped when to run with the ball and when to release it at the right moment, but he can go past players with ease, and that's something we lack within this group. If we can get him the ball in the final third of the pitch, I feel he can create something for us.

As an international manager you have very little time to work with the players. The idea that you can improve a player's technique in a two-day training routine is hogwash. You accept the limitations of the squad, build up a powerful team spirit, give players confidence to play, rehearse set pieces both offensively and defensively, and inspire them to win football matches against opposition that, on paper, may look vastly superior. If you have some proper talent in the team, as the Republic of Ireland have had through the decades, you allow it to flourish.

On a temperate evening in Tbilisi, the players are warming up on the pitch and I have just about finished pre-match interviews. I have about fifteen minutes to myself and all manner of thoughts run through my mind. Are the players prepared for the challenge ahead? Do they realize how important this game is in the context of qualification for France? Have I emphasized this enough, without making them feel too nervous? And of course, won't it be just princely if we're toasting victory while travelling back to Dublin in the dead of night.

I am jolted out of this self-absorption by the sound of the

players' boots clacking down the tunnel as they come back into the dressing room from their warm-up. It's time to deliver.

It's a tentative start by both teams, with a few goalmouth skirmishes but no immediate breakthrough. Then McGeady pounces on a through pass by James McCarthy and glides the ball into the Georgia net. We are in the lead. This brings temporary joy, but within minutes a defensive mix-up allows Georgia in for the equalizing goal. At half-time we have to regroup. It was a sloppy goal to concede and we need to refocus, be more aggressive and take the game to Georgia.

In the second half we are far from being a cohesive unit but we are certainly more aggressive in our play, able to quell dangerous Georgian counter-attacks. Can we muster some meaningful strikes ourselves? Both teams are starting to tire in the late September evening. But just when a draw looks most likely, McGeady scores a wonder goal to secure all three points. This victory in Georgia will prove vital come the final reckoning. It's not an easy place to win football matches, and I know that the Georgians will take some points off other countries.

By the time we get to Tbilisi airport, we've learned that Germany have beaten Scotland and Poland have demolished Gibraltar. If, as expected, Germany top the group come next October, then Scotland's loss seems like a good result for us. The trip back to Dublin may be long but the players are in high spirits. The squad is galvanized by this hard-fought victory and next month cannot come quickly enough for all of us.

In our next game, Robbie Keane's hat-trick helps us secure a big win against Gibraltar and sets the scene for our trip to Gelsenkirchen to face Germany. Unfortunately, we have to deal with a number of injury problems – not ideal when facing the world champions on their own soil. With Séamus Coleman injured, I decide to play David Meyler, the Hull City midfielder, at right back. I know David well from our Sunderland days together. He will play anywhere he's asked if it means donning a green shirt. He is fearless and committed.

Our game plan is simple and clear: we cannot afford to lose an early goal. We need to frustrate the opposition, cover gaps as quickly as possible, close players down and force them to go sideways. However, I know from experience that Germany have the ability to overcome a carefully planned strategy by even the most talented of teams. For seventy long minutes we hold firm, Meyler doing exceptionally well for us in his unaccustomed role at right back. But having chased and harried the opposition all evening, we are getting tired. Our own chances have been limited but a point against World Cup holders would be priceless if we can hold out. Toni Kroos, of Real Madrid, decides otherwise. He drives home a goal which looks to have won the game for Germany – but they have not reckoned on the determination that we have tried to foster within our group since we joined forces.

I push John O'Shea forward from centre back to centre forward. I don't care if we have left ourselves open for Germany to exploit defensive gaps and score a second or perhaps a third goal. We need a goal ourselves, and that's all that matters to me. And just when it seems that this massive frontal attack is thwarted, up steps O'Shea, on his one hundredth appearance, to score the equalizing goal. There are incredible scenes on our bench, on the pitch and in the stands. Our supporters who have travelled over to Germany are hugging each other in total disbelief.

It is a magnificent achievement, and most importantly, it gives us seven out of nine points in our opening matches. Nevertheless, apparently a draw against the world champions on their home patch hasn't satisfied every critic. Viewers back in Ireland get in touch with RTÉ to complain that their coverage of the game tonight has been excessively negative.

The following morning, I am somewhat taken aback to hear that an ex-manager in the League of Ireland has claimed in a newspaper column that the players got me out of jail with their last-minute equalizer. This individual is also a football agent. In fact, he is actually the agent for one of our players, Shane Long.

I wonder if Toni Kroos's agent is writing newspaper articles criticizing Joachim Löw.

We head to Glasgow in November. Hampden Park is not available. Press reports suggest that because the game is now at Celtic Park, the crowd will be empathetic towards me and McGeady. That couldn't be further from the truth. In fact, the fiercely partisan Scottish supporters boo McGeady constantly throughout the game because as a young Scotsman he chose to play for the Republic of Ireland.

It's a frenetic game from start to finish and there is no time to dwell on the ball. Thunderous tackles are made with no quarter asked nor given. We just have to get through this battle. With twenty minutes left in the game, we are still holding firm and Scotland force a corner. They play it short; we take too long to sense the danger, and much too long to close the Scottish players down.

Their sharp forward, Shaun Maloney, to whom I gave a debut at Celtic over a decade ago and whom I took to Villa Park, scores a terrific goal for Scotland and undoes the gritty, sterling work we have put into this match so far. We apply some relentless pressure on their goal and hit the bar, but when the final whistle blows we have lost the game. Our fierce rivals are back in contention for France in 2016.

The post-mortem on this game is inexhaustible in the Irish press and we don't have another European qualification match until March 2015 – far too long to brood over defeat. Four months in football management without a game is interminable, particularly after a loss. Reminders are constant. Scottish players' TV interviews around Christmas time send my mind back to Celtic Park. Twenty-two seconds elapsed from Scotland forcing a corner until they took it. We must surely react more quickly to potential danger. Just twenty-two seconds and the game was lost.

We play Poland, and defeat cannot be contemplated. Victory would be a major boost towards qualification. A draw does not end hopes, but it will be a setback. The Aviva Stadium is full to capacity but there are thousands of roaring Polish supporters inside, giving their team a big morale boost. Their players respond by taking an early lead, and we have to work hard for every play we make. But our team, imbued by a never-say-die attitude, conjure up a last-minute equalizer, thoroughly deserved for the sheer pressure we exert on the Polish defence in the last half-hour. It is only a point, but it keeps us in contention. Everything is now focused on our home game in June against Scotland.

The atmosphere in the Aviva Stadium at the Scotland game is electric. With eight points from five games before today's, we sit two points behind Scotland and Germany, with Poland leading the group on eleven points. It's clear that a victory for us is imperative. We put Scotland under enormous pressure in the first half and deservedly take the lead through Jon Walters, who is becoming our go-to guy in these qualification group matches. A second goal looks inevitable but doesn't materialize. I don't want half-time to come, so much do I feel we are bossing affairs. But it arrives, to the relief of Scotland.

Within a minute of the second half beginning, Scotland equalize. We should have cut out the danger at least three times before they score. Shaun Maloney – yes, him again – scores a deflected goal to level the game. Like a giant balloon being burst, the stadium deflates and it is some time before we regain a semblance of composure. When we do, we stage a grandstand finish that delivers everything but a goal. Scotland force the draw and keep the two-point gap between us in the table. Poland and Germany both win to increase their points tally, and we are left wondering what might have been. Criticism in the Irish media is heavy and I need to remind myself that we have lost only once in six competitive matches, although the narrative in the press seems to be telling a different story. We are being written off, and the prevailing view is that our chances of reaching France have receded, if not completely evaporated.

A few days later, I have an opportunity to become a Premier League manager once again. But despite the lure of a longer, much more lucrative contract should I choose to go, I tell John Delaney that I want to stay. I just cannot leave this job unfinished. We will still qualify, I tell him. I believe that Georgia can get a result against Scotland. But most importantly, I know that we will have to get some points ourselves from our home game against Germany or away to Poland.

First up is a warm September evening in the Algarve, where we play Gibraltar. The team leaves the hotel knowing that Georgia have taken the lead against Scotland. They are still in front when the coach arrives at the stadium. I spend the next fifteen minutes looking anxiously at the TV screen with John Delaney as they hold on to win. It's a brilliant result for us and our players, buoyed by the news, beat Gibraltar comfortably. Qualification is back in our own hands. Next, we follow up our victory with a crucial win over Georgia in Dublin. We are right back in contention.

Two games remain, and Germany are in town. We are ready for the game of our lives. Inevitably, they will have more possession than us during the course of the game, so knowing how to play without the ball will be the key this evening.

And when we do get possession, we have to be confident and take advantage. We can't let the reputation of the opposition frighten us into making silly mistakes. We need to believe that we belong on the same pitch as these proven superstars. That has been the message in our training sessions, to be emphasized in the dressing room.

As expected, Germany hog possession, but we thwart them. Great teams will inevitably cause you problems and Germany certainly do, but the crowd's enthusiasm and passion help us greatly. Then, with twenty minutes to go, I bring on Shane Long. Within minutes he scores a goal that he himself will never forget, nor will those supporters behind Manuel Neuer's goal. It is one of the most iconic moments in Irish football history.

The world champions are beaten, and we are assured of at

least a play-off place. Considering the majority of our starting line-up do not even play at the top tier of club football, this achievement cannot be overestimated.

After such a victory the country is abuzz; now is the time I would have liked three or four months of inactivity, just to gloat over the result. Unfortunately we are in Poland in a few days' time, vying with them for that automatic qualifying spot for France 2016. We lose a tight game but will play Bosnia in the play-offs for the right to go to France. A couple of weeks later, in a fog-bound stadium in Zenica, we play out a 1–1 draw. Now it's all or nothing in Dublin in the second leg. We have three days to prepare for the most important international game of my tenure to date. In a pulsating game, we prevail, winning 2–0.

I have been fortunate enough in this prized game of football to experience some wonderful times: European Cup victory, some magnificent results against all odds with Northern Ireland in Spain in 1982, but tonight's victory over Bosnia ranks alongside those cherished moments. The scenes at the end of the game, after Jon Walters's two goals take us to France, are everything I thought they might be. For Roy, Steve Walford, Steve Guppy and Seamus McDonagh, it's a wonderful summation of our efforts and application. This is why I took the job. Our supporters will have their day in the French sun come June and, knowing them, will make France more than memorable. And for some of the players tonight in this dressing room, France will represent the best moments of their footballing careers.

In the meantime, our kit man Dick Redmond surprises us all by donning a Superman outfit and running round the dressing room shouting, 'I can't believe I'm going to France.' His words echo how we all feel at this moment. It's my opportunity to say a big thanks to my own backroom staff: Walford, Guppy and McDonagh have all been as good at international level as they have been working for me at club level.

Roy Keane has played a major role in getting us to France. His presence around the training camp has been hugely positive. His training routines, particularly the quick-fire shots, blocks and saves involving all players, have been highly productive. The players revere him and he is witty and self-deprecating when he chooses to be. Most of all, though, it has been his driving determination and enthusiasm that has set him apart. Although quick to praise, he sets exacting standards and does not tolerate half-hearted attitudes either on the training field or on the playing field. He has strong, sometimes implacable opinions on many subjects, which makes for interesting debate.

In Ireland's entire footballing history, dating back almost a century, they have qualified only five times for major footballing tournaments. Tonight is the sixth. Victory against Bosnia and Herzegovina even has one or two reporters backpedalling just a little from their trenchant reproval of me. Bizarrely, one journalist in particular lists all the things I would have been criticized for had we not made it to France. It puts a wry smile on my face.

As for me, I have something to look forward to in the coming summer. Those heady days that Jack Charlton brought to this country, with euphoric scenes playing out in Dublin streets, could be re-enacted. But that can wait until the time comes.

We will be stationed in Versailles, outside Paris, for our campaign in France – a stone's throw from the storied Palace. Having the players together for, by international standards, quite a number of days makes for more of a club football atmosphere.

We have time to work on set pieces and time to do proper homework on the opposition we will be facing. We are in a tough group, with Belgium, Italy and Sweden our opponents, but we naturally want to do better than the squad did four years ago in Poland when the team was found wanting in so many ways.

I ask some of the players who participated then what had happened, and they mention that the preparation was all wrong. Wives and families were staying too close, and the players were even staying with families when they should have been in their own hotel. It isn't the first time that players have blamed off-field issues for their on-field inadequacies, but I am determined to eliminate as many excuses as possible from the players' agenda and concentrate on trying to qualify for the second stages of the competition.

I tell the players they will get a chance to see their families when the time is right, but that they will need to stay as a team group until I say so. Aiden McGeady must have cotton wool in his ears as I announce this, because he brings his family to our very hotel. I get to hear about it and ask him to follow the protocol.

Outside these little hiccups, there is a buoyancy within the group. It is a chance for young players like Robbie Brady and Jeff Hendrick to showcase fledgling talent, but I'm particularly pleased for Séamus Coleman, who deserves such days, fleeting though they may be. A quality player with Everton whose attitude is second to none, Séamus is never afraid to shoulder big responsibilities on the field. One of the most colourful sights I have seen in football awaits me as we walk out of the tunnel for our first match against Sweden, as the green of Ireland contrasts wonderfully with their yellow kit.

We are dominant and play some excellent football against a strong Swedish team which includes Zlatan Ibrahimović. We should be in front but spurn some chances. There is a freedom to our game, as a result of our hard-earned points in the qualifying rounds. Now is the time to express ourselves fully. Wes Hoolahan scores a magnificent goal just after half-time to give us a deserved lead, but I know we need the second goal. Although we are dominating, the game is still in the balance. As time runs down we drop a little deeper, trying to protect our lead. Sweden get a chance and an own goal allows an equalizer. It is an excellent performance overall, but a disappointing result.

Belgium, one of the best teams in Europe if not the world, are our next opponents. They beat us convincingly as expected by many pundits, but we allow them too much room throughout the match. The result means we have to beat Italy to qualify for the knockout stages.

And what an evening is in store. We display the willingness to go that extra yard when everything in your body is saying no, the determination to come out off the line to prevent a shot on goal when the easier thing to do is stay put. Robbie Brady's courageous header to win the game epitomizes everything about us over the last two years. We beat Antonio Conte's Italy to earn the right to play the host nation, France, in Lyon. The reception we receive from the fans in the stadium is uproarious. I hear that the scenes back in the Republic of Ireland were astonishing. We are still in the competition and the team have advanced past the group stages of a UEFA European Championship for the first time.

We travel to Lyon in two days to meet France, who have had a week to recover from their own exertions in the competition. It's an unfair advantage for the host nation but sadly, there is nothing we can do about it. Although we take the lead against them it's a tough physical struggle and eventually France triumph. They will go on to contest the final against Portugal and we will travel back to Dublin, with a lot of goodwill from the Irish people to greet our return. I do feel disappointment that we were not given the opportunity of a day or two's extra rest to take on the French on their own doorstep; but to achieve what we have done in France has been remarkable.

I have a conversation with my backroom staff. Have we taken the team as far as we can? The general consensus is that the World Cup in Russia in two years' time is attainable, and we decide to go for it. We are fourth seeds in a group which contains Serbia, Austria, Wales, Moldova and our old foes, Georgia.

I am in the middle of Belgrade, looking out the window of our hotel at the unrelenting rain. Belgrade has had its historic moments but right now it looks like any other city on a drab, dank September morning.

Tonight's game is hours away but I'm already feeling the nervousness that match day always brings. Maybe I should have considered my future after I came home from France. The fans have been given what they wanted and Ireland's world rankings have vastly improved. My family and friends think that a new club challenge might be more suitable, pointing out that if I can't win the media over after the amazing time the fans have had in France, perhaps I never will. My relationship with the press in Ireland is not good at the best of times. With any poor result it can only worsen, and constant critical reproof can be draining.

I have an excellent relationship with the fans, but during these two years as manager of the Republic of Ireland, I feel I have been viewed as an outsider. Early on I told Roy that the press thought of me as an interloper, and occasionally I was being referred to as 'the Northerner' by the media. Originally he didn't agree with me, but more recently he's come round to my viewpoint.

I have a feeling that our game against Serbia will be difficult tonight. It's still raining when we reach the stadium but on a very heavy pitch we get a terrific draw, 2–2, to start our qualification campaign. We do not lose an away game in the group, which shows the character within the team. However, we falter at home to Serbia – but then we win a dramatic game in Wales to finish second in the group on nineteen points, making the play-offs.

Denmark are our opponents. A 0–0 draw in Copenhagen gives us the chance to beat them at the Aviva Stadium. If we can do so, we can feast in Moscow next summer. We take the lead early on and miss two chances to put the game beyond them. But minutes before half-time they strike twice to take the lead. Only a win for us will be good enough to get to Russia.

At half-time, we have forty-five minutes of football to score at least two goals. I tell McGeady and Hoolahan to get ready, as we will need creativity to conjure a victory. I know that their introduction will not only weaken us physically but will also allow gaps to appear all over the pitch; however, it is a risk I must take. I cannot visualize the present team being able to produce enough chances to score the necessary goals. The substitutes enter the fray but within minutes, Denmark score a third goal and effectively finish the game. We concede two more in trying to chase the game, Eriksen of Tottenham scoring a hat-trick. Denmark will go to Russia. We won't.

It's the perfect magnet for more opprobrium to come my way. The RTÉ reporter questions me on whether this result is a sackable offence, forgetting that this is a play-off game for the World Cup. We have already finished second, with nineteen points from ten games, in a group where we were fourth seeds. Clearly the knives are out, as they say – and they are especially sharp.

A competition is brought into being called the UEFA Nations League. No one is exactly sure how it works, but in effect it takes the place of friendly games and becomes a gateway to the next European Championship. Two defeats against Wales and, ironically, two draws against Denmark are enough for John Delaney to bid goodbye to both me and Roy.

The night before my final game in charge against Denmark, there is the obligatory press conference. For the umpteenth time I'm quizzed about Declan Rice, a young West Ham United player who was born in England and may well choose to play for the country of his birth. It is a decision entirely for him and his family to make. I have visited him at his dad's house and have actually capped him three times at senior level in friendly games, but the choice is his; I cannot understand the continual harassment of me on this issue.

I finish the interrogative press conference and start to walk outside. Witnessing all of this is a gentleman acting as Denmark's press officer for the evening. He asks to speak to me for just a moment. He tells me that he's been working in football for a long time and has never seen a manager treated in the manner in which he has witnessed tonight. He's embarrassed for me. That shouldn't happen, he adds, to any coach, let alone to someone with decades in the top tier of football. I thank him for his comments and tell him that tonight's debacle is a walk in the park by contrast to a couple of weeks ago when one reporter, who I used to think was quite fair, had me down as some superannuated Luddite not equipped to deal with the modern world.

It sometimes seems to me that there is a revisionist colour painted by the Irish media with regard to our amazing adventure in the European Championships, perhaps even an attempt to airbrush those experiences from the history books. I'm not sure that those fans who had a wonderful time following the team around the French countryside, witnessing Wes Hoolahan's magnificent goal in Paris and Robbie Brady's courageous goal in Lille, would necessarily agree that those events didn't actually happen.

And for me it was a phenomenal privilege to lead the Republic of Ireland to those European finals and bring joy to so many Irish people, both at home and abroad. The fans will hope to experience such jubilation again, hopefully soon.

Stephen Kenny and his assistant Keith Andrews are the men charged with doing so now. The hopes and expectations of the Irish fans now rest on their shoulders. Stephen's lieutenant finds himself in a hotter seat in the dugout than the one he occupied in a TV studio when he was an excoriating critic of mine. He is finding out that winning football matches is more difficult to execute on the field of play than fidgeting about with a remote-control button. Such pontification in the studio hasn't so far achieved the desired effect on the playing field. Luckily he's getting plenty of opportunities to put things right.

As the great Humphrey Bogart says to Ingrid Bergman in *Casablanca*, 'We'll always have Paris'. I know that France did exist and that I'll always have it.

Perhaps I'll leave the last word to someone who knows something about winning major trophies. For all his successes in a stellar career, Roy Keane often says that our experiences in France rank alongside the best of those achievements.

POSTSCRIPT

I started out in the professional game with a pocketful of dreams – to reach the top and win medals along the way. If that happened, surely everything else, like happiness and wealth, would follow. When I scored that goal against West Bromwich Albion eleven minutes after coming on the field for my Nottingham Forest debut and followed it up a few weeks later with another goal at Old Trafford, my did I think I was going to conquer all before me in football.

As I view my life in this arena I have few regrets. Of course, in *Sliding Doors* moments it would have been Celtic, not Porto, as victors of the UEFA Cup in extra time in Seville 2003. But I have been blessed with so many other successes that may not have occurred had that same door slid in another direction. Brian Clough might have snubbed Nottingham Forest's offer to come back into football management and gone elsewhere. Kenny Swain may not have changed his mind about managing Wycombe Wanderers, and had Dermot Desmond decided to appoint another manager instead of me then Celtic would have remained an ambition instead of a reality.

I have always wanted to put into writing some of the experiences in my football career that bring some resonance, and reference and state them with more than a degree of authenticity.

I have had a footballing life that I could seriously not have imagined when that tennis ball kept falling off my foot before I reached ten keepy-ups. Places that I have seen and people that I have met are due in large parts to belonging to this game of football. How else would I have been able to converse, if only fleetingly, with Bobby Moore, Martin Peters and Geoff Hurst had it not been for football?

People often say that writing can be both therapeutic and energizing. Therefore to write about a subject of which you have been a part for fifty years and that still exists in your very consciousness is an overwhelmingly enjoyable undertaking.

For me football is an addiction that I have been unable to shake off. So I am looking forward to the next chapter . . .

ACKNOWLEDGEMENTS

To my mother and father for everything they did for me, and my brothers and sisters for such a wonderful childhood.

To Jimmy McAlinden. Without his encouragement at Distillery, who knows?

To the footballers I have worked with both as a player and a manager, particularly those at Wycombe Wanderers, without whose spirit, dedication and determination I may not have had the opportunity to write the second half of this book.

To Alan Hutchinson and J. D. Taylor for retaining the soul of Wycombe Wanderers Football Club.

To Professor Linch and his magnificent cancer care team at the University College Hospital, London, and the miracle workers at the Intensive Care Unit. My daughters and I owe you everything for what you did for Geraldine.

To Steve Kutner, football and music agent. I've known Steve for over twenty years and have never done one solitary piece of business with him in all that time. Now that's being a proper friend.

To the brilliant Pat Murphy, encouraging from beginning to end.

To that wonderful radio commentator, Mike Ingham, now enjoying retirement.

To Clive Tyldesley, as good as ever.

To Luke Edwards, that terrific journalist, for being . . . Luke Edwards.

To Matt Dickinson. Some months ago I read some scribblings to him, thus prompting his article in *The Times* which led to this book.

To Peter Lansley, that brash young journalist that I have known since our days at Wycombe Wanderers. He was a big source of encouragement and enthusiasm when the book was in its embryonic stage.

To everyone at Pan Macmillan, but particularly to three extremely talented individuals. Reading out loud to Lucy Hale can be an exhilaratingly unnerving experience, but I was allowed to continue and this is the result. A young man, Matthew Cole, was also at that reading. He had followed up his interest from Matt Dickinson's article in *The Times*, and his continued interest gave me the spur to continue the scribblings. He became an encourager, a listener, a reader, a discerner, a cajoler, and many other nouns I won't mention. His partnership with Mike Harpley became a real driving force.

Mike's brilliant talent became more evident by the day, and he became relentless in his motivation – actually just to get me to write, I think. Thanks, Mike, for your massive input.

To Seamus McDonagh, the best goalkeeping coach in football.

To Steve Guppy, a successful footballer and now an innovative coach both in Europe and the USA. He and his manager Gary Smith won the Major League Soccer Cup with the unheralded Colorado Rapids a few years ago.

To Jim Henry, probably the best fitness coach in Europe, and Stuart Walker, my great friend from the Aston Villa days.

To Roy Keane, an exceptionally gifted individual with an insatiable appetite for winning. I loved working with him – maybe because I wasn't going to see him every day. Brilliantly witty, and a major reason why the Republic of Ireland enjoyed such heady days in France in 2016. And, talking of the Republic of Ireland, thanks to the players for our days back then.

To John Robertson and Steve Walford. As a trio, we were

inseparable. Steve, as a coach, was ahead of his time. John was ahead of everything to do with football as a player and as an assistant manager. Unforgettable days with both of them. Major parts in our successes.

To John and Kathleen Keane at Celtic, two of the best people who have ever walked this planet.

To Paul Gilroy KC. A brilliant mind, a magnificent barrister and the most generous man with his time I have ever known. I owe him so much over the last decade it would be difficult to repay him.

To Mick McGuire, one of my very best friends in football.

To Martin George, John Elsom and, of course, Dermot Desmond.

And to the fans of football everywhere in the world. I'm sure you are aware that the game wouldn't exist without you.

To Geraldine, Aisling, Alana and my nephew Niall Swaidani. Niall's technical nous knows no limits. Trying to read my writing, let alone understand my sentences, became such a chore to him that he ended up with appendicitis. Thanks for all your help.

The three women named above must have the final word, which never belonged to me even when my daughters were children. Aisling and Alana gave up their precious time to do just about everything possible to keep me at this task. But, more than that, they were inspirational, motivational, forceful – much too forceful for their father's liking – but boundlessly energetic and insightful. Without them I would still be at page three and Pan Macmillan would have given up on me.

Thanks also to my daughters' husbands, Benan and James, for patient perseverance while Ash and Alana get on with the most important business of looking after their father.

What can I say about Geraldine that hasn't been written? A little more direct in her comments than her two daughters would be one way of putting it, but always delivered with the charm that I know exists permanently in her heart. Having had her own big cancer battle, she's ready for anything that life throws at her now. And doesn't she let me know about it – every day!

PICTURE ACKNOWLEDGEMENTS

1. Courtesy of the author.
2. Courtesy of the author.
3. Courtesy of the author.
4. Keystone / Getty Images.
5. Dick Williams / Mirrorpix / Getty Images.
6. Courtesy of the author.
7. *The Evening Standard* / Getty Images.
8. Bob Thomas Sports Photography via Getty Images.
9. PA Images / Alamy Stock Photo.
10. PA Images / Alamy Stock Photo.
11. Bob Thomas Sports Photography via Getty Images.
12. PA Images / Alamy Stock Photo.
13. PA Images / Alamy Stock Photo.
14. Bob Thomas Sports Photography via Getty Images.
15. (*top*) Michel Barrault / Onze / Icon Sport via Getty Images. (*bottom*) Bob Thomas Sports Photography via Getty Images.
16. Bob Thomas Sports Photography via Getty Images.
17. Michel Barrault / Onze / Icon Sport via Getty Images.
18. Courtesy of the author.
19. (*Vauxhall Conference*) Professional Sport / Popperfoto via Getty Images. (*FA Cup trophy*) PA Images / Alamy Stock Photo.
20. Courtesy of the author.
21. Professional Sport / Popperfoto via Getty Images.
22. Paul Popper / Popperfoto via Getty Images.
23. Ross Kinnaird / Allsport via Getty Images.
24. Popperfoto via Getty Images.
25. (*top*) Stu Forster / Allsport via Getty Images. (*bottom*) SNS Group via Getty Images.
26. Michael Steele / Getty Images.
27. Chris Furlong / Getty Images.
28. Andrew Yates / AFP via Getty Images.
29. Stu Forster / Getty Images.
30. Jamie McDonald / Getty Images.
31. Sportsfile / Corbis / Sportsfile via Getty Images.
32. PA Images / Alamy Stock Photo.
33. Ian Walton / Getty Images.
34. Matthew Ashton – AMA / Getty Images.

INDEX